T
4.00

The Autonomy of Reason

Books by Robert Paul Wolff

Kant's Theory of Mental Activity (1963)
Political Man and Social Man (editor, 1965)
A Critique of Pure Tolerance (with Barrington Moore, Jr., and Herbert Marcuse, 1965)
Kant: A Collection of Critical Essays (editor, 1967)
The Poverty of Liberalism (1968)
Kant's *Groundwork*: Text and Commentary (editor, 1968)
The Essential Hume (editor, 1969)
The Ideal of the University (1969)
Ten Great Works of Philosophy (editor, 1969)
In Defense of Anarchism (1970)
Philosophy: A Modern Encounter (1971)
The Rule of Law (editor, 1971)
Styles of Political Action in America (editor, 1972)
1984 Revisited: Prospects for American Politics (editor, 1973)

THE AUTONOMY OF REASON

A Commentary on Kant's Groundwork of the Metaphysic of Morals

ROBERT PAUL WOLFF

Harper & Row, Publishers
New York Evanston San Francisco London

And again, for Cindy

LIBRARY OF CONGRESS CATALOG CARD NUMBER: 73–9083

STANDARD BOOK NUMBER: 06–131792–6 (PAPERBACK)

STANDARD BOOK NUMBER: 06–136113–5 (HARDCOVER)

Designed by Ann Scrimgeour

Contents

Preface

With the publication of this commentary on the *Groundwork of the Metaphysic of Morals*, I bring to a close two decades of intense study of the philosophy of Immanuel Kant. I first conceived the plan of writing a commentary on the *Groundwork* during the fall of 1965. I had recently joined the philosophy department of Columbia University with the assignment of "covering" ethics at the graduate level, and in working up a course of lectures on the history of ethical theory, I allotted two weeks to the *Groundwork*. The two weeks stretched into four as I struggled with the deceptively brief text, and by the time I had finished, I knew that I wanted to attempt a full-scale interpretation of the *Groundwork*.

The first 125 pages of the commentary came easily enough, and I began to hope that I might complete the book in little more than a year. But when I reached the twelfth paragraph of Chaper 2, I ground to a dead halt. There were simply too many things that I did not at all understand about Kant's conception of will, maxims, rational agency, and therefore about the Categorical Imperative. I put the unfinished manuscript aside and turned to other projects, hopeful that sooner or later I would be able to make some progress toward a more satisfactory interpretation of the text.

In 1967–68, when I visited Rutgers University, again in the summer of 1969, and yet again during a sabbatical semester in the fall of 1970 I worked over the *Groundwork*, each time taking another step forward. Finally, during the sprng and summer of 1972, I completed a first draft of the manuscript.

In the Preface to my book *In Defense of Anarchism*, I observed that the argument of that work presupposed a moral theory which I was not then in a position to expound or defend. I knew that the first step toward the articulation of such a theory would be a satisfactory resolution of my struggle with the *Groundwork*. The concluding chapter of this book makes it clear how much further I have yet to go.

Once more, let me acknowledge my debt to Clarence Irving Lewis, with whom I had the great good fortune to study during my last undergraduate year at Harvard College. I do not know whether he would approve of my interpretation of the *Groundwork*, were he still alive, but I should like to think that he would approve of the effort to come to terms with Kant's moral philosophy. Let me acknowledge also my intellectual debt to the dean of American Kant scholars, Lewis White Beck, whose many writings on Kant's moral philosophy have been of repeated assistance to me. And finally, my thanks to Ms. Toby Rood, who typed much of the manuscript of this work while fulfilling her other duties as a member of the staff of the Philosophy Department of the University of Massachusetts at Amherst.

A Note about
References and Editions

All quotations from the *Groundwork* are from the translation by H. J. Paton (New York: Harper & Row, Publishers, Harper Torchbooks, 1964). Where I have altered the translation or have substituted my own, I have so indicated in the text.

Page references to the *Groundwork* are to Volume IV (1911) of the Preussische Akademie der Wissenschaften edition of *Kants Gesammelte Schriften*, 23 volumes, 1900–1956. *Grundlegung zur Metaphysik der Sitten*, edited by Paul Menzer.

References to the *Critique of Pure Reason* are to the first edition (A) or the second edition (B) as is customary. All other references to Kant's writings are to the appropriate volume and page of the Akademie edition.

Introduction

1. Some Remarks on Styles
of Philosophical Commentary

Groundwork of the Metaphysic of Morals is probably the most difficult short work in modern philosophical literature. Despite its great popularity—it is, after the *Critique of Pure Reason*, the most widely read and oft-commented upon of Kant's writings—scholars and philosophers have arrived at no common agreement about what it seeks to prove, what arguments it employs, or whether it is successful. Even the careful reader is baffled by complex chains of reasoning compressed into brief paragraphs and then beguiled by a series of surprisingly concrete examples which prove sadly misleading as clues to the more abstract doctrines surrounding them.

Some of the obscurity of the text is caused by the unfamiliarity of Kant's terminology, particularly in the area of psychology. Considerable confusion, too, is created by Kant's penchant for mixing up different and opposed methods of exposition, so that at one time he will merely explore the connections among concepts hypothetically, at another attempt a formal proof from premises to conclusions. But when the confusions have been sorted out, and we have, in W. S. Gilbert's words, "got up all the germs of the transcendental terms," we are still left with the root difficulty of the work: Kant's own unclarity, and inconsistency about the doctrines he wishes to expound. It is simply not possible to fit all of the principal doctrines of the *Groundwork* into a single coherent chain of argument, despite the most generous allowance for lapses of clarity, momentary vagary, or even inconsistency.

For example, no interpretation of the text, however vigorous and imaginative, can obscure Kant's deep-rooted conviction that the moral life is a continuing struggle between the call of duty and the lure of inclination. Now, Kant did not believe that an action must be wrong merely because I am inclined to do it. He did not even think that an action toward which I am inclined thereby lacks moral merit. But after these and other familiar errors of Kant interpretation are routed, still there remains a picture of the conflict within each man between duty and inclination. No one could do justice to Kant's moral philosophy without setting this conflict at the center of his account. And yet, strange as it may seem, if the central argument of the *Critique of Pure Reason* is correct, then such a conflict as Kant describes is absolutely impossible! In order for it to take place, the real, or noumenal, self would have to step into the temporal order of appearances and do battle with phenomenally determined inclinations, now defeating them, now being in turn defeated. But no coherent account can be given of such a struggle within the framework of the Critical Philosophy, as Kant from time to time reminds himself in the *Groundwork*. Any conflict about which we could speak significantly or whose episodes we could witness internally would have to be fought between mere appearances. It could only be a conflict of inclinations of the sort described by Hobbes and Hume.

What are we to do in the face of inconsistencies of this nature? The problem raises very general questions about the purposes of commentaries upon philosophical texts, and I can best indicate the aims of the present work by addressing myself for a moment to those questions.

One might suppose that there are at base only two ways of dealing with a text: historically or philsophically, exegetically or critically. Either one can strive to clarify what the author intended to say, drawing upon his other published works and even his unpublished papers as supporting evidence, in which case one preserves in the exegesis all the contradictions and confusions which are genuinely contained in the author's thought; or else one can treat the text as an argument and, after discovering its premises and the sequence of its steps, subject it to a critique in order to determine whether it is valid. The former approach is historical for though it may involve a great deal of logical analysis, its aim is to establish the historical proposition that the author thought or intended to assert a certain set of propositions. The latter is philosophical, for though it in turn may benefit from historical explanations of the author's intentions as a way of discovering missing steps in the argument or supplying suppressed premises, its aim is to evaluate the validity of an argument. If, for example, the historian of ideas successfully establishes that Kant believed *both* in the conflict between duty and inclination *and* in the total separation of phenomena from noumena, he will as historian merely record the fact of these two inconsistent beliefs. The philosopher, discovering that a valid argument which he had thought to be contained in a Kantian text was, in fact, not intended by Kant, will simply remove Kant's name from it and preserve it for what it is, a valid argument. In short, the history of philosophy is either philosophy or history, but never both at once. Only errant philosophical curiosity could lead the historian to criticize the texts he expounds, and only filial piety would encourage the philosopher to puzzle over texts whose arguments he thinks are wrong.

Or so it would appear. But in the present essay I have set out to combine exegesis with critical analysis, and I shall try to justify this hybrid enterprise by describing a third, intermediate way of dealing with certain texts, which I shall call philosophical reconstruction.

Within the ranks of the great philosophers, there are a few whose insight into the most profound problems goes so deep that it seems to outreach their capacity for clear, coherent exposition and argument. Kant is such a philosopher. He perceives underlying connections among certain features of our cognitive or moral experience and strives to explicate them within the confines of his system of critical philosophy. Out of his attempts to do justice to the complexity of his insight there arise formal contradictions and incoherences of exposition which the reader is quick to notice. Kant's thought grows and changes as he struggles to formulate his driving ideas, and his writings reflect this growth in untidy ways. To the dismay and exasperation of readers, Kant clings to old ideas long after he has himself refuted them, and when two insights will not cohere, he sometimes carries them both along rather than neatly pruning one to make place for the other. Confronted with writings of this sort, the historian can record the diversity of arguments and reproduce their inconsistency; the philosophical critic can evaluate the arguments as stated, rejecting those which fail and taking from the text whatever can be validated. But there may be some readers who are dissatisfied with both responses, who are convinced that Kant was right in his original philosophical insights, and who hope that by a critical reconstruction of the text they may be able to carry to completion the enterprise begun by Kant himself.

Obviously, no one will devote himself to such a task unless he has reason to hope that the outcome will be valuable in itself as an addition to our understanding of some philosophical problem. The willingness to attempt a philosophical reconstruction of a text, therefore, springs from the conviction that its author possessed genuine insight into his problems and that because, in a manner of speaking, he saw more deeply than he was able to say, it would be fruitful to study even his obscurest passages in an effort to wring from them the truth he dimly perceived. Philosophical reconstruction is a gamble in which the reader wagers his time and energy on the text, hoping to win from it results that he could not have discovered by his own unaided efforts.

Of all the great philosophers, there is none so rich in insights and so plagued by inconsistency as Kant. Despite his oft-stated intention to create a throroughly interconnected philosophical system, he time and time again refused to stifle his deeper reflections in the interest of systematic coherence or architectonic symmetry. Nowhere are his insights deeper or his systematic conflicts starker than in his attempt to establish connections between theoretical cognition and moral choice. The elaborate distinction between appearance and reality, which serves both to dissolve antinomies in theoretical philosophy and to make a place for practical freedom, must somehow be made to cohere with the sensitive account of moral experience on which the *Groundwork* is itself based. Because I believe that Kant correctly identified the principal problems of moral philosophy and that he had some genuine insight into their solution, I am prepared to gamble on the *Groundwork* as a worthwhile text for the enterprise of philosophical reconstruction.

In what follows, I shall comment upon the text and interpret it with an eye to discovering the most promising lines of argument, following them out as far as I am able. At some points I shall rather ruthlessly reject portions of Kant's theory which, though undoubtedly to be found in the text, are wrong-headed or unproductive. Obviously any such sorting out must be based upon my own judgment of the importance of Kant's doctrines. Hence this commentary is very much *an* interpretation of the text. It would make no sense to say that it is the only, or the right, interpretation, for from the same materials a number of alternative philosophical reconstructions could be made. In the end, the value of this enterprise will depend on the answers to two questions: does the interpretation developed here illuminate the text, so that at least some of what Kant says is clearer and more plausible in the light of it; and, more important still, does the interpretation result in an argument whose independent philosophical merit justifies the effort spent in grappling with Kant? I hope there will be at least some readers who will be able to answer both questions with a yes.

2. The *First Critique*
Background of the *Groundwork*

It is a commonplace among students of the *Groundwork* that one must master the *Critique of Pure Reason* before Kant's ethical teachings can be fully understood. This advice is issued with particular reference to the famous resolution of the conflict between freedom and natural determination set forth in chapter 3 of the *Groundwork*. With rare exceptions, however, it is advice more ignored than heeded. Commentators who treat the text of the *Groundwork* with admirable subtlety and insight revert to a superficial copybook rendering of Kant's doctrines when they allude to the arguments of the *First Critique*. Partly, of course, this is because one book by Kant is more than enough to understand at a time, but a more serious reason is that Kant's philosophy proceeds at two semidistinct levels, and the superficial level is far more readily accessible than the deeper, philosophically important level to which on occasion he descends. The *Groundwork* must remain a mystery so long as this split in Kant's philosophical system is ignored.

On the surface, Kant's philosophy is a systematic, exhaustive, critical inventory of the powers, possessions, activities, and propensities of the mind. As such, it is, Kant assures us, complete and final, for while experience may throw up an endless variety of objects, the mind which encounters them is once-for-all fixed and thoroughly knowable. The three major works in the Critical corpus correspond to the major faculties or powers of the mind: Understanding (or Reason in its theoretical function), Practical Reason, and Judgment. Even the subsections of the several books have their counterparts in subsidiary mental functions. To the Aesthetic of the *First Critique*, for example, there corresponds the capacity of the mind to be sensibly affected by objects; and to the Analytic of Concepts there corresponds the mind's ability for concept formation.

The system as a whole was sketched before the first work was published, and Kant thought so well of it that he clung to it, elaborated upon it, and returned to it again and again, despite the fact that his own later arguments frequently threw into doubt the assumptions on which it was based. The critical system was his guide in the immensely complicated development of his philosophy, and whatever the doubts he may eventually have felt about its adequacy, he was incapable of discarding it and building a new structure from the elements of his most mature thought.

Consequently, a curious pattern emerges in Kant's writings. When his attention is concentrated upon some particular segment of the whole, he does not permit himself to be constrained by the architectonic demands of the system. If his arguments carry him beyond the assumptions on which the section was originally posited, Kant follows wherever they lead. But as soon as he is done with that section, he is liable to revert or relapse into the old, simpler way of thinking; later on, when referring back to what he has written, he will frequently completely ignore the contradiction between the original view and his own deeper conclusions.

What is more, he will use the superficial version of the earlier section as a building block in some later argument. As a result, one cannot easily distinguish a complete superficial Critical Philosophy and a complete deeper theory underlying it. Rather there are complexly interwoven strands of profound and superficial argumentation, the complete unravelling of which is probably an impossible task.

An important instance of this confusion of superficial with profound doctrine is Kant's account of the problematic applicability of the categories to things-in-themselves. His original view was that the forms of sensibility constituted the principal constraint upon the extent of our knowledge. Pure concepts, he thought, were potentially universal in their range of application, but concepts required an object to which they could be applied, and the forms of space and time set limits to what could be given in experience as an object of knowledge. On this theory, statements about the causal connections or substantial character of noumena were meaningful but empty, that is, they inevitably lacked the sensible evidence which could confirm or disconfirm them. Hence, so long as we took care to guard against formal inconsistency, we were free to formulate as unprovable postulates what we could not empirically verify. In Kant's famous phrase we could limit knowledge (of things in themselves) to make place for faith (in the existence of God and the freedom and immortality of the noumenal self).

This simple, schematic account was worked out by Kant very early in his formulation of the Critical Philosophy. It represented only a short step beyond the semi-Critical doctrine expounded in the *Inaugural Dissertation* of 1770. However, when he came to investigate the nature of the categories more closely, in the Transcendental Analytic, Kant realized that his early theory wouldn't do. The categories were seen to be *rules for the organization of a manifold of sensibility*. As such, even their merely problematic applicability was limited to such a manifold. In other words, the categories, no less than the forms of sensibility, were inherently restricted in their sphere of application to appearances. The most that could be said for the categories was that they might hypothetically apply to manifolds of sensibility with a form other than our own (to a non-spatio-temporal manifold). *But since the entire elaborate resolution of the conflict of free will and determinism depended upon hypothetically applying the category of causality to noumenal action, Kant had, in the deeper investigations of the Analytic, undermined the foundations of his ethical theory.*

Kant never faced this problem. Indeed, it seems likely that he never even knew it existed. His references in the *Groundwork* to the *First Critique* doctrine are all steadfastly at the superficial level. In reading the *Groundwork* we are therefore faced at the outset with a choice. We may follow Kant in setting its argument in the framework of the more superficial version of the *First Critique*, or we may test its argument against the deeper doctrines of the *First Critique* and reject as misguided whatever hopelessly conflicts with them. I have chosen the latter course because I am convinced that the most advanced teaching of the *Critique of Pure Reason* is too valuable to be ignored, even though Kant himself frequently did just that. In addition, I hope to be able to show that the argument of the *Groundwork* is actually strengthened by conforming it to the line laid down in the *Critique*. Indeed, some of the most serious weaknesses in the *Groundwork* argument can be eliminated by assuming (contrary to the textual evidence) that Kant always had his deeper *First Critique* doctrines in mind when he developed his ethical theory.

There are three topics which require some special discussion before we launch into a detailed commentary on the text of the *Groundwork*. Two of these, Kant's theory of causal connection and his wavering commitment to the doctrine of psychological determinism can, I think, be fairly decisively dealt with by a sufficiently vigorous interpretation of the *First Critique*. The third topic, Kant's theory of the self, presents a somewhat different problem. Despite the obvious centrality of the self for the Critical Philosophy, Kant never drew together the several divergent lines of his thought into something resembling a coherent theory of the self. Consequently, I shall be forced merely to raise a series of difficult questions which Kant never answered and to indicate how this failure influences the ethical theory of the *Groundwork*. A fourth topic, the famous resolution of the conflict between determinism and free will, can most conveniently be discussed when we come to chapter 3 of the *Groundwork*.

A. The Four Selves of Kant's Philosophy

The Critical Philosophy is preeminently a philosophy of the self. As Kant says repeatedly, the proper subject-matter of transcendental philosophy is the element in experience, judgment, aesthetic appreciation, or action which is contributed by the mind itself. It is surprising, therefore, that we cannot find any extended discussion in Kant's writings of the relations among the several selves, or functions of the self, which people his theory.

In the doctrines of the *First Critique*, there are at least three different "selves" whose relations to one another must be established. First in the order of knowing is the empirical or phenomenal self. This is the self in whose empirical consciousness one finds the diversity of sense perceptions, feelings, and thoughts which constitute the matter of experience. My empirical self has the best claim to be identified as *me* or so it would seem, for when I introspect, it is the contents of my empirical self that I encounter; when I act in the world, it is the purposes of my empirical self that I accomplish. It is the empirical self that can be said to doubt, hope, fear, love, expect, believe, desire, intend, approve, and disapprove. It is my empirical self that takes a walk, does a sum, gives a speech, performs an experiment, makes an observation. My virtues and vices, my strengths and weaknesses of character, the idiosyncrasies that make me the person I am, are all dispositions and characteristics of my empirical self.

But according to Kant, this empirical self is merely the appearance of my true, real, rational, or noumenal self. What I know as the empirical self is myself as I appear to myself under the form of inner sense. The mind, Kant says, "intuits itself not as it would represent itself if immediately self-active [which it is not], but as it is affected by itself, and therefore as it appears to itself, not as it is."[1] Since time is the form of inner sense, I appear to myself as an empirical consciousness spread out in a temporal ordering. This

---

[1] *Critique of Pure Reason,* B69. For an explication of this difficult passage and the theory of inner sense which it expounds, see my book *Kant's Theory of Mental Activity* (Cambridge, Mass.: Harvard University Press, 1963), pp. 191–202, esp. pp. 197ff.

appearance, which I know as the empirical self, is composed of perceptions, thoughts, feelings, and so forth. Like all other appearances in the realm of phenomena, it is governed by causal laws upon which a science of psychology (or anthropology, as Kant calls it) can be erected. My real self, on the other hand, is atemporal and stands outside the causal order of nature. All the causal and other judgments that I make about my character, experience, and activity, like the analogous judgments that I make about the behavior of things in nature, are limited by the condition that they are true only of the self as appearance.

The noumenal self, according to Kant, is the seat of the rational faculty. In contrast with the flux of perceptions and thoughts in empirical consciousness, its consciousness is described by Kant as "pure, original, and unchanging" (A107). Sometimes Kant seems to assign the faculty of Reason to the noumenal self and the faculty of Understanding to the empirical self. At other times, he treats these two faculties merely as titles for distinct powers of one and the same intellectual faculty, whose activities are manifested now in the guise of the empirical self, now as the real self-in-itself. It is a little difficult to tell just exactly what the relation might be of one noumenal self to another; indeed, Kant does not even offer any principle of individuation of noumenal selves, a fact which led to considerable confusion in the Idealist metaphysics of his nineteenth-century German followers. It seems even a little odd to speak of *my* noumenal self, although it is perfectly natural to speak of my empirical self or personality.

Thus far, we have dealt with only two of Kant's selves, the empirical and the noumenal, but a third self dominates the argument of the *Critique*, namely, the transcendental ego. According to the theory set forth in the Deduction of the Pure Concepts of Understanding, the mind comes into relation with objects and brings those objects under concepts in conformity with certain rules (the categories) which lie ready in the mind. The active imposition of these a priori rules is called synthesis, and the locus of the activity of synthesis is the transcendental unity of apperception or *transcendental ego*. The entire world order, including both the objects of nature *and the empirical self that perceives them*, is produced by the mental activity of synthesis. The active, knowing mind or transcendental ego, knows things as they appear rather than as they are in themselves, including of course itself, which it knows only as appearance.

Now, what is the relation among these three selves according to Kant's theory? The most natural answer is that the noumenal self and transcendental ego are one and the same entity and that the empirical self is its (their) appearance in the realm of phenomena. Since the transcendental ego is described functionally—that is, Kant speaks of it always as *that which does* this or that—it might be more accurate to say that the transcendental ego is the name given to the noumenal self insofar as it is engaged in certain activities which generate empirical consciousness, objective unity, and the experience of a world of objects. This alternative characterization has the virtue of leaving it open whether the noumenal self has other functions beside those discussed in the *First Critique*. So the most plausible interpretation of the *Critique* on this matter would be that there are two selves, noumenal and phenomenal, and that the noumenal self is the seat of the transcendental faculties which generate the phenomenal world including the phenomenal self.

Unfortunately for Kant's theory, this natural solution to the problem of the three selves creates a great many more complications than it avoids. The difficulties begin as soon as we raise the question of other empirical selves and their relationship to the world order. The transcendental ego is supposed to be the creative source of the unity and structure of the entire natural world. As Kant makes clear in the Transcendental Deduction and later in the Second Analogy, this means that the synthetic activities of the mind literally generate an objective order of nature in contradistinction to the subjective order of awareness. But if the transcendental ego, as seat of these synthesizing activities, is identified with my noumenal self, then there would appear to be room in the phenomenal world for only one empirical self, namely, myself. Suppose, after all, that there were two persons in the world, myself and Smith. If Smith is merely an appearance, then no difficulties arise, but then, too, he is not really a person, anymore than a tree or a dog or a robot is a person. But if Smith is a conscious, rational mind, if, that is to say, Smith is also the appearance of a noumenal self, then what is *his* relation to this synthesizing transcendental ego? Either he and I are appearances of the *same* noumenal self (transcendental ego), in which case Kant is reduced to some kind of transcendental solipsism; or else each of us is the appearance of a separate noumenal self, in which case it is impossible to explain satisfactorily how both of us independently synthesize the same phenomenal world order or how each of us manages to be an appearance in the other's field of consciousness. Of course, we might retreat to the ancient Protagorean doctrine that each man lives in his own separate world, but that is scarcely more satisfactory than the other two solutions.

Since this point is vitally important and perhaps a bit difficult to grasp, let me try to clarify it by means of an extended analogy. Imagine a group of persons who, as a game, decide to sit down and write stories about the group. Each person is to write a story in which he and the others appear as characters. Now, a given person stands in the relation of *author* to each of his characters, of course, but he stands in a special relation to the character in his story who represents himself. That character is not identical with him, but is, so to speak, his *appearance* in the story. Every member of the group will stand in this special sort of relationship to one and only one character in the entire collection of stories, namely, the character who represents him *in the story he himself has written.* Needless to say, a character representing him will appear in each of the stories, but only the one in his own story can be spoken of as his *appearance.*

Obviously the stories written by the several members of the group may differ widely, but suppose that by some miracle the stories were all word for word identical.[2] Smith says and does exactly the same things in Jones's story, in Black's story, and in his own story. Even under the conditions of this remarkable assumption (which, in the terms of the analogy being developed here, corresponds roughly to Leibniz's postulate of preestablished harmony), Smith will still bear that special relationship of *appearance* only to the character who represents him *in his own story.* It is

[2]Let us ignore the complexities of first-person reference. This example is complicated enough as it is!

not the *content* of the characterization but its formal relation to the authorship of the story which defines the relation of "appearance of."

It should be clear that there can never be two characters *in the same story* who are both *appearances* of members of the group (omitting for simplicity the case of joint authorship). In each story only one character will be an appearance of the author, and that one different in each story. In order for two characters to be appearances in the same story, it would have to be the case that two members of the group had independently written numerically the same story, and that doesn't make sense. They might of course write exactly similar stories, but they could no more write literally the same story than they could both sneeze a single sneeze or utter numerically the same token of some sentence-type.

Now let us draw the obvious analogy. Each author is like a transcendental ego or noumenal self, and each story is like a complete order of nature synthesized by the transcendental ego. The characters in the story are like people in this order of nature, and the character representing the author is like that empirical self which is the appearance in the phenomenal order of the transcendental ego. Just as there cannot be two characters in a single story both representing authors, so there cannot be two noumenal selves or transcendental egos who encounter one another as empirical selves in the same phenomenal order. In short, Kant seems committed by the logic of his position to a radical solipsism.

The truth of the matter is that Kant never adequately faced this problem of many minds, as we may dub it. In the *Critique* he managed to ignore the issue by vacillating between a psychological and an epistemological interpretation of the theory of the categories. When he was hard at work analyzing the origins of unified consciousness, he gave a thoroughly psychologistic account of the synthesizing activities of the transcendental mind, but as soon as he was done, he retreated to the more cautious position that he was merely exploring the epistemological grounds of our knowledge claims.[3] The result is that we are invited to draw from

[3]For a striking instance of this vacillation within the confines of a single passage,

Kant's theory the extremely powerful conclusions which are entailed by his psychological doctrine of synthesis while at the same time we are spared the painful recognition of its manifest drawbacks.

The full complexity of the problem is not yet before us, however, for in his moral philosophy Kant makes essential use of the distinction between noumenal and phenomenal self in order to resolve the dilemma of freedom and determinism. To the empirical self, the noumenal self, and the transcendental ego Kant adds yet a fourth self, the *moral self*. As appearance, I am sensuous, passionate, causally determined, a mere thing in the realm of things; but as noumenon, I am rational, free, a person worthy of respect and capable of according respect to other rational agents.

Now, the resolution of the antinomy of freedom and determinism, as we shall see, turns on the fact that the causally determined order is mere appearance and that the laws governing my behavior as phenomenon are imposed by my own mind in its synthesizing activities. I can consistently maintain that I could have acted differently in some situation and, hence, that I am genuinely responsible for my act even though such an alternative action would have had to issue from a preexistent sequence of causes, only because it is my own noumenal or transcendental mind that has imposed the causal order on experience.

In short, Kant's moral philosophy depends essentially on the supposition that the synthesizing, nature-creating transcendental ego *is* the maxim-forming, morally acting noumenal agent, of which my empirical personality is the appearance. But now Kant's dilemma should be apparent. According to him, some of my moral obligations are to other persons; I am bound to treat them as ends and not merely as means, to refrain from lying to them, to keep my promises to them, to further their happiness, and so forth. It

see A117, *n*. a. Commentators are in complete disagreement over the proper way to read Kant on this central matter. In my commentary on the Analytic, I flatly adopt the view that the psychologistic variant of Kant's theory must be taken seriously if we are to make any sense out of his philosophy at all. Peter Strawson, in a brilliant commentary on the *Critique*, adopts the diametrically opposite view. According to Strawson, the psychological theory of Transcendental Idealism is complete nonsense and should be cleanly excised from the otherwise healthy body of descriptive metaphysics to be found in the *Critique*. See P. F. Strawson, *The Bounds of Sense* (New York: Barnes & Noble, 1966), part iv.

follows that there *must be* other persons appearing in the natural world—other persons, not simply other bodies. Hence, there are other noumenal agents, other transcendental egos. But if we can resolve the conflict between determinism and freedom only by identifying the transcendental ego with the noumenal moral self, then we are left with the absurd conclusion that many independent noumenal selves are all simultaneously synthesizing the one nature in which they all appear and are doing so in such a way that we may consistently ascribe freedom of the will to each of them.[4]

There is, to my knowledge, no adequate solution to this problem within the framework of the Critical Philosophy. Even if we could work out the rather tricky relations among the several rational faculties of the mind—Understanding, Pure Reason, Practical Reason, Reason in its real and in its merely logical employments—we would still have no consistent account of the way in which several rational agents encounter one another in the natural world and establish moral relationships to one another. When we come to discuss Kant's doctrine of the Kingdom of Ends, we shall find this problem reappearing. Despite his overriding concern for moral matters, Kant seems never to have asked himself the fundamental question, What is it for one man to stand in a real relation to another man?

B. The Critical Theory of Causal Connection

The most important element in Kant's Critical epistemology, for purposes of understanding the *Groundwork*, is the theory of causal connection and causal inference developed in the Second Analogy of the Transcendental Analytic.[5] Kant accepts Hume's

---

[4]Kant seems in this way to have returned, by a very circuitous route, to the Leibnizean doctrine of preestablished harmony that he strove so hard to overturn. Leibniz thought it was necessary to posit such a God-imposed harmony among the experiences of the several centers of consciousness in order to account for our possession of a priori knowledge. Kant very early rejected this ad hoc solution as philosophically unworthy, but he seems here to have arrived at a contradiction in his theory which can be eliminated in no other way.

[5]For a detailed commentary on the Analogy, including textual justification for the interpretation expounded here, see *Kant's Theory of Mental Activity*, pp. 260–283.

critical arguments against the rationalist account of causal connection. As Hume saw the matter, previous philosophers had sought illegitimately to assimilate causal inference to logical deduction; they claimed for both general causal principles and particular causal laws a kind of certainty which properly attached only to statements expressing mere "relations of ideas." Causal judgments asserted a necessity of connection between two events which neither reflection nor experience could warrant. Both the causal maxim, which claimed that every event must have a cause, and particular causal judgments, which attributed a necessity of connection to specific pairs of events, were without rational justification, according to Hume.

Kant agreed with Hume that the essence of a causal judgment was the assertion of a connection (a "synthetic" connection) between discrete events bearing no logically necessary relationship to one another. He agreed also with Hume's claim that the mind is inclined to assign a causal connection to types of events which have been repeatedly conjoined in experience. He set himself the task of demonstrating, contrary to Hume, that this subjective propensity has its ground in an *objective* connection of events.

The law of causation, as stated by Kant in the second edition of the *Critique,* is : "Everything that happens, that is, begins to be, presupposes something upon which it follows according to a rule." When we abstract from all the particularities of experience which differentiate one causal connection from another, we are left with *regular succession* as the essence of causal connection in general. Mere succession, indeed even mere repeated succession, is not causal connection, for in repetition by itself there is no necessity. But succession governed by a rule possesses the necessity of causation. It is the rule which distinguishes "B must follow A" from merely "B follows A."

The key to Kant's proof that everything that happens follows upon something else according to a rule is the distinction between the subjective order of our awareness and the (possibly different) objective order of events in the natural world. It is a commonplace that the order of events in the world is not always exactly mirrored in the order of our awareness of those events. I hear the sound of a distant drum seconds after I see the drummer move his arm, but in the real world the events are simultaneous. More generally, I may learn of events in an order bearing no similarity to that of their actual occurrence. One way of describing the difference between the objective order of events and the subjective order of experience or awareness is to say that the objective order is necessitated while the subjective order is variable, contingent, merely accidental. The defining characteristic of the objectively real is its unalterability, its independence of my will or perception. I may *learn* of two events in any of a variety of sequences—one first, the other first, or both at once—but once they have actually occurred, there can be only one correct way to portray them as having happened.

According to Kant, events can be located in objective time only by relating them forward and backward to other events in the same objective time. Time, after all, is not like a clothesline strung from eternity to eternity on which we can hang an event by a hook. Time itself cannot be perceived, it is a dimension, not a container. We fix the time of an event by ascertaining that it happened *after* a set of events and *before* another set of events. Ultimately, of course, the whole endless time sequence of objective events is established by the totality of back and forth relations of before and after. To *date* events, we merely select some special event as our zero point (such as the birth of a god) and some convenient sequence as our unit.

Now, according to Kant, the mind *creates* the objective order of events by taking up the materials of subjective consciousness and reordering them according to a set of rules which lie ready in the mind. The materials are sense perceptions or "a manifold of sensuous intuition" as Kant calls them. The rules are the Pure Concepts of Understanding, more familiarly the *categories*. The new order of consciousness established by the mind is a *necessary* order, because it is governed by the mind's rules rather than merely being haphazard. The content of the objective order of events is no different from that of the subjective order of apprehension (Kant is, in that sense, a direct realist, oddly enough); but the *order* or form is different, and, what is more important, the objective order is a necessary succession. Since necessary succession according to a rule is precisely *causation*, the objective time order of events *is* a causal order.[6]

If we put the pieces of this theory together, we find that according to Kant it is one and the same thing *to happen, to occupy a moment in objective time, to be caused,* and *to follow upon something else according to a rule.* Two important consequences can immediately be drawn from this theory. First, everything that happens in the natural world *must* have a cause, for to say that anything happens is to say that it happens at some time or other, and that is the same as saying that it presupposes something upon which it follows according to a rule. Second, causal laws will, as Hume claims, assert regular successions among types of events; for rules are implicitly general in their form, and temporal succession is the common ingredient of all rules which establish a temporal order. Later on, we shall find that these implications of Kant's theory of causation help to explain such things as Kant's claim that the principle, "He who wills the end, wills the means" is analytic.

C. Psychological Determinism

Kant never quite made up his mind about the status of mental events in the phenomenal order of nature. At several points in the *Critique of Pure Reason,* he suggests that a science of empirical psychology is indeed possible, perhaps even that it has a necessary position in a complete system of knowledge of nature. Thus in the opening section of the Paralogisms of Pure Reason, he writes:

> [If] we . . . made use of observations concerning the play of our thoughts and the natural laws of the thinking self to be derived from these thoughts, there would arise an empirical psychology, which would be a kind of *physiology* of inner sense, capable perhaps of explaining the appearances of inner sense. (B405)

---

[6]Strictly speaking, there are some contents of subjective consciousness, such as feelings of pleasure and pain and sensations, which have no representative function. They are mental events but not also representations of events other than themselves. In the objective reordering of the contents of subjective consciousness, they appear as (objective-time-located) states of the empirical self.

Later, in the last pages of the *Critique*, Kant reiterates his conviction that there is a place in the science of nature for a system of laws of the mind. Empirical psychology, he says, "belongs where the proper (empirical) doctrine of nature belongs, namely, by the side of *applied* philosophy, the a priori principles of which are contained in pure philosophy" (B876). The time will come, he concludes, when empirical psychology "is in a position to set up an establishment of its own in a complete anthropology, the pendant of the empirical doctrine of nature" (B877).

Unfortunately for the student of the Critical Philosophy, these statements are by no means the only pronouncements on the status of empirical psychology to be found in Kant's writings. In the Introduction to the *Metaphysical First Principles of Natural Science*, in the course of what is perhaps his most sophisticated and carefully thought out discussion of the structure of the natural sciences, Kant delivers himself of the opinion that there can never be a science of psychology. He offers several arguments in support of this thesis. The principal obstacle is that a true science, grounded in a pure a priori set of fundamental principles, must deal with objects which are capable of being represented a priori in intuition. In short, science must be mathematical in order to achieve the requisite necessity. But Kant believes that the single dimension of time cannot support a mathematics, and time is the form of inner sense. Hence, there can be no mathematical foundation for psychology and so no true science of psychology. His other reasons are somewhat more familiar, including the difficulty of conducting experiments in psychology and the problem that introspective observation of psychological events alters them. Kant concludes that psychology is doomed never to rise even to the humble status of chemistry, let alone to achieve the full scientific splendor of mathematical physics.

There is little to be gained from buttressing these passages with others drawn from more and more peripheral Kantian sources. Since Kant himself was of two minds on the subject, we must ask which view is consistent with his general theory or even perhaps whether one of the alternatives is logically entailed by the rest of his epistemology. I think it is fairly easy to see that Kant's *First Critique* theory of synthesis requires him to treat psychology as a science fully as well-grounded as physics, although it is rather difficult to see just how such a view can be made to fit into his already complicated account of the processes of synthesis. Since the subject turns out to be crucially important to a correct interpretation of the *Groundwork,* I shall devote the next few pages to tracing out the lines of the argument, at the risk of offending those readers who have taken up this book in hopes of finding an explication of Kant's ethics rather than of his theory of knowledge.

To see that Kant is committed to psychological determinism, we need only recall that, for him, location at some objective point in time is literally equivalent to being both effect of what preceded and cause of what follows. The synthesizing process whereby an event is assigned an objective time position *is* the process of establishing a succession according to a rule, which is to say, establishing a causal order. Now the thoughts and perceptions of my mind are as much events as are physical movements in space. My perceptions can be dated ("When did that idea pop into your head?" "How long did your glimpse of him last?") and according to physiological psychologists, they have causes and effects. My mental life history is an objective subsequence in the total sequence of natural events. Hence it must, in principle, be possible to find causes for the events in my mind, to establish laws of thoughts *(not* laws of thought, which are something very different), and to predict the occurrence of states of empirical consciousness in just the way that states of physical matter are explained and predicted by physics.

How can we integrate this conception of the empirical self as a causally determined phenomenon into the general theory of the natural world as a conceptual reordering of the contents of subjective consciousness? How, for example, can we maintain the ordinary view of thoughts and perceptions as caused by neurological events, while at the same time holding Kant's Critical theory that physical events, including brain states, are in some sense constructs from those self-same perceptions? How can the contents of subjective consciousness be *both* the material from which the natural world is constructed *and* a subset of the events in that world?

To begin, let us note that perceptions have, as it were, a double nature, or rather can be viewed in two ways: either as contents of consciousness *simpliciter,* or as representations of something other than themselves. Insofar as perceptions are contents of consciousness, they constitute the matter or content of the knowing mind. Insofar as they are representations, on the other hand, they constitute the matter of material objects. According to Kant, the distinction between the two lies not in the content of the perceptions, but in the *manner* in which they are organized. Objects are *ways* of reordering the contents of consciousness. Now the mind has, strictly speaking, no spatial extent. The spatial terms which we employ when we describe perceptions as being "in" the mind or as undergoing a "rearrangement," are metaphors which must be given a literal interpretation. According to Kant, it is *time* which, as the form of inner sense, provides the order of mental contents. Hence, if a manifold of perceptions is worked up into an object by means of a rule-governed reordering, a *temporal* reordering must be involved. For this reason, in the section of the *Critique* entitled Analytic of Principles, Kant interprets the categories as rules for imposing a temporal ordering on a manifold. All twelve categories receive a temporal interpretation, but the main portion of the discussion is contained in the Second Analogy, which treats the category of cause and effect. The category of cause and effect is a general rule-type which dictates that particular concepts of causal influence must have the form of the rule for necessary succession. In other words, when the mind reorders its perceptions, it does so by formulating rules which prescribe that certain perceptions (those of the cause) must precede certain other perceptions (those of the effect). In the famous examples of the house and the moving boat, Kant shows that we make a distinction between the subjective temporal order in which perceptions enter the mind and the objective temporal order of causality which we ascribe to those same perceptions when we reorder them according to the category of causality.

The distinction between the subjective and objective temporal orders of perceptions corresponds to the distinction between perceptions considered as contents of consciousness and as representations of objects. The objectivity, or necessary unity, of perceptions in their representative capacity, it will be recalled, is due to their having been reordered, or synthesized, according to a rule.

In terms of this analysis, we can give a general account of what it means to say that one event causes another. When I say that event A caused event B or that state A of object O caused state B of object O^1, I am asserting that no matter in what temporal order the perceptions of those events and states enter my mind, I must in reorganizing them assign the perceptions of A to a temporally earlier location than the perceptions of B. When we try to apply this analysis to the causal relation between objects and our perceptions of them, however, we encounter trouble, for in order to assert that an object O caused my perception of it, P, I apparently must assign my perception of the object, namely, that same P, to an earlier time than I assign to its effect, which is P again. So I encounter a problem that is characteristic of phenomenalist analyses of objects and the self, namely, that they seem to require something to be viewed as cause of itself and, hence, to occur before itself.

The solution to this puzzle lies in the fact that perceptions actually have a *triple* nature, not a double nature as stated above. Perceptions are, it is true, both contents of consciousness and also representations of external objects; this much Kant recognizes explicitly. But in addition, perceptions are themselves the states of an empirical object, namely, the mind. As such, they have an objective time position *which may be different from the objective time position to which they are assigned as representations of other events.* For example, consider a perception in consciousness which is the sight of smoke rising from a distant chimney. When I synthesize my perceptions, I assign that perception a position in the objective time order which I am constructing, and that position is the objective time of the event itself, that is, the time of the rising of the smoke from the chimney. But since my own mind is one of the empirical objects being constructed by the synthesizing process, I must also assign that perception to an objective time position as a state of my mind. Since light takes a finite time to travel from the object to my eye, the occurrence of the perception in objective time will be slightly later than the occurrence of the event of which it is a perception. That, indeed, is precisely what we mean by saying that the event *causes* the perception. Now, every perception both *represents* an objective event and itself *is* an objective event. Hence, every perception will be assigned to two objective time positions, and, generally speaking, those two positions will be different.

To summarize, the mind is presented in subjective apprehension with a variety of contents of consciousness. The mind now synthesizes this manifold, which means reordering it according to rules. The outcome is a temporal sequence of contents of consciousness in which each element of the original ordering appears *twice*. The new ordering is the objective time order of events, and the number of events is, as it were, twice the number of original perceptions, because each perception both *is* and also *represents* an event. Now the objective time order of states of my mind is identical with the subjective time order of apprehension; hence the new, objective sequence consists of the old sequence interlarded with the same elements rearranged. The only rule is that for any perception, P, its occurrence qua mental event must be later than its occurrence qua representation of an event: for otherwise we would be involved in the false assertion that the sight of the smoke causes the smoke, rather than vice versa.

As an example, consider a manifold of just three perceptions, A, B, and C, all of a boat moving down a stream. A is a view of the boat upstream, B is a view of the boat slightly downstream of A, and C is the sound of the boat's whistle, originating from a point father upstream than either A or B. Since sound travels slower than light, let us suppose that the order in which the perceptions actually occur in consciousness is ABC. The objective order of events which the perceptions represent is CAB. There are, in all, six events which must be assigned objective time positions in the final rearrangement or synthesis, namely, the three positions of the boat and the three mental events of perceiving. The correct ordering might be something like the following, with primes indicating the perceptions qua mental events: $CAA^1BB^1C^1$. That is, first the whistle blows; then the boat gives off light; then I perceive that light; then the boat gives off light again; then I perceive *that* light; and finally I hear the sound of the whistle.

Thus far we have been discussing cases of psychophysical interaction, in particular, cases of perception. But the analysis sketched here can easily be extended to cover all cases of causal interactions between mental events and other events both mental and physical. Nothing in Kant's theory prejudges the question of whether ideas cause ideas or whether ideas can produce changes in the physical world. As Hume argued, there is no way of telling a priori what sorts of events will turn out to be causally related. One point, however, must be very strongly emphasized, for it will later emerge as a key to the interpretation of the argument of the *Groundwork*: ideas are phenomenal causes and effects *only* insofar as they are datable events in the mental history of an empirical self. *The cognitive or intensional import of mental contents plays no role in their phenomenal causality.* For example, there might be a cognitive relation between my idea of some bodily movement and my performance of that movement, but, so far as an empirical science of psychology would be concerned, that intensional relation could have nothing to do with the possible causal connection between the two. To put the point somewhat differently, the science of psychology can make no scientific distinction between rational action and irrational behavior. That, as we shall see, is in Kant's philosophy a distinction which divides the phenomenal from the noumenal, and hence it can play no positive role in a science of the phenomenal.

3. The Structure of Kant's Exposition

One of the sources of the complexity of Kant's exposition is the fact that there are actually three layers of argument which proceed simultaneously. In a manner of speaking, the *Groundwork* is directed at three distinct audiences. Significantly, the same layering of argument can be found in the *Critique of Pure Reason*. In both cases, Kant fails to make entirely clear the demarcations between the layers, with equally confusing consequences for even the alert reader. It is worth comparing the two works for the light that is shed on Kant's general philosophical method.

In the *Critique*, the most superficial layer of argument, directed at what we may consider the least critical audience, begins with the unquestioned assumption that we possess valid a priori knowledge in the form of mathematics and physics. In the *Prolegomena to Any Future Metaphysics* and in certain sections of the Introduction to the *Critique*, Kant says, in effect, to this first audience: "You and I, we know that we possess a priori knowledge, for the manifest success of physics and mathematics proves as much. But we may nevertheless wonder how mathematics and natural science are possible." In reply to this question, Kant offers his theory of categories, forms of intuition, and synthesis. His conclusion is expressed in the form of a hypothetical proposition:

> If we possess valid a priori knowledge, then the theory of categories and forms of sensibility must be correct.

Such a conclusion will presumably satisfy many in his audience who have no serious doubts about the validity of the received science nor any sceptical questions about our everyday experience of the material world. But we may imagine, scattered through the audience, Locke, Berkeley, and others who have called into question precisely the assumption with which Kant begins his first level of argument. To this select and more sophisticated audience, the conclusion stated above is no better than a begging of the question. They wish to know not *how* science and mathematics are possible, but *whether* they are possible.

For these doubters, Kant has a much deeper argument. Again, it is in the form of a conditional proposition (for every argument must have premises), but this time the validity of mathematics and physics is the conclusion, not the premise. The difficulty of the argument makes it somewhat awkward to state the conclusion as a simple conditional, but roughly speaking, Kant's thesis is: "If we do have experience of a world of objects, and if the familiar distinction between subjective apprehension and the independent objective world order is legitimate, then mathematics and physics are valid." The protasis of this conditional is considerably weaker than that of the first proposition, and the argument is correspondingly stronger. There are presumably many people who grant the reality of our experience of the natural world but are not willing simply to assume the validity of mathematics and physics.

But loitering at the fringe of the audience, looking on with amused disdain may be David Hume. His sceptical doubts cut so deep that he can plausibly be read as denying even the reality of our experience of objects and the legitimacy of the distinction between subjective apprehension and the objective world order.

For him, Kant presents his deepest and most powerful argument. Grant merely that you are conscious, Kant says to Hume, and I will endeavor to prove to you the existence of a world order of objects standing in necessary and universal causal connection. Going all the way back to the premise of Descartes's *Meditations,* Kant asserts: If I am conscious, then mathematics and physics are valid.

Now, this most powerful and profound layer of Kant's argument is still conditional, and hence it would seem logically possible for a sufficiently persistent sceptic to deny the premise and, thereby, to deny the conclusion. But the premise has now become the mere assumption that I am conscious! To deny that, as Descartes showed, is to involve oneself in an immediate contradiction. Even Hume must grant that he is conscious, if he is to engage in argument at all. Thus Kant's argument at its very deepest level is a dialectical *ad hominem,* designed to force his opponents either to assent to his conclusions or to remain silent.[7]

We find the same three levels of argument and the same division of the audience when we turn to the *Groundwork of the Metaphysic of Morals.* The great mass of the audience, to whom Kant addresses himself in the first chapter of the *Groundwork,* consists of those good people who know perfectly well what is right and how they ought to act, even though they may not be able to formulate with any precision the principles which guide their decisions. In talking with them, Kant wishes merely to persuade them that they have all along had something like the Categorical Imperative in mind. As in the *Prolegomena,* so in the first chapter of the *Groundwork* Kant's conclusion takes a conditional form:

> If our (this first audience's) ordinary moral convictions are true, then the Moral Law is unconditionally binding upon all rational agents.

As we shall see, this conclusion is a kind of a reconstruction of a body of beliefs, and for those who have no doubts about the truth of those beliefs, it serves the purpose of rationalizing them and ordering them into a system.

---

[7]The conclusion of Kant's argument in the *Critique* is that mathematics and physics have a *conditionally* a priori validity, but that fact has no connection with the conditional form of the argument by which it is established. In the *Groundwork,* Kant's conclusion is that the Moral Law has *unconditionally* a priori validity, but the argument still has a conditional form.

Here, as in the case of the audience of the *Critique*, we may discern doubters scattered among the good, simple North German peasants by whom Kant set such store. But whereas in metaphysics one must contend only with *theoretical* sceptics who doubt the conclusions of science on principle, however incapable they are of actually giving up such beliefs in their daily practice, in morals one must acknowledge the existence of genuine disagreement issuing in concrete differences of behavior and belief. Hume admits that when his theoretical speculations grow tedious, he quits his closet and goes out into a world of objects and causes. But the utilitarian is no closet philosopher; he genuinely believes in and acts on moral principles which Kant insists are wrong. To rebut him, Kant must present a more powerful argument.

In chapter 2 of the *Groundwork*, Kant sets about developing a direct justification of the Moral Law and, thereby, a refutation of all the moral philosophies which, he says, suffer from the flaw of "heteronymy." His argument, supported by the analysis of freedom which is developed in the *Critique* and rehearsed in chapter 3, is that if man's pure reason is capable of moving him to action —if, in the language of the Critical Philosophy, pure reason can be practical—then the one and only valid law of such a motivating reason is the Moral Law. Should his opponents deny that pure reason can be practical, Kant argues, they will find themselves esteeming or condemning actions for which the agents are not responsible. Since it only makes sense to esteem or blame men for actions for which they *are* responsible, the utilitarians and others must either acknowledge the validity of the Moral Law or else cease making moral judgments altogether.

The conclusion here is obviously analogous to the second-level conclusion of the *First Critique* argument. Just as Kant there showed that those who granted the reality of a world of objects must also grant the validity of mathematics and science, so here he shows that those who grant the legitimacy of moral discourse must grant as well the supremacy of the Moral Law.

But here, as there, Kant may encounter a *third* audience, the stubborn sceptic who, faced with the choice, forswears all moral discourse and retreats to a denial of the legitimacy of moral judgment in general. To deal with this denial, Kant needs an even stronger argument. Implicit in his theory of rational willing is the thesis that if man is capable of action at all, if, again in the language of the Critical Philosophy, reason can in any manner be practical, then pure reason must be capable of moving him to act. From this, it follows that the moral law is valid. So against the amoralist, Kant, in effect, argues that if man is capable of action at all, then he is bound by the Categorical Imperative.

Now the total sceptic is pushed to an extreme position. If Kant's argument is right, then he must either grant the validity of the Moral Law or else deny the possibility of any action (that is, rational conduct) at all, *even action of a prudential nature.* But this latter would be a very drastic claim. Indeed, we can even charge anyone who denies that he can *act* with a kind of practical contradiction, for asserting is a species of action. Hence, the assertion that I cannot act provides its own refutation. Dialectically speaking, Kant's most powerful argument is designed to divide the world into two groups: those who grant the truth of his conclusion and those who may not consistently speak at all.

In a sense, Kant's entire theoretical and moral philosophy is a return to the *cogito* of Descartes. In Meditation II, Descartes argued that the one undeniable fact is my ability to make a conscious assertion. From the *conscious* nature of that act, Kant in the *Critique* infers the validity of all theoretical knowledge. From the *active* character of assertion, he infers the validity of the Moral Law in the *Groundwork.* No one can consistently *deny* the possibility of making a conscious assertion, for any such denial *is* a conscious assertion. Hence, if Kant is successful, he has reduced his opponents to silence. It is difficult to imagine what more one could hope to accomplish.

4. A Cautionary Word about Reading Kant

Kant's moral philosophy, like the other parts of his Critical System, poses considerable problems for the contemporary student. The unfamiliar terminology, the outmoded psychological theories, the rigid Germanic moral attitudes, all conspire to give Kant's ethical writings an air of archaic impenetrability. To the student weaned on Hume or Bertrand Russell, Kant is nigh on indigestible. As though these difficulties were not formidable enough, Kant indulges in a practice which is calculated to mislead even the most dedicated reader: he persists in claiming, as logical consequences of his argument, doctrines which are both manifestly false in themselves and *not even implied by his philosophy*. Kant had a number of very strong convictions in the fields of mathematics, physics, and ethics. He confidently believed that his Critical System would, once and for all, certify them as a priori valid. But he repeatedly failed to notice that his philosophical arguments, powerful as they were, did not come close to establishing his pre-philosophical convictions. The effect of this confusion on modern readers is something like this: they begin with the text of, say, the *Critique of Pure Reason*, which they really can't make heads or tails of. Casting about for something they can understand, they come upon Kant's claim that the argument in the text proves the a priori validity of Euclidean mathematics or Newtonian physics. Now, on quite independent and sufficient grounds, the baffled readers are sure that Euclidean geometry is *not* a priori valid. So, converting the conditional, they conclude that Kant's argument must be wrong. They take Kant's word for it that his theory has the implications he claims; who, after all, should know better what an argument entails than the author of the argument himself?

Kant lays this trap again and again. In the Transcendental Aesthetic of the *First Critique*, for example, not a word is said about the axioms of Euclid's system of geometry. Kant merely advances very general considerations designed to show that there must be some mathematics of space or other; then he draws the natural but quite unwarranted conclusion that Euclidean geometry must *be* that mathematics. Since he knew of no other, it never occurred to him to question the leap from "there must be a mathematics of space" to "Euclidean geometry is valid." Any modern reader who is acquainted with the modern development of mathematics will conclude that something (he isn't quite sure what) is wrong with Kant's argument. There is probably not a college course on Kant in which someone doesn't sooner or later say with an air of weary superiority, "Of course the discovery of non-Euclidean geometries proves Kant wrong."

Nowhere does this problem cause more trouble than in the

Groundwork of the Metaphysic of Morals. By the time the reader has worked his way into the midst of the second chapter, he is more than likely totally at a loss. Not only the individual steps of the argument, but even its broad outlines have become obscured from view, and he is as parched for an illustrative example as a desert traveler for water. Suddenly the haze clears, and before him are four lovely clear exemplifications of the Categorical Imperative. It is a rare reader who does not fall upon those famous four examples as the key to interpreting the surrounding text. Instead of asking, "Do these four moral judgments (Don't commit suicide, Be generous, and so on) follow from the Categorical Imperative?" he is liable to ask, "What meaning can we ascribe to the doctrine of universalizability which will make it imply these four conclusions?" The result is some manifestly implausible doctrine, which he rejects out of hand. Worse still, the modern reader, less addicted to certain moral dogmas than Kant's contemporaries, concludes that any principle that entails the absolute wrongness of taking one's own life or of breaking a promise *must* be invalid.

It cannot be too strongly stated that *Kant frequently makes false claims about the implications of his own theories.* Therefore, we can never judge the truth of the theories merely by examining the consequences Kant claims for them. In the *Groundwork,* for instance, we shall find that two of the supposed examples of duties have no legitimate claim at all to be derived from the Categorical Imperative, a third turns out on close examination not to be derivable, and only for the fourth can any real case be made out. Difficult as Kant's argument is, we must try to understand it without benefit of those deceptive illustrations.

An Apology to the Reader

Before beginning my commentary on the text of the *Groundwork*, I should like to say a few words about the awkwardness of the order of my exposition. Kant's thought is so difficult that a commentary must strive before all else for absolute clarity and simplicity of organization. Since I have been unable to comply with that prime exegetical directive, some explanation is owing to the reader.

As I have already indicated, the *Groundwork* contains several layers of doctrine, each of which has its own premises, its own arguments, and its own imagined audience. The version which I have characterized as superficial appears principally in chapter 1, where it is directed at an audience of decent, unsceptical men and women. This first version is by no means simple, but it can be explicated adequately enough without detailed appeal to other portions of the Critical Philosophy and without elaborate philosophical analysis of key concepts and inferences. The deeper version of Kant's doctrine, however, requires commentary of a very different sort. In order to do a satisfactory job of interpreting the eleven pages of chapter 2 in which that argument is set forth, we must go at great length into a number of matters which will carry us very far from the actual text of the *Groundwork*.

Now, in organizing the exposition of my commentary, I have found myself forced to choose between two alternatives, neither of which is truly satisfactory. The first possibility was to place all the philosophical analysis of a nontextual sort in the Introduction. I would then ask the reader to work his way through it "on speculation," as it were, assuring him that it would all be useful when we reached the commentary on chapter 2. This course would permit the actual commentary on the text to flow quickly, without interruption, for at each relevant point I could simply refer back to the appropriate section of the Introduction. But it would place on the reader a double burden which seemed to me well-nigh intolerable. First he would have to read a great deal of philosophical argument without any clear idea how it was going to help him to understand the *Groundwork* (and there is already too much material of that sort in the Introduction). Then he would have to try to recall it to mind when he reached the commentary on chapter 2. The net result of such a mode of exposition could only be confusion twice compounded.

The second possibility, which I have chosen, is to defer the supplementary philosophical analysis until we arrive at that portion of chapter 2 where it is actually needed. So, after a brief commentary on the Preface and a longer but relatively straightforward exegesis of chapter 1, you will come upon a long, complex, many-sided discussion of the first third of chapter 2. The exegesis, in effect, comes to a dead halt, while a variety of matters are gone into. After I have disassembled, clarified, reorganized, and reassembled Kant's theory to the best of my ability, I pick up the thread of the exegesis and continue on to the end of chapter 2. The result, I am afraid, is a commentary whose shape somewhat resembles Antoine de Saint-Exupéry's picture in *Le Petit Prince*, of a boa constrictor digesting an elephant.

As the picture suggests, the boa found the elephant a trifle indigestible. I sincerely hope the reader will not suffer the same problem with my treatment of chapter 2.

The Structure of the Argument
of the *Groundwork*

Although the *Groundwork* is a baffling and elusive work, the underlying structure of its argument is actually quite simple. The major sources of obscurity are two in number: first, Kant shifts from a regressive or explicative to a progressive or synthetic mode of argument, thereby leaving the reader somewhat in doubt at each point as to what has been proved and what is merely being assumed; and, second, the argument as a whole is less than totally conclusive because of the impossibility, already demonstrated in the *First Critique,* of having theoretical knowledge of things in themselves. Nevertheless, it is possible to indicate quite succinctly the line along which Kant develops his argument.

In the first chapter Kant proceeds regressively, beginning with the assumption that our ordinary moral convictions are correct and seeking in them the organizing principle or highest standard which we implicitly invoke when we make moral judgments. No attempt is made to *prove* the conclusions to which Kant comes, if by that is meant a demonstration of the validity of the principle from some higher and more certain premises. Although Kant's analysis of ordinary moral consciousness is quite profound, at least in my opinion, it is entirely open to a reader to deny that he shares the convictions cited by Kant and hence to reject the analysis as in any way a reconstruction of *his* moral opinions. The central purpose of the section is to formulate a series of propositions about duties and obligations, culminating in the statement of the Categorical Imperative, which Kant hopes to demonstrate as universally and unconditionally valid for all rational creatures: *"Act only on that maxim through which you can at the same time will that it should become a universal law."*[1]

[1] I give the formulation which appears at Ak. 421 in the second chapter, rather

In the second chapter Kant begins again, this time with the concept of a will. His aim is to establish, through a series of conceptual analyses, the hypothetical proposition that *if* man is capable of being determined to action by reason, *then* he stands under the absolute and unconditional obligation to conform his action to the moral principle enunciated provisionally at the end of chapter 1. Using the label "Moral Law" to refer to that principle, we can rephrase this hypothetical judgment thus: If man is capable of being moved by reason alone, then he stands under the Moral Law. Strictly speaking, Kant completes his argument for this conclusion in the first third of the chapter (by Ak. 421), although a number of later passages, including some in chapter 3, are useful as additions to and clarifications of the basic argument. The remainder of the chapter is devoted to the elaboration of a number of alternative formulations of the Moral Law, which Kant claims are analytically derivable from the first and fundamental formulation, as well as to discussion of a number of related topics. Included in the supplementary portion of chapter 2 are the famous four examples of the Categorical Imperative.

Obviously, one would like the third chapter to prove the protasis of the conditional proposition demonstrated in chapter 2: Man is capable of being moved by reason alone. Combining the conclusions of chapters 2 and 3, it would then be possible for Kant to assert categorically: Man stands under the Moral Law. Unfortunately, it turns out to be impossible to prove that man is capable of being moved by reason alone, for that is equivalent to proving that his acts are determined independently of phenomenal causes. Since the *Critique of Pure Reason* has already established the conclusion that every event in the phenomenal world, including human behavior, is completely determined by universal and necessary laws, man could only be moved by reason insofar as he is a noumenal agent, or self-in-itself. Consequently, Kant must settle in the third chapter for a pair of propositions which, taken together, are weaker than the protasis of the conditional proved

than as it is first stated at Ak. 402 in the first chapter. The earlier formulation is not couched in the imperative mood, but I do not think there is any significant difference between them.

in chapter 2. Drawing on the famous resolution of the antinomy of freedom and determinism in the *First Critique* and on the analysis of action and obligation in chapters 1 and 2 of the *Groundwork,* Kant proves the following propositions: First, there is no logical contradiction between the principle of phenomenal determinism and the assertion that man is capable of being moved by reason, and second, a rational agent must assume that he can be moved by reason if he is to act at all.

In summary, the structure of the *Groundwork* can be represented as follows, where P=Man stands under the Moral Law and Q=Man is capable of being moved by reason.

Chapter 1: We all actually believe that P.

Chapter 2: If Q then P.

Chapter 3: It is logically possible that Q,

and

we must assume that Q if we are to act at all.

Commentary
on the
Groundwork

Preface

The Preface of the *Groundwork* is only fourteen paragraphs in length. It raises no major philosophical issues and poses no serious problems of interpretation. Nevertheless, it is worth a few pages of exegesis, for by glossing Kant's introductory remarks we can conveniently sketch the central problem of the work and indicate a few of the difficulties which lie in store for us.

The text divides naturally into three sections. The opening five paragraphs define the place which ethics occupies in the total system of man's knowledge of himself and the world. Kant draws on an ancient Greek division of all learning into logic, physics, and ethics, which actually represents his own philosophical position better than the elaborate architectonic classifications with which he usually opens his philosophical arguments. Paragraphs 6–10 explain the general enterprise of what Kant calls a "metaphysic of morals," which is to say a demonstration of the principles forming the a priori part of ethics. Paragraphs 11–14 conclude with Kant's justification for writing this preliminary *Groundwork of the Metaphysic of Morals* rather than launching directly into the Metaphysic of Morals proper.[1]

---

[1]The *Groundwork* was published in 1785. *The Critique of Practical Reason* appeared three years later in 1788, and the book which eventually bore the actual title *Metaphysics of Morals* was not published until 1797, when Kant was seventy-three years old.

Some of Kant's remarks in the second and third sections of the Preface reveal a deep and potentially serious confusion about the relationship between the empirical and the a priori portions of ethics, and I shall have something to say on that subject presently. Most of our attention, however, should be directed to the opening paragraphs, in which Kant defines the proper place and subject matter of ethics.

1. The Place of Ethics in the Critical Philosophy (Ak. 387–388)

According to Kant, all cognition of whatever sort involves two elements. There is first an object which is in some way presented to the mind, and there is then a thought directed to it. Kant describes the given object as the *matter* of cognition, and the thought directed to the object as the *form*. This description, he thinks, is perfectly general. It applies to mathematical cognition (in which the mind constructs its own object), to scientific cognition (in which the object is presented through the affection of our sensibility), and even to practical cognition, or moral judgment (in which, as we shall see, the notion of an "object" of cognition takes on a somewhat different meaning).

In the light of this general characterization of cognition, we might suppose that there would be three possible kinds of knowledge: First, knowledge which concerns itself solely with the form of thought without attention to the matter or object of thought, second, knowledge which concerns itself with thought in its application to some object, and finally, knowledge which concerns the matter of cognition without reference to or attention to the form. The first sort of knowledge does indeed exist, according to Kant. It is logic, and its subject is the laws of thought in general. The second sort of cognition also exists. It has two branches: theoretical knowledge, or what the Greeks called physics, and practical knowledge, or ethics. But there is, Kant tells us, no knowledge of the third sort, nor could there be. Since all knowledge is expressed in judgments, it is impossible to abstract from the judgmental form of knowledge and attend purely to its material content. In modern jargon, Kant's position is that there can be no sense-datum reports, no knowledge of the pure given. (The asymmetry of the relation of form to matter in cognition reflects the rationalist presuppositions which persist in Kant's philosophy even after his conversion to the distinctively "critical" standpoint. The same asymmetry, of course, is to be found in any philosophy which grounds its analysis of knowledge or the universe in a form-matter distinction.)

In the second category of knowledge, Kant distinguishes the two major branches—theoretical cognition and practical cognition—according to the aim of the cognitive activity. If our purpose in thinking about the object is to find out what it is and what is true about it, then our cognition is theoretical. Under this heading fall the sciences, both theoretical and descriptive, and also the variety of our ordinary knowledge of the world around us. If our aim, on the other hand, is to bring the object of our thought into existence, to "make it actual," then our cognition is practical. Any act of thought which is purposive, directive of action, prescriptive in any of the modes in which we may prescribe, falls under this second heading. Kant draws the distinction between theoretical and practical cognition in the Preface to the second edition of the *Critique of Pure Reason* in the following way:

> Now if reason is to be a factor in these sciences, something in them must be known *a priori*, and this knowledge may be related to its object in one or other of two ways, either as merely *determining* it and its concept (which must be supplied from elsewhere) or as also *making it actual*. The former is *theoretical*, the latter *practical* knowledge of reason.

Material knowledge, which is to say knowledge of objects rather than merely of the form of thought, may yet have a formal part concerned with what can be known independently of the objects to which it is directed. To such knowledge, whether theoretical or practical, Kant attaches the adjective "pure." His concern throughout the Critical Philosophy is thus with "pure cognition" in all its varieties and modes.

Now logic is possible as a pure or formal discipline precisely because it abstracts from the objects of thought and restricts itself to explicating the laws of any correct thinking in general. Its power, as Kant several times points out, is precisely proportional to its emptiness. But on first examination it is not at all clear how material philosophy—physics and ethics—could ever discover substantive truths which are also "pure," for insofar as they make nontrivial assertions about their objects, it would seem that they must depend for their evidential ground on some experience of those objects. We might say, therefore, that Kant's entire philosophy is an attempt to analyze and justify the formal portions of physics and ethics. The *Critique of Pure Reason* deals with the former, and the *Groundwork*, together with the *Critique of Practical Reason*, deals with the latter.

The formal or conceptual element in cognition, since it originates in the mind's own activity, can be called a priori, in the sense that is is independent of and, hence, logically prior to its object.[2]

In the search for a priori cognition, we must distinguish three senses in which the term "a priori" may be predicated of knowing.

[2]As I pointed out in my book *Kant's Theory of Mental Activity* (Cambridge, Mass.: Harvard University Press, 1963), p. 113*n*, students of the Critical Philosophy are sometimes not entirely clear about the pair of distinctions analytic-synthetic and a priori–a posteriori. "Analytic" and "synthetic" are adjectives which modify "judgment" or "proposition." They divide the class of propositions exhaustively and exclusively. According to Kant, it is at least in principle possible to determine whether a proposition is analytic or synthetic by inspection and analysis of the component concepts. "A priori" and "a posteriori" are adverbs which modify such verbs as "to know." They define the two ways in which a proposition can be known: independently of experience of the object of the judgment or not independently. There is no such thing, strictly speaking, as an a priori judgment, and Kant never, to my knowledge, writes "synthetic a priori judgment." He always writes "synthetic judgment a priori," which is elliptical for "synthetic judgment known a priori." Hence it is not possible to determine whether a judgment "is a priori," that is, can be known a priori, merely by inspecting the judgment. Such a determination requires an epistemological inquiry into the nature of the grounds for the judgment and the evidential relation between those grounds and the assertion of the judgment, an inquiry of the sort carried out in the *First Critique*. Kant's problem is not whether there are any synthetic a priori judgments, but whether there are any synthetic judgments which can be known a priori. He phrases the problem more felicitously in his 1772 letter to Marcus Herz when he asks, "How the understanding can . . . formulate . . . principles which are independent of experience, but with which experience must exactly conform." (Translated in N. Kemp Smith, *A Commentary to Kant's "Critique of Pure Reason,"* 2d. ed. [New York: The Humanities Press, 1923], p. 220.)

This three-fold division applies both to theoretical and to practical cognition. In the case of theoretical cognition:

1. If a cognition is logically prior merely to certain particular instances to which it is applied, as in the case of a scientific law known prior to some of its instances but ultimately based on experience, then we may call it *relatively* a priori.
2. If a cognition is logically independent of every particular instance of it and even of all evidence or experience so that its validity is relative only to the general conditions under which objects can be presented to the mind, then we may call it *conditionally* a priori.
3. If a cognition is completely independent of particular experiences and even independent of the conditions under which something can be an object for our minds, then we may call it *unconditionally* a priori.

Kant's concern and ours is not with cognition of the first sort—*relatively* a priori cognition. All the knowledge whose a priori validity Kant demonstrates in the *Critique of Pure Reason* comes under the second heading, the *conditionally* a priori. For example, the law of causality, according to which every thing which happens follows upon something preceding it according to a rule, is valid for all objects of experience. It can be known to apply necessarily to all experience (and known a priori so to apply) just because it states one of the conditions under which anything can be brought to consciousness as an object of cognition *for me*. As Kant puts it in the Introduction to the *Critique*, the conditions of experiencing anything as an object of knowledge serve as the bridge which connects the terms of the synthetic judgment expressing the causal maxim. Since the human mind is such that objects can be objects for me only insofar as they exhibit the connection asserted in the causal maxim, I can be certain a priori that *for me* the judgment will be universally valid of all objects.

So far as cognition of the third sort is concerned, Kant's conclusion in the *Critique* is entirely negative. Save for the assertion of analytic judgments, all attempts to acquire *unconditionally* a priori knowledge lead to contradictions and confusions. In terms of this three-fold division of theoretical judgments known a priori, we can summarize Kant's view as follows: All *relatively* a priori cognition rests on a system of *conditionally* a priori cognition, and no substantive *unconditionally* a priori cognition is possible. To put the point somewhat differently, science rests upon a metaphysics of experience, and transcendent metaphysics is impossible.

When we turn to practical cognition, an analogous division of a priori judgments appears, with differences resulting from the different character of practical judgments.

All cognition has some object, Kant holds. In the case of practical judgments, to what does the term "object" refer? Since the practical employment of reason is its use as a guide to action, the object of our thought is not some existing thing whose nature we seek to determine, but rather the end or goal we are attempting to bring into being through our action.

As Lewis White Beck explains with characteristic lucidity in his Commentary on the *Critique of Practical Reason:*

> An object of practical reason is an effect possible through freedom. . . . "Object" must be taken in a sufficiently broad sense to cover two things: states of affairs produced by action and action itself. It must not be thought that "object" means only a thing in the world created by action. . . .
> The concept of the object of practical reason is the object's representation regarded as an efficient cause of the action that is to produce the object. Object of practical reason and purpose of the will are thus identical.[3]

The distinctive feature of rational action is that its cause is a representation of its end, or, as Aristotle would have said, its efficient and final causes are identical in form.

Theoretical cognition tells me what the objects of my *thoughts* are. In other words, it tells me what the world *is*. Practical cognition tells me what the objects of my *actions* are. In other words, it tells me what the world *ought to be*. Theoretical cognition is expressed in the form of descriptions; practical cognition finds

[3]Lewis W. Beck, *A Commentary on Kant's "Critique of Practical Reason"* (Chicago: University of Chicago Press, 1960), pp. 129–130. My experience is that Beck is always the clearest and the most helpful of the commentators on Kant's ethics. Even when I depart very considerably from his reading, I am conscious of having learned from him.

expression in injunctions or imperatives.[4]

We can now distinguish practical judgments which are asserted with *relatively* a priori, *conditionally* a priori, or *unconditionally* a priori validity.

1. A *relatively* a priori practical judgment takes the form of a conditional command. It commands me, on condition that I actually take some particular end as my end, to do a certain sort of action which is calculated to achieve that end. It commands this independently of the instance actually before me but, of course, not independently of the general knowledge of causes and effects presupposed by the judgment nor independently of the end being an end for me. Kant calls relatively a priori practical judgments Rules of Skill.

2. A *conditionally* a priori practical judgment is also a conditional command, but it posits as an end something that, as a human being, I cannot help but seek, namely, happiness. Kant believed it to be a fact that all men pursue happiness, and, contrary to the popular view of his moral philosophy, he thought it right that they do so. Because of the peculiar nature of happiness as an end, Counsels of Prudence, as conditionally a priori practical judgments are called, do not take the form of simple commands to adopt specific means in pursuit of posited ends. Rather, they have more the character of homilies or adages. Nevertheless, in logical form they are identical with Rules of Skill.

3. An *unconditionally* a priori practical judgment would be a command which did not rely for its validity upon the condition that the agent adopt certain ends as his own. Such a judgment would command absolutely, and, hence,

---

[4]We shall have a good deal to say later on about imperatives. At this point, it might just be helpful to note that even so-called hypothetical imperatives are expressed in the imperative rather than the declarative mood. For example, a practical judgment directing my efforts to obtain shelter would be, "Desiring shelter as you do, build a lean-to!" not "If you wish to obtain shelter, the best way in the situation is to build a lean-to." The latter judgment is a product of theoretical reason. It is relatively a priori, and states a fact about the world. Needless to say, it is the basis of the practical injunction.

if it were binding on any rational agent, it would be binding on all rational agents. Kant calls such judgments Moral Laws.

It is easy enough to see how Kant could have developed a moral philosophy along lines strictly parallel to those of his theoretical philosophy. Just as the *Critique of Pure Reason* demonstrates the validity of a system of conditionally a priori theoretical judgments which depend for their truth on their limitation to conditioned human experience, so in a *Critique of Practical Reason* or a *Metaphysic of Morals* Kant could have elaborated a system of conditionally a priori practical judgments which would depend for their truth on their limitation to the conditions of human willing. Taking the affective, purposive character of the human personality as given, Kant might have discovered some sort of proof that all men seek a rationally integrated harmony of affective satisfactions (that is, happiness). Then he could have derived some very general propositions, valid for all human beings, concerning the best way to achieve that goal. In short, Kant could have written an eighteenth-century version of the *Nichomachean Ethics*.

But while Kant was prepared to accept conditional a priori validity in the realm of theoretical philosophy, insisting indeed that anything more was dialectical illusion, he rejected out of hand the attempt to exalt Counsels of Prudence to the status of Moral Laws. To Kant, the philosophy of eudaimonism and all its variants, including even the philosophy of self-perfection, was the epitome of moral confusion. Morality must either issue in unconditionally a priori judgments or else quit the field all together. The task of moral philosophy could only be to explain how unconditionally a priori practical judgments were possible, to discover their proper formulation, and then to demonstrate their validity. In short, moral philosophy must be like Logic in its universal and absolutely unconditional validity.

The manifest difficulty of this enterprise, which proved impossible in the realm of theoretical philosophy, accounts for the genuine philosophical difficulty of Kant's writings on moral philosophy. In order for reason to be *unconditionally* practical, it must issue judgments (laws) which abstract from all matter (ends) and yet are not merely analytic. The analogue in theoretical philosophy would be universally valid judgments, known a priori, which asserted synthetic connections among concepts. Since it appears on first consideration impossible to discover judgments which combine the certainty of Logic and the significance of Science, Kant has the obligation of showing us that morality really does demand such judgments. This, as we shall see, he attempts in the first chapter.

2. The Relation of the Formal to the Material Elements in Ethics (Ak. 388–392)

". . . the whole of moral philosophy is based entirely
on the part of it that is pure. . . ." (Ak. 389)

As I have already indicated, Kant's discussion in paragraphs 6–14 does not call for much in the way of comment. A good deal of it is occasioned by his need to explain why he is presenting this *Groundwork of the Metaphysic of Morals* rather than the expected *Critique of Practical Reason*. At one point, however, Kant offers a rationale for writing a Metaphysic of Morals which reveals a very deep confusion lying at the heart of the Critical Philosophy. Since this confusion, concerning the relation between the formal and the material elements in cognition, runs all through the *Groundwork,* this is a good place to make some general remarks about it.

In the realm of theoretical cognition the problem of the formal and the material arises in connection with the role of sense perception in science. Superficially, Kant is quite clear and unambiguous: All scientific knowledge has a formal or conceptual component provided by the mind itself (the Categories) and a material or perceptual component given to the mind through sensibility (the manifold of empirical intuition). Against the rationalists, who sought to reduce all cognition to conception, and the empiricists, who attempted a reverse reduction of cognition to perception, Kant asserts his famous principle: "Thoughts without content are empty, intuitions without concepts are blind" (A51 = B75).

On closer examination, however, Kant's position becomes quite unclear. His language naturally suggests to the modern reader some sort of cooperation between general principles (perhaps, like the causal maxim, of a methodological nature) and experimental evidence. In the *Metaphysical Foundations of Natural Science* (1786), Kant offers his version of the "material" part of the metaphysics of nature. It turns out to be a collection of theorems in Newtonian physics ostensibly derived from the *First Critique* System of Principles of the Pure Understanding by means of the addition to the *Critique* of a single empirical concept—the concept of *matter* (Ak. iv, 476–477). Disciplines based upon observation and the accumulation of data, such as chemistry, Kant says, do not deserve the title of science (Ak. iv, 468). Nowhere in the Critical writings do we get a satisfactory account of the relationship between concepts and perceptions, between the formal and the material, the a priori and the a posteriori.

The problem is compounded in the ethical theory. As we have seen, Kant clings to the formal-material distinction which he employed so extensively in the *First Critique*, but he will not permit a merely *conditionally* a priori status for the principles of ethics. Hence, he must alter his conception of the relationship between the *formal principles* and the *objects* of practical cognition. He has a choice between two alternatives. *Either* he must show that we can, from some independent source, deduce objects, or *ends*, of practical reason which are *unconditional* so that all rational agents are objectively obliged to choose them (unlike happiness, which is an end only for creatures constituted as we men are); *or else* he must show that the objects, or ends, of practical reason can be deduced from the purely formal principle of practical reason. In short, either there are obligatory ends of conduct, or else the Categorical Imperative is a sufficient as well as a necessary criterion of the rightness of our maxims of action.

Kant chooses *both* alternatives! In the *Groundwork* and again in the *Metaphysic of Morals*, he offers a theory of obligatory ends designed to complement the Categorical Imperative, just as the concept of matter in the *Metaphysical Foundations of Natural Science* complements the system of Principles of the *Critique of Pure Reason*. But at the same time in the elaboration of the several formulations of the Categorical Imperative, Kant tries to derive a theory of obligatory ends ("Man as an end in himself") directly from the purely formal moral law.

The theory of obligatory ends in the *Metaphysic of Morals* is so feeble and ad hoc an affair that it has long since sunk into well-deserved obscurity. Kant introduces the notion in the Introduction to the second half of the *Metaphysic of Morals*. After arguing that there must be some obligatory ends or other if we are to be said to have duties at all (an argument which cuts two ways, of course), Kant poses the question: "What are the ends which are at the same time duties?" (Ak. vi, 385). He replies, "they are these: one's own perfection and the happiness of others." Kant appears not to have thought it necessary to offer any argument for this conclusion, and so we are left to imagine that he merely consulted a faculty of rational intuition or perhaps asked one of the good, simple peasants of north Germany.

There follow in characteristic fashion all the old prohibitions—against suicide, self-mutilation, sexual self-abuse, lying, avarice, servility, pride, intemperance—and the familiar virtues—beneficence, gratitude, sympathy, friendship. The details are brilliantly complex, as we would expect from Kant. But the whole has an air of one of those meticulous stories of space travel, complete in every particular, which begin, "Lothar pushed the ship into hyperdrive, and it sped forward faster than the speed of light. . . ." The story is fascinating, so long as one does not balk at the initial impossibility. Kant can offer no grounds for attributing unconditional obligatoriness to *any* set of independent ends, and the entire *Metaphysic of Morals* must therefore be set aside as a mere exercise in hypothetical possibilities.

Nor are there adequate grounds for the second alternative open to Kant, namely, the derivation of the obligatory ends from the highest principle of morality itself. On the face of it, deducing substantive obligatory ends from the purely formal Categorical Imperative seems as impossible as deducing substantive empirical propositions from the law of contradiction. And in this case appearances are *not* deceiving. The Categorical Imperative defines the *necessary conditions* for the unconditional validity of our principles of action. Like the law of contradiction, therefore, it can be used to *rule out* those maxims, or subjective principles, which are in a sense yet to be explicated, inconsistent. But there is no legitimate way to deduce from the Categorical Imperative those maxims which are to be *ruled in* as objectively binding substantive moral principles.

Kant fatally obscures this limited power of the Categorical Imperative first by the examples which he offers as supposed applications of it and then by his very moving presentation of the notion of man as an end-in-himself. The fact is that only one of the four examples can genuinely be construed as an application of the Categorical Imperative, and the formula of man as an end-in-himself, although clearly expressive of a profound and important moral insight, can in no sense be derived from the Categorical Imperative in its first, canonical formulation.

It is easy enough to see what sort of trouble Kant has created in the exposition of his moral philosophy by his persistent and conflicting attempts to introduce the notion of objective or obligatory ends. As we proceed through the *Groundwork*, particularly chapter 2, I shall call attention to such confusion on several occasions. But there is a problem much larger than mere expositional incoherence that we must at least take notice of. If the Categorical Imperative is a purely formal principle, a negative or merely necessary criterion of the bindingness of moral principles, and if no sufficient criterion of the right ends of action can be derived either from some independent source or from the Categorical Imperative itself, then what becomes of Kant's claim to have established ethics on an a priori and unconditional foundation? Is the entire enterprise simply a failure? In my opening remarks on styles of philosophical commentary, I defended textual commentary of the sort presented here on the grounds that it offered a reasonable hope of advancing our understanding of some important philosophical problem. But it would now appear that we can expect only negative results. Why go on with the commentary?

I have reserved for my concluding chapter a fuller answer to this perfectly legitimate question, but I must make some reply here if I am to keep you with me through the remainder of this book. Briefly then, I am persuaded that major portions of Kant's moral philosophy are fundamentally true, *even though his claims for it are quite false.* The Categorical Imperative is the unconditionally valid formal principle of reason in its practical employment. Insofar as we undertake to *act,* we are bound by its strictures, just as we are bound by the strictures of the law of contradiction insofar as we undertake to *judge.* But the Categorical Imperative does not command any particular, substantive principle of action, any more than the law of contradiction entails any particular, substantive empirical judgments.

What is more, and I give voice here to moral convictions of my own which I shall try to justify in a subsequent work, *there are no* substantive principles of action which are objectively binding on all rational agents. Substantive obligations can arise only from free acts of commitment by which groups of rational agents collectively bind one another to a set of principles of action. In thus commiting themselves and in the carrying out of their commitments, men are bound by the dictates of reason to conform to the formal requirements of the Categorical Imperative. But this constraint does not rule out collectively agreed upon practices involving, for example, competition or mutual hostility or even killing. What makes murder wrong is not that it is an instance of killing, but that it is an instance of killing someone who has not accepted a practice of mutual hostility and could not reasonably be expected to accept it if offered a chance to choose. Where such a practice has been tacitly or explicitly agreed upon, as in the case of dueling, then there is nothing at all immoral about killing.

In short, Kant fails to discover an a priori ground for substantive moral principles because there is no such ground. Here, as elsewhere, he does better than he says. Despite the confused and contradictory claims which he makes for the Categorical Imperative, it remains a valid but purely negative criterion of the formal correctness of principles of action. Kant's distinctive contribution in the *Groundwork* is to show us how to derive the Categorical Imperative from an analysis of rational agency itself. If that seems a meager result for so great an effort, we might reflect that he was the first philosopher even to understand the need for such a derivation, as well as the philosopher who achieved it.

chapter one

Passage from Ordinary
Rational Knowledge of Morality
to Philosophical

1. The Rational Reconstruction
of Ordinary Moral Beliefs

The discussion of chapter 1 is entirely explicative or regressive in
logical form.[1] Kant assumes that he and his readers are in agreement about what sorts of things are good or bad, right or wrong.
His aim is to show that our ordinary moral judgments implicitly
presuppose a very general and abstract moral principle, whose
validity he will later try to prove. Hence his argument is by example, and his final appeal is to the convictions of his readers. Kant
quite clearly understands that such a mode of discussion proves
nothing to the sceptic, but he thinks, nevertheless, that it is a good
way to begin an examination of moral philosophy. Before embark-
ing upon an analysis of the text, it might be worthwhile to say a
few words about this sort of enterprise. Following the terminology
of twentieth-century phenomenalists, I propose to label the contents of chapter 1 a *rational reconstruction of ordinary moral
consciousness.*[2]

---

[1]For an explanation of the distinction between explicative and ampliative, or
regressive and progressive, exposition, see *Prolegomena* and also my *Kant's Theory
of Mental Activity* (Cambridge, Mass: Harvard University Press, 1963), pp. 44–56.
[2]For an account of a somewhat similar notion, see John Rawls, *A Theory of Justice*

The aim of a rational reconstruction of a body of beliefs is to reorganize them into a system which reveals their logical interdependence and, if possible, their derivability from some small set of very general premises. The reconstruction proceeds by a sort of shuttling back and forth between provisional formulations of the premises and testings of them against particular cases. In the case of a reconstruction of moral beliefs, we begin with some strongly held convictions, such as that it is wrong to inflict needless suffering or that one should be honest and keep one's promises. Then a stab is made at a general principle from which these convictions can be derived. The principle is tested by inferring new particular moral judgments from it and then asking whether they, too, accord with our presystematic convictions. As we draw more and more beliefs into the system, the accuracy and scope of reconstruction increases. Eventually, the whole spectrum of moral convictions is exhibited as the systematic application of a set of principles which are then proclaimed the fundamental axioms of our morality.

Although a rational reconstruction takes our presystematic convictions as its ultimate evidential base, there may, nevertheless, be a certain amount of rectification and revision in our moral judgment as a consequence of the process of systematization. At the very least, we may become aware of inconsistencies among strongly held beliefs, and the attempt to eliminate this irrationality will inevitably result in the giving up of some convictions which were previously thought to be inviolable. For example, a man who simultaneously holds to the moral equality of all men and also to the legitimacy of a system of slavery may find himself hard put to defend both convictions when they are brought forward clearly and laid side by side.

More generally, rational reconstruction may produce a broadening and sophistication of moral outlook. Prejudice all too often masquerades as conviction, and the effort of restating our beliefs in a general form can have the effect of separating true commit-

---

(Cambridge, Mass.: Harvard University Press, 1971), on "reflective equilibrium." Rawls considers the process to confer some measure of validity on the principles arrived at. I do not.

ment from parochial bias. Thus, the dedicated advocate of personal liberty who nevertheless feels himself offended by nonconforming young people may be forced to give up this prejudice when he fails to find a justification for it that will comport with his higher beliefs.

There are two very different sorts of rational reconstruction, which we may label "real" and "virtual." A *real rational reconstruction* seeks to uncover the principles which actually, though perhaps unconsciously, guide our moral judgment. It proceeds on the assumption that such principles must exist, and that when we find them we will recognize them as *more certainly true* than the particular judgments in which they find application. The ultimate aim of a real rational reconstruction is an independent proof of the basic principles, from which we can then descend once more to particulars but with vastly greater assurance and understanding.

A *virtual rational reconstruction,* on the other hand, proceeds *as though* our moral judging involved appeal to underlying principles, but it does not assume that such an appeal actually takes place. What it seeks is merely a way of organizing the variety of particular convictions by exhibiting them as virtually or apparently the applications of higher principles. A virtual rational reconstruction forswears any hope of producing an independent proof of the principles it discovers, and hence, logically, it remains entirely dependent upon the presumed correctness of the presystematic beliefs.

A real rational reconstruction gives insight into the reasons for the presystematic beliefs, while a virtual rational reconstruction merely achieves a useful systematization. For example, a utilitarian might undertake to show that all of our beliefs actually can be brought under the principle of the greatest happiness for the greatest number. If he seeks a real reconstruction of moral belief, he will then attempt to justify the greatest happiness principle in order to lay a firm foundation for our ordinary convictions. This will enable him to infer new conclusions from his principle, some of which may even be directly contrary to our original beliefs. He may, for example, try to show, as Mill did, that retributive punishment has no rational foundation in morality or that complete liberty of thought and expression should be guaranteed because of the good results it brings rather than because of any supposed natural law.

A utilitarian who advanced his greatest happiness principle as a merely virtual reconstruction, on the other hand, would never be justified in drawing from it conclusions which flew in the face of presystematic conviction. If he came upon a strongly held belief, such as the retributive view of punishment, he would have to alter his reconstruction to fit the belief, rather than the belief to fit his principle.

Kant in chapter 1 of the *Groundwork* is engaged in a *real rational reconstruction* of the ordinary moral beliefs of himself and his first, most superficial audience. He clearly thinks that the Moral Law in some way lies implicit in our moral consciousness and that when even the simple, good man makes moral judgments, he appeals to it in some manner. Thus, after finally stating the Moral Law, Kant writes: "ordinary human reason ... admittedly does not conceive [this principle] thus abstractly in its universal form; but it does always have it actually before its eyes and does use it as a norm of judgment" (Ak. 403). Furthermore, Kant's purpose in eliciting the Moral Law from our beliefs is to prepare the way for an independent justification of it. For that reason, he need not despair of convincing those readers whose initial moral convictions differ widely from his own. The arguments of chapters 2 and 3, he hopes, will bring them around or at least reduce them to so unsatisfactory a position that they no longer can defend a genuine alternative to the moral philosophy Kant espouses.

2. The Structure of Chapter 1

Chapter 1 consists of twenty-two paragraphs. The discussion proceeds quite straightforwardly in four stages:

    1. Paragraphs 1–7 (Ak. 393–396). Kant opens with the statement that a good will is the only thing that is good without

qualification. In the next four pages he defends this claim or, rather, defends the assertion that all of us already believe it. He also takes the opportunity to fire some passing shots at the competing philosophies of self-realization and utilitarianism.

2. Paragraphs 8–16 (Ak. 397–401). The concept of a good will leads Kant into a discussion of the concept of duty. After a lengthy distinction between action *from* duty and action *according to* duty, he formulates and defends three propositions about duty and the moral worth of human actions.

3. Paragraphs 17–19 (Ak. 401–403). The outcome of the discussion of duty is a formal statement and explanation of the Moral Law or Categorical Imperative, which makes its first appearance at Ak. 402.

4. Paragraphs 20–22 (Ak. 403–405). Kant closes with an explanation of the need for a theoretical defense of the Categorical Imperative, a principle supposedly so well-known and widely acknowledged.

The entire section is barely 6,000 words long, but Kant manages to introduce in it a number of the central notions of his moral philosophy.

3. Paragraphs 1–7 (Ak. 393–396):
The Unqualified Goodness
of the Good Will

"It is impossible to conceive anything at all in the world, or even out of it, which can be taken as good without qualification, except a *good will*."

With this flat assertion, Kant begins his discussion of moral philosophy. It is noteworthy that the philosopher most completely identified with the doctrine of stern duty should begin, not with a statement about what we ought to do, but rather with a judgment of what is unqualifiedly *good.*

At the outset, Kant assumes that we are all able to make a distinction between the various "pro-attitudes" of admiration, love, desire, or appreciation which we adopt from time to time toward objects or persons and the specifically moral attitude of esteem or *moral approval.* He assumes also that we can distinguish between conditional approval, of the sort we give to things which are good in certain circumstances or good under certain conditions, and the unconditional approval we accord to the one thing which is always and everywhere deserving of esteem—a good will.

There are many qualities which excite our admiration, envy, desire, or love. Physical beauty, technical virtuosity, the tasteful display of great wealth, all draw us naturally to them. But although we may admire a handsome man, we do not imagine him to be worthy of moral esteem for being handsome. Nor do we consider a skillful craftsman to be deserving of moral approbation merely in virtue of his expertise. To someone who might question these judgments, we can offer thought experiments designed to show him that he really does agree with us. For example, would anyone think a skillful torturer deserving of our esteem because of his deftness with the rack?[3]

The Renaissance was the age that elevated to a principle the confusion between aesthetic admiration and moral approval, if Burckhardt is to be believed. In his book *The Civilization of the Renaissance in Italy,* he offers us a portrait of the renaissance man, accomplished, confident, idiosyncratic, aristocratic, possessed of that variety of skills and talents which, properly integrated, constitutes what Machiavelli called *virtù.* Toward such a man we may

[3]It must be remembered that we are not *arguing for* the moral judgments invoked here but rather are appealing to them as evidence in support of our rational reconstruction. There are, alas, all too many people in the present age who have become so intoxicated with sheer technique, so enslaved by the idol of efficiency, that they seem genuinely to approve of any expert skill, however evil. Appalled by ordinary personal brutality, they cannot quell a covert admiration for anything so rationally organized as the Nazi's extermination of the Jews, or the CIA's adroit overthrow of some Latin American government. The principal criticism of the abortive invasion of Cuba by American-supported forces, for example, was that it was clumsily executed.

feel many sorts of positive sentiment, but to imagine that he thereby deserves moral approbation is, Kant would insist, the very deepest confusion. As Machiavelli himself reveals, such a great-souled man may nonetheless commit evil (though, we may be sure, *great* evil) and deserve our severest condemnation.

In the eighteenth century the moral sentiment school in England also encouraged a confusion of aesthetic appreciation or sympathetic identification with the strictly moral judgment of goodness. Hence, Kant is concerned to point up the distinction in order that his readers not fall into that error. More important for his own purposes, however, is the distinction between the unconditional goodness of the good will and the merely conditional goodness of every other object, event, or disposition of character to which we might on occasion apply the term "good." Kant quickly canvasses several classes of candidates which vie for the honor accorded a good will. Gifts of nature, or natural talents and abilities, gifts of fortune, such as wealth and position, even happiness, are all of them good under certain conditions or in certain circumstances but not good always and unconditionally.

Or so Kant says. He scarcely pauses to justify these assertions, apparently thinking them too widely accepted to need discussion. Nevertheless, we may try for a bit to develop the sorts of evidences by which he might have argued his case. The question Kant seems to be asking is this: of anything we wish to name, would we say that everywhere and under any conditions it is good that it should exist? A good will, he says, is such a thing, and we shall have to return to that claim presently. But what of courage or temperance or wealth or health or happiness itself?

Talents and abilities enable one to accomplish some end more efficiently. The goodness of the talent is, therefore, conditioned upon the goodness of the end. Bad as a burglar is, a courageous and agile burglar is worse still. If we disapprove of Napoleon's imperial designs, then we can only deplore the military genius with which he pursued them.

There is a certain ambiguity in Kant's brief discussion. In considering a talent, we may ask ourselves whether it is a good thing that someone possess it. The answer, of course, is that it depends on what use he puts it to. When we consider a good will, on the other hand, the question is not precisely whether it is a good thing that someone have a good will, but rather whether that good will, *which in a sense is the very person himself,* deserves our approbation everywhere and always. The answer, I would agree, is that it does. But from this we cannot infer that it is always a good thing that someone have a good will. For example, suppose a situation in which a man, by steadfastly doing what he has every reason to believe is his moral duty, produces through no fault of his own an unimagined harm; suppose further that were another man to take his place, corruptible and heedless of duty, he might in an equally unintended manner effect great good through succumbing to the basest of temptations. We would certainly not blame the good man for his steadfastness; indeed, we would admire the goodness of his will and praise him for it. Were there a God to requite men for their endeavors, we would all agree that the man of good will should be rewarded despite the unfortunate outcome of his actions, and some among us might agree that the evil man should be punished for having intended no good. But all the same, would any of us wish to claim that it was *a good thing* that at that place, at that time, there was a man of good will?

Kant's point, as he very quickly makes clear, is that when we talk of responsibility, we must all grant on reflection that it is intention rather than outcome which determines praiseworthiness and blameworthiness. The reason for this, of course, is that a man can only be held responsible for what is within his power, and at best it is his intention and not its outcome that he controls.[4] Kant holds that one and only one thing is everywhere and under any conditions worthy of esteem, and that is the attempt to do what one ought. It is, I take it, generally granted that the intention to do the right deserves approbation. What is novel in Kant's assertion, if

[4]This is not at all to say that the only thing anyone ever intends is the muscular contraction which initiates the action or, perhaps, even only the effort of will which mysteriously activates the innermost muscle. When I undertake to shoot a man, it is true that the means I choose is to crook my index finger at just the moment when it is bent around the trigger of a loaded gun pointed at my target. But, believing as I do that the crooking of the finger will accomplish his death, it *is* his death that I intend and *not* the crooking of the finger. When the Judgment Day comes, I can hardly plead my innocence on the ground that I merely intended to agitate a muscle with what turned out to be unhappy consequences. Of course, if I did *not* intend thereby to kill him, I *can* legitimately enter such a defense, and that is just the point.

anything, is the claim that *only* such an intention is unconditionally good. Strictly speaking, as we shall see, a good will is the only thing which is morally estimable at all, for everything else which we might be tempted to esteem acquires its merit from its relation to or furthering of a good will. Needless to say, this still leaves quite open the question *what* we ought to do.

The most popular alternate candidate these days for the title of unconditional good is pleasure or, more generally, happiness.[5] Many modern philosophers since Bentham have claimed that pleasure, whenever and wherever it appears, is unconditionally good, and that pain is unconditionally bad. Just as bad consequences may flow unintentionally from a good will without thereby diminishing its moral worth, so these philosophers have argued that the pain which sometimes results from pleasure in no way diminishes the worth of the pleasure itself, though of course it may constitute a good reason for not doing whatever produced the pleasure. Thus, the joy of a night on the town is intrinsically good, it is said, while the hangover is intrinsically bad. The latter may be causally consequent upon the former, but that does not alter the goodness of the binge.

Kant offers the briefest of replies to this view. He says at the end of the first paragraph of the section: "a rational and impartial spectator can never feel approval in contemplating the uninterrupted prosperity of a being graced by no touch of a pure and good will." If we are offered two worlds, the second of which differs from the first solely in that in it some sinner flourishes, we should unhesitatingly choose the first. In general, the world is a better place when the wicked are punished or, at the very least, do not enjoy the fruits of their evil doing and when the good are rewarded or, at least, do not suffer.

This, I am afraid, is one of those "ordinary" moral judgments which Kant's modern readers will not so readily accept. Oddly enough, there seem to be more people willing to agree that the good should prosper than there are people who insist that the wicked should suffer. For all those who question Kant's judgment,

---

[5]Kant has a rather complex analysis of the concept of happiness, which differentiates it very sharply from pleasure. For present purposes, however, there is no harm in the utilitarian's confusion of the two.

I offer the following case. It is not an argument, but I have some hope that it will convince at least some of the doubters. Imagine a sadist whose pleasure is not merely a *result* of another's pain but is actually pleasure *taken in* someone else's suffering. His pleasure, to put the point abstractly, involves another's pain *essentially* rather than *accidentally*. I suggest that a world in which such a man causes pain to others and enjoys doing so is a worse place than a world in which he causes the pain and reaps no satisfaction from it. (Needless to say, it would be a good deal better if no pain were inflicted at all.) To those who regard even this judgment as a piece of harsh and retributive rigorism from a happily departed Puritan past, I can only say, wait until chapter 2. As I pointed out at the beginning of this discussion, Kant is engaged in a reconstruction of beliefs which he assumes to be universal, and if, in fact, they are not, he has no arguments in the present section to alter the disagreement.

Even if we eschew the retributive spirit of Kant's moral outlook, there are still other reasons for doubting that pleasure is everywhere and always good. Utilitarianism assumes that men have an obligation to increase the pleasure experienced by others and to, diminish their pain. One familiar argument for this claim is that pleasure is intrinsically good and that we all have a standing obligation to bring into existence or to sustain in existence that which is intrinsically good. But if this argument were valid, then it would follow that we ought to persevere in pleasuring others even if those to whom we were ministering did not want to experience pleasure. Were human nature to undergo a transformation which left men regularly inclined to seek pain and shun pleasure, would it still seem plausible that we had an obligation to inflict upon them quantities of unwanted pleasure?

Of course, one can redefine the terms "pleasure" and "pain" so that they come to mean merely "the feeling which accompanies the fulfillment of a desire" and "the feeling which accompanies the frustration of a desire." Such definitions are neutral with respect to the felt quality of their designata. But it would then become clear that utilitarianism, insofar as it is plausible at all, rests on the higher principle that we should assist our fellowmen in the satisfaction of their (legitimate) desires. Such a principle might perhaps be derived from an analysis of the nature of purposive action and the universalizability of the principles which govern such action. Indeed, we shall find Kant attempting an argument very like that in later chapters. Nevertheless, pleasure remains a conditioned rather than an unconditioned good, for its goodness is a consequence of its being an object of universal desire. If George Bernard Shaw is to be believed, even so indefatigable a pleasure seeker as Don Juan would find an eternity of satisfaction Hell and would soon strike out for the Heaven of eternal struggle.

In Ak. 394–396 Kant appends an argument based upon teleological considerations. Its tone seems to me to be ironic rather than literal, although Kant elsewhere appeals quite seriously to teleological principles. Suppose, Kant argues, that we grant the familiar claim that each faculty of the mind has some natural function and, hence, that reason does also. May we conclude that reason's purpose is to aid man in the pursuit of happiness? Reason has the power to guide the will, it is true. But surely had nature intended man to seek happiness as the highest good, instinct would have been a better guide than reason. Indeed, those in whom reason flourishes are so far from finding themselves more contentedly happy that they characteristically envy the simple folk whose ordered lives are not disturbed by the reflections of reason.

Three-quarters of a century after Kant published the *Groundwork,* John Stuart Mill was to write that it is better "to be a human being dissatisfied than a pig satisfied; better to be Socrates dissatisfied than a fool satisfied." Kant would have agreed with these sentiments. He would have added that it is not only better, but also more likely, that one will be dissatisfied if one is Socrates.

4. Paragraphs 8–16 (Ak. 397–401):
The Concept of Duty

After the discussion of the unconditional goodness of the good will and the brief detour into teleological reasoning, Kant makes an abrupt shift of direction. In order, he says, to develop the concept of a will which is to be esteemed good of itself, "we will take up the concept of *duty.*" The rationale for this move, at which Kant only hints, is that the concept of duty is the key to the analysis of that species of good will which men are capable of possessing.

According to Kant, a good will is a will moved by the idea of the good. There are, he thinks, two species of good will. A *holy will,* of the sort supposedly possessed by God or by any perfectly rational being, is a will which cannot be moved by anything but the idea of the good. Its subjective constitution is such, in other words, that it is incapable of doing wrong. To put the same point yet another way, it naturally desires the good.

Men do not have holy wills, unfortunately. They are subject to the temptations and pressures of sensuous motives or inclinations. Hence, they sometimes fail to be moved by the idea of the good. For Kant, the moral life of men is an unending conflict between the pressures of inclination and the motivating power of the idea of the good.

Since Kant thinks of inclination on the analogy of sensibility as a kind of limitation or condition placed upon the will, we can speak of a holy will as an "unconditioned will" and of a human will as a "conditioned will." In these terms the central question of the *Groundwork* then becomes: How can a conditioned will stand under an unconditioned moral law? This characterization of the moral condition and of the nature of holy and human wills conflicts. with the deeper metaphysical doctrines of Kant's philosophy. When we come to Kant's discussion of imperatives in chapter 2, we shall explore at length the nature of conditioned and unconditioned willing.[6]

Duty is simply the requirement that a conditioned will stands under to be moved by the idea of the good rather than by inclina-

[6]Kant's distinction between a holy will which naturally desires the good and a conditioned will which has a duty to do so, is a philosophical reflection of the contrast between man reborn through the Holy Spirit in the New Testament and man unregenerate in the Old. Those in whom the Spirit lives do naturally that which the Law of Moses commanded. As St. Paul says, "Christ has redeemed us from the curse of the law" (Gal. 3:13), and "But before faith came, we were kept under the law, shut up unto the faith which should afterward be revealed. Wherefore the law was our schoolmaster to bring us unto Christ, that we might be justified by faith. But after that faith is come, we are no longer under the schoolmaster" (Gal. 3:23–25). Kant's famous description of the "Kingdom of Ends" in chapter 2 of the *Groundwork* can be interpreted either as an account of an earthly community of men reborn through Christ or as an account of heaven.

tions. At this point, of course, Kant is assuming without argument that men actually can be moved by such a concept. Much of the argument in chapters 2 and 3 is devoted to an explication and defense of that pivotal assumption.

The discussion of duty is cast in the form of a justification of three propositions concerning duty and moral worth. The first proposition is not explictly labeled as such by Kant. He simply goes on for a while about action in accordance with duty versus action from duty. Then, suddenly, in paragraph 14 he asserts, "The second proposition is: . . ." leaving the reader to wonder what the first proposition was.

Most translators and commentators have assumed quite naturally that the unstated first proposition is the implicit theme of paragraphs 8–13, namely, some such statement as:

To have moral worth an action must be done from duty.[7]

Mr. A. R. C. Duncan has challenged this interpretation. In a rather tendentious book designed to throw doubt on customary interpretations of the *Groundwork*, Duncan argues that the first of the three propositions is *not* a statement connecting the notion of moral worth with the notion of action done for the sake of duty, but is instead simply the opening sentence of the entire chapter 1, namely, "It is impossible to conceive anything at all in the world, or even out of it, which can be taken as good without qualification, except a good will."[8]

Not a great deal turns on the resolution of this dispute, so far as I can make out, but Paton, Beck, and the others do seem to me to have the stronger case. Aside from considerations of style and textual orderliness, there is an internal logical argument in support of the Paton-Beck interpretation. The second and third propositions are explicitly stated as:

[7]Paton summarizes the passage in his preliminary analysis as: "A human action is usually good, not because it is done from immediate inclination—still less because it is done from self-interest—but because it is done for the sake of duty." H. J. Paton, *The Moral Law* (New York: Barnes & Noble, 1967), pp. 18–19. In his commentary, *The Categorical Imperative* (Philadelphia: University of Pennsylvania Press, 1971), he offers the briefer equivalent: "An action has moral worth only so far as it is done for the sake of duty" (p. 47).

[8]Cf. A. R. C. Duncan, *Practical Reason and Morality* (London: Nelson, 1957), chap. 4, esp. pp. 59, 70.

2. An action done from duty has its moral worth *not in the purpose* to be attained by it, but in the maxim in accordance with which it is decided upon.

3. Duty is the necessity to act out of reverence for the law.

Now Kant claims, at the beginning of paragraph 15, that the third proposition is an inference from the first and the second. If the first proposition is something like, "Only an action done for the sake of duty has moral worth," then it is possible to see how the third proposition might be thought to follow from it together with the second. The principal problem would be to introduce the notion of a law and connect it up with the more general concept of a maxim which appears in proposition 2. But if the first proposition is simply the opening statement about the unqualified goodness of the good will, it is not clear why Kant would have imagined proposition 3 to follow from propositions 1 and 2. In all events, I shall assume that Paton, Beck, and the others are right and that Duncan is wrong.

A. The First Proposition Concerning Duty
(Pars. 8–13)

"To have moral worth an action must be done from duty."

The six paragraphs in which Kant expounds the first proposition have given rise to more misunderstandings and absurdities than any other single passage in the *Groundwork*. Kant may have imagined himself merely to be rehearsing the common moral beliefs of decent men and women everywhere, but for his troubles he has got himself labeled a prig and a prude and a spoilsport.

His intention is quite modest and straightforward. He wishes simply to remind his readers of the commonplace distinction between the man who acts in *conformity* with the commands of morality and the man who acts out of a respect for, or for the sake of, those commands. Through a series of familiar examples Kant tries to show that we do not ordinarily consider an action to be worthy of moral approval *merely* because it conforms to the letter of the moral law. The grocer who is honest out of self-interest is not *thereby* worthy of our esteem, nor is the philanthropist motivated by natural generosity or the martially inclined warrior. Since inclinations, as elements of our empirical character, are causally determined, it makes no sense either to esteem or to blame a man for possessing them. We may deliberately cultivate inclinations which direct ourselves or others in right directions, but action done merely from such inclinations has no moral value at all.

Readers of this passage characteristically come away with two quite absurd misunderstandings of Kant's view. The simplest mistake is to suppose that Kant thinks an action is good if you hate doing it. A somewhat more subtle version has it that Kant thinks you shouldn't get any moral credit for an act if you like it. The result is to see Kant as a perverted misanthrope who preaches an ethic of dedicated masochism. The truth, of course, is quite otherwise. Actions done from inclination have no moral worth at all, positive or negative, for we are only accountable for what we can help, and we cannot help the direction of our inclinations. Actions which *violate* our duty must of necessity be morally wrong, assuming that we are responsible for them at all. On the other hand, actions done in *conformity* with our duty are praiseworthy only if their motive is duty itself rather than inclination. Now, when a man manifestly is inclined to do what his duty commands, it is very hard to tell whether he was nevertheless motivated by a sense of duty. So Kant concludes that the way to get really good examples of actions done for the sake of duty is to fix upon cases in which men's inclinations clearly urge them away from the dutiful action which they nevertheless perform. These are not the *only* cases of praiseworthy action, he thinks, merely the most nearly indisputable cases.

The misinterpretations of Kant are so obviously wrong and the correcting of them so easy and pleasant a task that the dedicated student frequently misses a much more serious error of which Kant really is guilty. As I indicated in my discussion of the implications of the *First Critique*, Kant is committed by his theory of knowledge to a doctrine of psychological determinism. Every state of the empirical self and, most certainly, every piece of behavior attributable to an empirical self is causally determined by some antecedent series of empirical states which lead up to and necessitate it. Now, inclinations are on Kant's view the sorts of events or states which cause behavior in the phenomenal world.[9] It follows, therefore, that on his view every action will have its antecedent determinants among our inclinations. Not merely the naturally generous philanthropist or the willing warrior, but also the reluctant philanthropist and dutiful soldier must be adequately inclined to behave as they do; for if they were not so inclined, then their behavior would not occur in the phenomenal world. Causal determination, on the theory of the *First Critique*, is identical with objective temporal location, which in turn is identical with simply occurring. Hence, every act which can truly be said to have happened must have been determined to happen either by inclinations or else by other sorts of phenomenal antecedents.

In short, Kant has himself demonstrated that there can be no *empirically verifiable* cases of action done from a sense of duty *rather than* from inclination. Indeed, his theory guarantees that if only we look hard enough, we must be able to find an inclination which accounts for the performance of the action. In characteristic fashion, Kant himself recognizes this implication of his theory only a few pages farther on. At the beginning of the second chapter of the *Groundwork*, after summarizing the conclusions of the first chapter, he states flatly:

> In actual fact it is absolutely impossible for experience to establish with complete certainty a single case in which the maxim of an action in other respects right has rested solely on moral grounds and on the thought of one's duty. (Ak. 406–407)

We see here the confusions which are generated by Kant's commitment to the view of the moral life as a struggle between duty and inclination. His image is that of a good man who must on occasion force himself to do what he knows to be right despite his lack of any natural inclination. Kant obviously thinks that his dis-

[9] If we give a dispositional analysis of inclinations, it may turn out to be a mistake to attribute causal efficacy to them. Nevertheless, *something* must stand as cause to bits of behavior as effects, and the argument developed here will simply apply to whatever is selected as the likeliest candidate.

tinction between the noumenal self and its phenomenal character, and the correlative distinction between acting from a sense of duty and acting from inclination somehow provides a philosophical analysis of the felt experience of internal moral struggle. His theory of knowledge, however, has the completely contrary implication that all such felt experiences are mere phenomenal conflicts whose origins can be traced to physiological, psychological, and cultural antecedents.

My own judgment is that Kant's philosophy is at this point closer to the truth than are his prephilosophic convictions. We are now in a much better position to give psychocultural explanations of such experiences as a sense of guilt or a struggle between conscience and inclination. Ironically, Kant's moral philosophy is improved by this rejection of his most deeply held belief; for if his theory depends on the assumption that all men experience the internal struggles of inner-directed Puritans, then obviously it must lack the requisite universal validity. But if the argument of the *Groundwork* can be developed without appeal to culturally relative phenomena of this sort, it will thereby be immeasurably strengthened.

B. The Second Proposition Concerning Duty
(Par. 14)

The second proposition about duty is: "An action done from duty has its moral worth *not in the purpose* to be attained by it, but in the maxim in accordance with which it is decided upon" (Ak. 399). Although this is by far the most important step in the argument of chapter 1, Kant offers almost no explanation or justification of it. Unfortunately, the proposition is stated in a most misleading way. It will be necessary, therefore, to plunge for some while into the tangled confusion of Kant's views on maxims, principles, reasons, and laws. I must confess that I find this entire subject very hard to sort out in any orderly way. Kant's own statements are puzzling and inconsistent. Commentators are frequently helpful up to a point, particularly Lewis White Beck in his brilliant commentary on the *Critique of Practical Reason*. But there is a hard core of sheer obscurity which seems to resist my powers of analysis. At any rate, here goes.

It is Kant's view that whenever a man acts—indeed, whenever any rational agent acts—he acts on the basis of a policy which he has adopted covering a class of relevantly similar cases. Examples of policies which a man might adopt and act on are: to maximize profits in economic transactions, to drink a quart of water a day, to revenge all insults (Beck's example), to commit suicide when continued life threatens more evil than satisfaction (Kant's example), and never to send a boy to do a man's job.

Despite some historical evidence that Kant actually went about formulating little policies to himself and invoking them as the occasion warranted, we need not construe him as claiming that every act is preceded by an interior monologue in which the proposed act is brought under a policy, which is then perhaps checked against the Categorical Imperative. Rather, we can interpret Kant as saying that acts strictly so-called—that is, genuine instances of rational agency—have that structure and that other bits of behavior qualify as acts only insofar as they can be analyzed, or rationally reconstructed, as having that structure.

The analysis here is analogous to the analysis of empirical judgments as implicitly inferential and predictive in nature. According to Kant (at least in his phenomenalist mood), a judgment that a given object is a house can be unpacked into a set of inferences from and predictions about certain sense experiences. On some occasions I may actually perform the inferences and make the predictions. But on all occasions these judgments are implicit in the simple statement, "that is a house."

Every action implies a policy under which it can be subsumed, because actions are guided and determined by reasons, and reasons are general in their nature. If I drink a glass of water to slake my thirst, it must be that I have a policy of drinking water to slake my thirst. For in the strict sense of "act," I can only be said to perform the act of drinking water if my doing so is determined by a reason. And if that reason is a good reason for drinking water in this instance of thirst, then it must be an equally good reason for drinking water in all relevantly similar cases. This, however, is just to say that insofar as I am rational enough to acknowledge the force of reasons, I have a *policy* of drinking water to slake my thirst.

My policies can be formulated or expressed as general propositions expressing my purpose in a certain class of situations. In that form they are suited to serve as the major premises of practical syllogisms. For example, Lewis White Beck, on whose account of maxims I am relying heavily, offers the following example:

> To avenge a wrong is always my purpose.
> To tell this lie would avenge a wrong.

Therefore,

> I propose to tell this lie.

Since the major premise of the first, or highest, syllogism in a syllogistic chain of reasoning is called *sententia maxima,* Kant labels these general policy statements *maxims.*

It is one thing to say that a certain policy actually is someone's policy, that he adopts it as his own and follows it in appropriate situations. It is a second thing to say that he would adopt it as his policy if he were rational. And it is a third and very different thing indeed to say that all rational agents whatsoever will adopt that policy insofar as they are rational. The first is purely descriptive. Leaving aside the subtleties and complexities inherent in the ascription of intentions, we say that a man has a policy when he actually adopts it, acts on it, acknowledges it as his policy, distinguishes it from other policies having similar implications for action, and so forth. But the second and third are in one way or another normative. When I tell someone that he ought, given his anxiety about financial security, to put a little money aside each month, I am not describing his behavior, but prescribing for him. To be sure, my prescription may be couched in an apparently descriptive mode ("if you are prudent, you will save some money"), but it will find its most natural expression in imperative form ("put aside some money each month").

In a footnote to the paragraphs we are now considering (Ak. 400), Kant says that a maxim is "The subjective principle of a volition." In short, an agent's maxim is the principle (or policy) he is actually acting on. By contrast, Kant goes on:

> an objective principle (that is, one which would also serve subjectively as a practical principle for all rational beings if reason had full control over the faculty of desire) is a practical law. (Ak. 400n)

In this way the terms "maxim" and "law" are introduced and connected. As Beck points out,[10] Kant's use of the terms is confusing. Strictly speaking, "maxim" or "principle" is the genus of which "law" is a species, the *differentia* being "objective." But Kant frequently talks as though "subjective principle of volition" were synonymous with "maxim" and "objective principle of volition" with "law." For purposes of clarity, let us follow the strict usage. "Maxim" will mean "a statement of a policy, or principle of volition." Then a subjective principle of volition will be a maxim which some agent is actually employing as his policy, and an objective principle of volition will be a maxim which that agent or any agent would adopt insofar as he is rational. Maxims which would be adopted by *all* rational agents insofar as they are rational will be called practical laws. It remains to be seen whether there are any such policies.

All of this is rather clumsy but not essentially obscure. So long as we ignore really hard questions, such as what it means to say that an agent would do such-and-such "insofar as he is rational," we seem to have a familiar and serviceable distinction. But at this point things become very confused. The problem begins with Kant's desire to talk about the "formal" and "material" components of a maxim. Let me quote at length from Beck, who is both very much superior to any other commentator on this subject and yet also fundamentally mysterious:

> if a rational being regards his maxims as universal laws, as he does when he says that some action that he does is the kind of action that all men (or other rational beings) should do, it cannot be by virtue of the material of the maxim, which refers to the object or the purpose of his will. This is true even if the maxim should, fortunately, in a person of benevolent or sympathetic disposition, be a desire for the general welfare or the happiness of others. If the material or goal of desire is presupposed in a principle, whatever it may be, there is no universality in the principle, and the corresponding imperative is not categorical. Besides the material of the maxim, however, there is only its form. The form of the maxim as expressed in an imperative is "ought," just as the form of any theoretical proposition is some mode of "is." As form, it is independent of any specific desire, which constitutes the content of specific maxims. If we abstract from an impera-

[10]Lewis White Beck, *A Commentary on Kant's "Critique of Practical Reason"* (Chicago: University of Chicago Press, 1960), pp. 80–81.

tive all content by virtue of which it is addressed to a person motivated by a specific subjective desire, we are left with only the form,
the skeletal "ought." What is derivable from this, unlike what is
derivable from any specific content, is addressed to all rational beings
who act, and the rules derived from it are fitted to be universal in
application. That is, the form of a maxim and not its content determines whether it is a law or a mere maxim.[11]

This gloss of Kant's argument is a great help for the puzzled
reader, since it identifies precisely what Kant is referring to when
he speaks of the form and matter of a maxim. But as I try to apply
these guides to an example, my momentary insight evaporates.
First of all, the example of a maxim given by Beck several pages
later ("to avenge a wrong is always my purpose") doesn't contain
any mode of the verb "ought." The policy announced by the
maxim is expressed in infinitive form ("to avenge a wrong"). As for
the matter of the maxim, I suppose we might say that avenging a
wrong is the "object or purpose" of my will when I act on that
maxim. But the example offered by Kant in the *Groundwork* ("for
love of myself, I make it my principle to shorten my life when by
a longer duration it threatens more evil than satisfaction") is significantly different. Kant not only offers us the policy ("to shorten
my life when . . .") but also gives us the reason ("for love of
myself"). In the very next sentence, he refers to "this principle of
self-love," suggesting that it is the goal or object of self-love, rather
than anything mentioned in the maxim itself, that most appropriately could be called the "matter" of the maxim.

The source of the trouble here, so far as I can see, is that one and
the same policy can be adopted by an agent for any number of
reasons. To follow Kant's example of the honest grocer, suppose
that I adopt it as my policy *always to give the correct change when
concluding a sale.* One possible reason for choosing this policy
might be the belief that honesty in such dealings offers the best
prospect for personal gain ("honesty is the best policy"). A second
reason might be a desire to avoid the feeling of self-loathing which
past experience has taught me to expect on the occasions when I
cheat customers. Still a third reason might be that it is right to be
honest.

[11]Ibid., p. 72.

At this point, the reader may be tempted to ask, "Ah, but *why* is it right?" as though the mere fact that a policy is right couldn't by itself be a reason for adopting it. But although we are of course very interested to learn why honesty is right, it is totally wrong to suppose that "because it is right" is not by itself an adequate or complete reason. In order to see this, compare the first reason offered for honesty, namely, that it promises the best chance for profit. We can obviously ask, "Ah, but *why* does it offer the best chance for profit?" The answer will involve facts of psychology and economics, but those facts are not my reasons for adopting the policy. My reason is because honesty pays off in profits.

Kant thought that honesty in financial transactions is the right, or morally obligatory, policy. Hence, actions guided by that policy are, on his view, right actions. But only right actions done for the right reason are morally to the credit of the agent. A policy of honesty adopted for reasons of profit or self-esteem confers no merit on an agent; but a policy of honesty adopted because of its rightness is morally estimable as well as right.

At this point, an obvious question arises. Why, we may ask the prudent grocer, does the expectation of profit move you? The answer is presumably that the grocer has some antecedent desire (for money itself or for the things money can buy or for the pleasure to be derived from consuming those things) which bids fair to be satisfied by the expected outcome of the policy. By the same token, we may ask the righteous man, "Why does the rightness of a policy move you to adopt it?" Kant, like most of us, seems to have thought the first question simply needs no answer, whereas the second needs one very badly. That is, my having a desire for something perfectly well explains my acting to get it, whereas my believing that a policy is right does not of itself explain my adopting that policy as my own. To put it another way, "because it will make me happy" is considered an adequate explanation for an action (although not necessarily an adequate justification). But "because it is right" is generally viewed as requiring something more by way of explanation (though it may be a perfectly adequate justification). In our discussion of chapter 2, we shall have to explore further this contrast between acts motivated by desire and acts motivated by the idea of their rightness.

I said earlier that a given policy could be adopted for any number of reasons, but, speaking generally, there are two fundamentally different sorts of reasons an agent might act on. Either he is moved by reasons which are good reasons for him only insofar as he is in a certain special condition which distinguishes him from at least some other agents, or else he is moved by reasons which would be good reasons for all rational agents insofar as they are rational. Kant completely confuses the issue by identifying reasons of the first sort as relating to the *matter* of the agent's maxim and reasons of the second sort as relating to the *form* of the agent's maxim. Actually, I should like to suggest, the form-matter distinction can be drawn with regard to *either* sort of reason.[12]

The obvious example of a reason of the first sort is a desire for the end or goal aimed at by the maxim. If my maxim or policy is to seek vengeance for wrongs done me, then my reason for adopting that policy may be that I desire vengeance. If I am asked *why* I desire vengeance, I may reply either that vengeance gives me a sort of pleasure which I desire or that I simply find myself desiring vengeance.[13] A reason of this sort would be a good reason only for agents having the desire. Since there is no desire which is necessarily possessed by all rational agents, it follows that no reason based upon a desire can be a good reason for all agents merely insofar as they are rational. Hence, no maxim adopted by an agent because of some desire is *thereby* shown to be a practical law. (It may, of course, be shown to be a practical law on other grounds.)

Another example of a reason of the first sort (but one which Kant seems not to have considered) is a taste or preference for consistent maxims. Later on, we shall have to explore this notion of the

[12]What follows in the text is an explication of the theory of desire, ends, reasons, and imperatives that seems to me to be implicit in the *Groundwork*. In terms of this explication, I believe we can make a good deal more sense of Kant's argument. But later on, I shall explain why I believe that even this clarification leaves Kant with a theory which is neither true nor compatible with the doctrine of the *First Critique*. I have chosen to advance my interpretation in this manner, by stages as it were, because the position I shall ultimately sketch as in some sense consistent with Kant's metaphysics takes us very far indeed from his expressed views. Even if the reader rejects that later revision of the theory, he will I hope find the present explication a help in reading the *Groundwork*.

[13]It makes no difference to this analysis whether or not Kant thought that every desire for an object, experience, or state of affairs must at base be a desire for the pleasure expected from it. Beck, *Commentary*, p. 101, suggests that Kant did not know Joseph Butler's famous discussion of the question in his Sermon on Self-Love, but he points out that Kant could have encountered the same arguments in works by Christian Wolff and David Hume with which he was familiar.

logical consistency of a maxim: roughly speaking, inconsistency is a matter of simultaneously adopting a general policy and deviating from it in particular instances. But there is no reason why I shouldn't have a taste for consistency which moves me to act on consistent maxims. My reason, then, would be, "because I prefer consistent maxims," of which this is one. Since a taste or preference for consistency, like a desire for vengeance, is not necessarily a characteristic of all rational agents, my reason could not be a good reason for all agents insofar as they are rational.

Now, my first example can plausibly be said to refer to the matter of the maxim, while my second example refers to the form. But both are examples of reasons of the *first* sort: that is, they are reasons which are good reasons for an agent only insofar as he is in a certain special condition (having a desire, having a preference) which distinguishes him from some other agents. So Kant is wrong to associate material reasons with subjective maxims and formal reasons with objective maxims.

The same formal-material distinction can be drawn in the second category of reasons, those which would be good reasons for all rational agents insofar as they are rational. But here, instead of two subclasses of reasons, we have just one reason of each kind. The only material reason for acting on a maxim that would be a good reason for all rational agents insofar as they are rational is: Because the state of affairs proposed or intended by the maxim is good. This is what Kant calls "being moved by the Idea of the Good." The only formal reason for acting on a maxim that would be a good reason for all rational agents insofar as they are rational is: Because the maxim is logically consistent. A maxim which is consistent and which aims at an end that is good is a practical law, for it is a maxim which all rational agents would adopt as their own insofar as they are rational.

As I have several times remarked, it is a much-debated question whether anyone can be moved by the mere idea of the goodness of the goal of a proposed action. It is, I suppose, even more debatable whether anyone can be moved by the bare thought of the logical consistency of a policy. If one assumes, with psychological theorists like Hobbes and Hume, that desire and aversion are the sole moving forces in the self, then one will conclude that the second category of reasons is simply irrelevant to an account of the sources of action. Thus far in the *Groundwork* Kant has said nothing about this question but it would be a very bad mistake to accuse him therefore of begging it or even of being unaware of its importance. Quite to the contrary, we shall see that Kant's entire theory of morality turns on an analysis of rational willing or what he calls Practical Reason. He himself formulates his central question as, How pure reason can be practical!

The Categorical Imperative, which Kant is preparing to introduce shortly into chapter 1 is a general statement of that purely formal reason for adopting a policy which would be a good reason for all agents qua rational. Its direct analogue in the area of the theoretical use of reason is of course the law of contradiction. The law of contradiction is a merely negative or necessary condition of the truth of a theoretical judgment. It rules out those judgments which are self-contradictory but does not discriminate between true and false consistent judgments. Experience of an object is required to draw that distinction. One might naturally suppose, therefore, that the Categorical Imperative would only suffice by itself to rule out inconsistent maxims, while requiring supplementation by a theory of objective or obligatory ends in order to identify particular objectively binding practical laws. As I have already indicated, that is precisely the line Kant takes half of the time. But the other half of the time he tries to perform the impossible feat of deriving substantive practical laws from the purely formal Categorical Imperative. It cannot be done, any more than we can derive the laws of nature from the law of contradiction alone. I shall repeat this point a number of times throughout my commentary, for it is one of the principal sources of the confusion in Kant's moral theory.

We are finally ready to return to the brief bit of text that prompted this lengthy excursion. You will recall that Kant had just enunciated the second of his three propositions concerning duty:

> An action done from duty has its moral worth, *not in the purpose* to be attained by it, but in the maxim in accordance with which it is decided upon. (Ak. 399)

It should now be clear that this is a quite inadequate expression of the idea Kant has in mind. In particular, we cannot tell from this formulation whether Kant is concerned with the policy of which the action is an expression or whether he is rather concerned with the reasons for which the policy has been adopted. Since, as we have seen, the right policy can always be adopted for wrong or morally neutral reasons, the moral worth of an action cannot reside in the policy. An action "done from duty," however, is an action done *for a certain reason,* and we may tentatively conclude that Kant meant to say:

> An action done from duty has its moral worth not in any character of the purpose to be attained by it, but in some character of the reason for which it is done.

When the full significance of this proposition is understood, it will be seen to imply a complete rejection of all forms of utilitarianism and eudaimonism. In order to grasp Kant's justification for this step in his argument, let us raise the general question: *what is it in virtue of which an action is judged morally estimable?*

We all agree that the actual consequences of an action cannot be the ground of its moral worth; for a man can only be esteemed or blamed for what is within his control, and men do not have complete control over the outcome of their actions. But, says Kant, it cannot even be the *intended* outcome of an action which confers moral worth upon it. The goodness of a morally worthy act *cannot* consist in the goodness of the end which it strives to bring about. For consider: if it were *merely* the goodness of the goal of an act which conferred moral worth on the act, then by parity of reasoning *any* act which aimed at the same goal, no matter for what reason or from what cause, would possess an equivalent moral worth. Suppose, for example, that I plunge into an icy river to save a drowning child. Now, if the moral worth of the action derives solely from the goodness of its end (namely the saving of a life), then the act will have that moral worth whether I was motivated by a sense of duty, a love for children, or a malevolent desire to thwart the child's benevolent uncle who will inherit a vast fortune on the child's death and give it all to meritorious

charities. Similarly, if the moral worth of honesty lies in the goodness of its aim, which is to render to each man his due, then there
can be no moral difference between the man who is honest from
a sense of duty and Kant's grocer who is honest from calculation
of self-interest.

Needless to repeat, Kant does not think that a right action done
from nonmoral motives is bad or reprehensible. It simply lacks any
moral worth at all. A world in which the drowning child is saved
by a Boy Scout in pursuit of merit badges is obviously better than
a world in which the child drowns, but the quantity of *moral*
merit, if we may use that phrase, is the same in both worlds. If this
seems quaintly puritanical or even harshly formalistic, one need
simply ask oneself whether it makes any sense to say that a world
without mosquitoes would be *morally* superior to the present
world. It would certainly be a more pleasant world in which to
live, assuming no obscure ecological blacklash, but it would have
no claim to moral superiority. Now for Kant, the presence or
absence of such inclinations as ambition is as completely causally
determined as is the presence or absence of mosquitoes. Since no
moral worth attaches to behavior which is causally determined, it
follows that the goodness of the badge-seeking Boy Scout's goal in
no way confers moral worth on his action.

This argument, so simple and yet so far-reaching in its consequences, is a particular application of the general principle that
what counts as adequate grounds for one judgment must count as
adequate grounds for all other judgments which are identical in
the relevant respects. Thus, "because he lit the fuse" cannot *by
itself* be an adequate explanation for a bomb's blowing up, for
under other circumstances (lack of oxygen and so forth) the bomb
might not blow up even after the fuse was lit. So, too, "because it
is a rectangle" cannot *by itself* be an adequate explanation for the
fact that the diagonals of a square intersect at right angles, for
there are (nonsquare) rectangles whose diagonals do not intersect
at right angles. On the other hand, "because it is a rectangle" *is*
in some manner of speaking an adequate explanation for the fact
that the diagonals bisect one another.

In the case before us, "because its intended effects are good"
cannot *by itself* be a sufficient ground for the attribution of moral
worth to an act. If it were, then it would be an adequate ground

for attributing moral worth to any action intending the same effects, even one done for the basest of motives. It may very well be the goodness of the end that makes an action *right,* but it cannot be the goodness of the end that makes the *performance* of the action morally worthy.

If not in some character of the end intended by the action, then wherein lies the moral merit? Clearly in some character of the reason for which the act is done. But no moral merit could attach to an act in virtue of a reason of the first sort distinguished in our discussion of maxims and reasons, for tastes and desires are causally determined elements of our phenomenal character and, hence, not within our control. So the moral merit of an action must lie in the fact that it was done for a reason that would be a good reason for any rational agent insofar as he is rational. Somewhat more succinctly, the moral merit of an action consists in its having been done for the sake of (for the reason of) a practical law. More succinctly still, an action has moral merit insofar as I do it merely because it is right.

In the paragraph under consideration, Kant confuses the matter by ringing in the form-matter distinction. The result is to make it seem that the merit-conferring reason must concern only the form of the maxim. But as I have tried to make clear, moral merit can perfectly well attach to an action by virtue of its being done *because its intended end is good.* That is a reason which refers to some character (goodness) of the matter (end) of the maxim, but it is nonetheless a reason which is a good reason for all agents insofar as they are rational.

There is a rather tricky point which must be cleared up here, for it may at first glance appear that I am directly contradicting what I said only a few pages ago. The goodness of the intended outcome of an action confers no moral merit on the actor, for his *reasons* for acting may have nothing to do with that goodness. But if his reason for acting is precisely that the intended outcome is good, then moral merit *does* attach to act. Thus, the honest grocer intends to return the correct change to his customers. It is good that the customers should receive the correct change (according to popular morality—we are still in chapter 1, remember). But it is still an open question whether the grocer is to be esteemed for giving correct change. To determine that, we must know *why* he did so. If he returned the correct change because he expected thereby to realize higher profits, then he is not deserving of our esteem (although he is not to be condemned either). But if he returned the correct change because it is good that the customers should be dealt with honestly or, what is the same thing, if he returned the correct change because that is the right thing to do, then he *is* deserving of our esteem.

We see then that the final sentence of that paragraph on which we are still commenting is wrong. Kant writes:

> Since [the action] must be determined by some principle, it will have to be determined by the formal principle of volition when an action is done from duty, where, as we have seen, every material principle is taken away from it. (Ak. 400)

He should have written:

> Since [the action] must be determined by some reason, it will have to be determined by a reason which would be a good reason for all rational agents as such when it is an action done from duty, where, as we have seen, every reason which is good only for some agents but not others has been taken away from it.

Before moving on to the third proposition concerning duty, it might be worthwhile to devote a few words to answering a famous objection to Kant's moral philosophy. As we have seen, Kant holds that an act is morally worthy or estimable only insofar as it is done from a sense of duty. W. D. Ross, in a much-quoted section of his influential book *The Right and the Good*, claims that it is logically absurd to suppose that we ought to act from a sense of duty. The argument is as follows:

> Those who hold that our duty is to act from a certain motive usually (Kant is the great exemplar) hold that the motive from which we ought to act is the sense of duty. Now if the sense of duty is to be my motive for doing a certain act, it must be the sense that it is my duty to do that act. If, therefore, we say "it is my duty to do act A from the sense of duty," this means "it is my duty to do act A from the sense that it is my duty to do act A." And here the whole expression is in contradiction with a part of itself. The whole sentence says "it is my duty to-do-act-A-from-the-sense-that-it-is-my-duty-to-do-act-A." But the latter part of the sentence implies that what I think is that it is my duty to-do-act-A simply. And if, as the theory in question requires, we try to amend the latter part of the expression to bring

it into accord with the whole expression, we get the result "it is my duty to do act *A* from the sense that it is my duty to do act *A* from the sense that it is my duty to do act *A*," where again the last part of the expression is in conflict with the theory, and with the sentence as a whole.[14]

The argument turns on Ross's interpretation of what it is, for Kant, to do the right act. Kant holds that we have a duty to do what is right, but Ross imagines that for Kant, the rightness of an act is determined by its motive. If that were true, Kant would indeed be caught in a vicious regress. What Kant actually says is that our acts have *moral worth* only insofar as they are done from a certain motive (namely, respect for the law). Their rightness is quite independent of their motive. We have, according to Kant, an obligation to do what is right. We do not have an obligation to perform morally meritorious acts. At this point in the exposition of the *Groundwork*, it is still an open question what makes some acts right and others wrong. For the time being Kant is merely concerned to discover what confers moral merit on our acts. His conclusion is that we deserve approbation for doing what is right *because it is right* rather than for some other reason.

C. The Third Proposition Concerning Duty (Par. 15)

"Our third proposition, as an inference from the two preceding, I would express thus: *Duty is the necessity to act out of reverence for the law*" (Ak. 400). With this brief statement Kant begins two exceedingly obscure paragraphs in which he introduces the central notion of a moral law and offers some reflections on what we would today call the phenomenology of moral experience. Most of the passage deals with the phenomenology of reverence *(Achtung)*, but the philosophical meat is in the idea of law.

We have already sorted out the notions of "maxim" and "law" as much as is necessary for an explication of chapter 1. The definition of "maxim" as "the subjective principle of volition" actually

[14](New York: Oxford University Press, 1930), p. 5.

appears for the first time here as a footnote to Ak. 400, but for reasons of expositional clarity I included my treatment of it in the commentary on the second proposition concerning duty. By pulling together material that has already been set forth, we can now exhibit the third proposition as indeed an inference from the first and second.

The first proposition was: "To have moral worth an action must be done from duty." Put somewhat differently, if an action has moral worth, then it is an action done from duty. Since it is of course also the case (according to Kant) that if an action is done from duty, then it has moral worth, we may express the first proposition as an equivalence:

1. An action is done from duty if and only if it is an action which has moral worth.

The second proposition, as stated by Kant, was: An action done from duty has its moral worth, not in the purpose to be attained by it, but in the maxim in accordance with which it is decided upon. This, as we saw, is a confused way of expressing what Kant has in mind. After much analysis and argument, I suggested that a better formulation would have been: An action done from duty has its moral worth, not in any character of the purpose to be attained by it, but in some character of the reason for which it is done. Further analysis of this proposition led to the formulation: the moral worth (or merit) of an action consists in its having been done for the sake of (that is, for the reason of) a practical law. Again adopting the form of an equivalence, this proposition becomes:

2. An action has moral worth if and only if it is done for the sake of the law.[15]

Combining equivalences 1. and 2., we infer:

3. An action is done from duty if and only if it is done for the sake of the law.

Compressing this somewhat, we arrive finally at:

3.[1] Duty is the necessity to act for the sake of the law.

[15]Permit me to glide over the distinction between "a practical law" and "the practical law."

In this form, proposition 3.[1] differs from Kant's third proposition concerning duty only by its lack of reference to the notion of reverence. Kant now adds this one further element to his formulation.

I stand in a peculiar and contradictory relation to the moral law. I am conscious of its absolutely binding character, its unconditional demand that I submit to it. This produces in me, Kant says, a feeling rather like fear. But at at the same time I recognize it as a law which I have given to myself. In submitting to the law, I am not submitting to another will, but to my own will insofar as it is rational. This awareness of my authorship of the law produces in me a feeling rather like love. The combination of fear and love or submission and domination is the distinctive emotion of *reverence*.

Considered philosophically, the introduction of the emotion of reverence is contradictory to the entire thrust of Kant's argument. Feelings of any sort are events of the phenomenal world and hence play no legitimate role in a theory of the moral law. Like all other feelings, reverence has its discoverable phenomenal determinants, both individual and cultural. In a long footnote Kant tries to avoid this conclusion by means of a dubious distinction between feelings which *produce* determinations of the will and feelings which *are produced by* determinations of the will. Since reverence is of the latter sort, it is supposedly admissible into moral theory. But of course this won't do. It is a fact about my *phenomenal* character that consciousness of submission to self-made law produces a feeling of reverence in me. As far as moral theory is concerned, this fact is no different from the fact that a malicious pleasure is produced in me by the awareness of my enemy's misery or the fact that a feeling of well-being is produced by the satisfaction of bodily needs.

But if Kant's account of reverence is inappropriate from the point of view of his moral philosophy, as an analysis of a central element in moral experience it is superb. When the child becomes an adult, the commands which he first heard from his parents and society are internalized as his conscience. If the internalization is achieved through the total suppression of instinctual drives, the result is a punitive superego which the individual hates and fears. If the internalization is incomplete or the guidance of the adult society confused and indecisive, the result may be an ego-destroying

84 THE AUTONOMY OF REASON

licentiousness which masquerades as unlimited gratification. But
if the internalization is accomplished in such a manner that the
self can identify positively with the voice of conscience then the
individual achieves a mature, self-regulated autonomy. Respect
for an external authority is transmuted into self-respect, and this
self-respect, I suggest, is the emotion which Kant calls reverence
(*Achtung*).

5. The Moral Law (Ak. 402–403)

We arrive finally at the moment for which the foregoing argument
has been merely preparation: the formulation of the moral law
that implictly guides us in our ordinary judgments of esteem and
disesteem, duty and responsibility. Kant's entire argument takes
up only one brief paragraph:

> But what kind of law can this be the thought of which, even without
> regard to the results expected from it, has to determine the will if this
> is to be called good absolutely and without qualification? Since I have
> robbed the will of every inducement that might arise for it as a
> consequence of obeying any particular law, nothing is left but the
> conformity of actions to universal law as such, and this alone must
> serve the will as its principle. That is to say, I ought never to act
> except in such a way *that I can also will that my maxim should
> become a universal law.* Here bare conformity to universal law as
> such (without having as its base any law prescribing particular ac-
> tions) is what serves the will as its principle, and must so serve it if
> duty is not to be everywhere an empty delusion and a chimerical
> concept. The ordinary reason of mankind also agrees with this com-
> pletely in its practical judgements and always has the aforesaid prin-
> ciple before its eyes. (Ak. 402)

I think it is not too strong to say that this paragraph and the
three paragraphs of exemplification and elaboration which follow
are a total mess. Kant compresses enough confusion and sheer bad
argument into these pages to provide object lessons for a semester
of introductory philosophy. Once more, therefore, we are faced
with a dilemma of textual commentary. Either we follow the line
of Kant's exposition, insofar as one can be discerned, and find

ourselves explicating what would better be forgotten, or we attempt to "rectify" the argument, thereby risking the charge that we are putting words in Kant's mouth.

By now, it will be obvious that I intend to choose the latter alternative. As a partial defense, let me remind the reader that we are still dealing with chapter 1, in which Kant imagines himself to be talking to a sympathetic audience that agrees with his own moral convictions. Much of what I seem to be imputing rather arbitrarily to Kant will appear in his own name in chapter 2. The first problem in the text is the confusion of self-interest with inclination. Kant presents us here with an image of moral deliberation as a struggle between the stern commands of duty and the siren lure of self-interest. Now, generally speaking, Kant is concerned with the conflict between duty and inclination. Since it is at least possible that a man might be inclined toward something other than his own self-interest, the two struggles are not identical. Nevertheless, in the example Kant offers of false promising, self-interested deviation from duty is taken as the prototype of immoral action, and so the confusion continues.

The second problem, to which we have already devoted some attention, concerns the whole matter of "expected results." As every beginning graduate student knows, Kant is classified as a "deontologist," not a "teleologist" in ethics. That is to say, he is thought to hold that morals is a matter of principles rather than of consequences. In a sense, of course, this standard view is correct, and certainly Kant encourages it by countless statements like those in the passage we are considering. But in another sense, Kant is totally concerned with consequences, for he believes that a moral agent should be moved by the thought of the good at which his actions aim.[16]

This problem, as we have already seen, originates in Kant's confusion of the form-matter distinction with the quite different

[16]Mary Gregor has made this point quite effectively in her fine commentary on *The Metaphysic of Morals*, entitled *Laws of Freedom* (New York: Barnes & Noble, p. 32). Gregor explains that the *Groundwork* was intended as an introduction to both Kant's theory of legal obligation, or *Rechtslehre*, and his theory of moral virtue, or *Tugendlehre*. Since it is precisely one's obligation to pursue certain ends, rather than merely to abide by certain rules, that distinguishes virtuous from merely right action, Kant naturally abstracts from all consideration of ends in the work designed to lay the foundations for both branches of moral theory.

distinction between reasons which are good reasons for any agent qua rational and reasons which are good for an agent only insofar as he is in some special condition. A reason based upon a desire or inclination is morally irrelevant, *not* because it refers to an expected result, but because it is a good reason only for those agents who have the desire or inclination. "Because the expected results are good" is a morally relevant reason (and a good reason, too) because it is an equally good reason for all rational agents. The fact that it refers to consequences in no way invalidates it.

Kant further complicates matters by being uncertain whether he wants conformity with the Categorical Imperative to be a sufficient or merely a necessary condition of the objective validity of a maxim. In the grand scheme of his moral philosophy, as we have already noted, the *Groundwork* was to establish the Categorical Imperative as the formal or necessary condition, and the Doctrine of Virtue of the Metaphysic of Morals was to complete the conditions of validity with a theory of obligatory ends. But the actual argument of the *Groundwork* again and again treats the Categorical Imperative as a sufficient condition of the validity of maxims. Consequently, Kant talks as though an agent who conformed his action to the Categorical Imperative would have thereby a sufficient reason for action. Thus, in the passage before us, Kant argues:

> Since I have robbed the will of every inducement that might arise for it as a consequence of obeying any particular law, nothing is left but the conformity of actions to universal law as such.

But this makes no sense at all. Having "robbed the will" of all reasons for action based upon some mere de facto condition of the self, such as its possession of certain desires or inclinations, Kant leaves nothing which could motivate the will save those reasons which are good reasons for any agent qua rational. Among those reasons for adopting and acting on a policy is the Categorical Imperative, to be sure. But as a merely necessary condition of the objective validity of policies (maxims), it can at most serve to *rule out* those proposed policies which are inconsistent. Something more, namely the Idea of the Good, will be needed to *rule in* certain specific policies as objectively valid for all rational agents.

Perhaps I can make this matter a bit clearer by developing an analogy with the functioning of theoretical reason. The making of objectively valid judgments is to theoretical reason what the adopting of objectively valid policies is to practical reason. The law of contradiction states the necessary condition of the validity of judgments, just as the Categorical Imperative states the necessary condition of the validity of maxims, or policies. The principles of evidence express the material conditions of the validity of judgments, as the Idea of the Good expresses the material condition of the validity of maxims.

Imagine that men were tempted by prejudice, superstition, or some material interest to assert judgments which violate the formal and material principles of theoretical reason, just as they are tempted by desire, inclination, or other material interest to adopt policies which violate the formal and material principles of practical reason. Then we might write a *Critique of Pure* (Theoretical) *Reason* in which we demonstrated those principles of theoretical reason and exposed the ways in which men are led to deviate from them. Instead of a grocer whose greed impelled him to cheat his customers, we might tell of a psychologist whose racial bigotry led him to misinterpret the results of intelligence tests. In place of the affecting story of a philanthropist, saddened by personal tragedy, who nevertheless continued his policy of generosity though his heart wasn't in it, we could offer the case of the historian who correctly inferred from his accumulated data results which contradicted his most cherished theories.

But in cautioning prospective scientists to shun all prejudice and *parti pris*, we could hardly advise them to be guided by the law of contradiction alone! Such advice, if taken, would limit them to the elaborating of sterile tautologies and the rejecting of internally inconsistent theories. To arrive at substantive, objectively valid scientific judgments, they would have to invoke the material rules of evidence as well as the formal law of contradiction.

By the same token, Kant cannot expect moral agents to adopt objectively valid principles of practical reason so long as they restrict themselves to the Categorical Imperative alone. Some appeal to the Idea of the Good or to a theory of obligatory ends must be conjoined with obedience to the Categorical Imperative, if substantive, objectively valid policies are to be chosen and acted upon. To be sure, it will still be a mystery how the Idea of the Good can move a man to action in the absence of any desire or inclination urging him in that direction. But it is a logical confusion, not a mere mystery, to suppose that the purely formal Categorical Imperative can dictate a substantive policy in the absence even of an Idea of the Good.

Kant's actual statements at Ak. 402 confirm this interpretation, even though he persists in claiming substantive implications for the merely formal Categorical Imperative. Formulating that principle for the first time in the *Groundwork*, he says:

> I ought never to act except in such a way *that I can also will that my maxim should become a universal law*.

Exactly so. The Categorical Imperative states a negative or necessary condition and the injunction, therefore, takes the form of telling us the sorts of policies we should *not* adopt. Kant goes on to say: "bare conformity to universal law as such . . . serves the will as its principle," which certainly sounds as though the Categorical Imperative were to be used as a *sufficient* condition of the validity of maxims. But immediately in the next paragraph, he offers an example, and sure enough, it is an example of an *invalid* maxim which is ruled *out* by the Categorical Imperative.

Before attempting a reconstruction, in the light of these comments, of Kant's argument for the Categorical Imperative, perhaps we ought to say a few words about the example offered in paragraphs 18–20 (Ak. 402–403). The passage has often been criticized and rightly so, for it is virtually a parody of Kant's real position. The question is, "May I not, when I am hard pressed, make a promise with the intention of not keeping it?" (Ak. 402). That is to say, I am asked to evaluate the policy of making false promises when I am hard pressed. Notice two facts about this case, both of which are important. First, it is a policy, not a particular act, which is to be evaluated. A great deal has been written in recent years about the fact that any individual act can be described in a multitude of ways and, hence, can be an instance of a number of different general rules or policies. Some authors have seen an objection to Kant in this fact, but its relevance is indirect at best, for Kant always considers policies (maxims), never individual acts.

Second, the policy under consideration, as stated, makes no

reference to the reasons for which it might be adopted. To be sure, the policy specifies false promising "when hard pressed," but it does not say, "because I am hard pressed." Nor does it say, "because I expect the false promise to relieve the distress." For reasons already given, I believe that we must distinguish sharply between the content of a policy and the reasons for which it is or may be adopted.

Kant begins his analysis of false promising well enough. He distinguishes prudential from moral reasons for adopting such a policy and observes that we might perfectly well choose a maxim of false promising from prudence, although rather more calculation of future consequences than is common among moral egoists would be required before that choice could be called even prudentially rational. But the question before us is whether false promising is *right,* not whether it is *prudent.*

Now Kant goes disastrously wrong. Here is the offending passage:

> Suppose I seek . . . to learn in the quickest way and yet unerringly how to solve the problem "Does a lying promise accord with duty?" I have then to ask myself "Should I really be content [*wurde Ich wohl damit zufrieden sein*] that my maxim (the maxim of getting out of a difficulty by a false promise) should hold as a universal law (one valid both for myself and others)? And could I really say to myself that every one may make a false promise if he finds himself in a difficulty from which he can extricate himself in no other way?" I then become aware at once that I can indeed will to lie, but I can by no means will a universal law of lying; for by such a law there could properly be no promises at all, since it would be futile to profess a will for future action to others who would not believe my profession or who, if they did so over-hastily, would pay me back in like coin; and consequently my maxim, as soon as it was made a universal law, would be bound to annul itself. (Ak. 403)

Students have a field day with this paragraph. Where shall we begin? It is a purely contingent empirical fact that men who are the victims of false promising tend to disbelieve future promises from the same source. Some such men retaliate with false promises of their own; others do not. Experience suggests that the practice of promising persists even in the face of widespread reneging. Compare the fact that Renaissance notables continued to accept dinner invitations even after the custom of poisoning one's enemies at table had taken hold. But all of this is irrelevant, for these considerations are patently prudential in nature. How can Kant have made such a mistake!

The concluding argument of the paragraph looks rather more like an appeal to logical consistency, but as phrased it is simply absurd. It may well be that a maxim of false promising "would be bound to annul itself" if universally adopted, but so would a policy of combatting racial prejudice: for if *everyone* undertook to eliminate bigotry, it would disappear. Are we to infer that it is wrong to fight prejudice? We find ourselves slipping into the sentimental notion that the poor ought to be preserved in their misery so as to be continuing occasions for charity.

Finally, Kant's paraphrase of the Categorical Imperative is singularly designed to mislead. Should I be content, he asks, that my maxim should hold as a universal law? This, we are to suppose, is equivalent to asking whether I "can will" that my maxim should be a universal law. But a wealthy and powerful villain might perfectly well be content to suffer the inconvenience of being falsely promised to, on the grounds that he can reasonably expect to gain more than he will lose from universal deceit. It is quite another question whether such a man can (consistently) will such a universal policy.

I shall attempt to sort out this business of false promising when we come to it again in chapter 2. We shall find that a policy of false promising can, under suitable interpretation, be shown to contain a formal inconsistency and hence to violate the Categorical Imperative. As for the paragraph now before us, I am afraid that Kant does his fellow Prussians no service by imputing such reasoning to them. I would hope that even simple, good peasants would do better than that.

Now let us see whether we can reconstruct the argument by which the Categorical Imperative is introduced. As expressed by Kant at Ak. 402, the principle states:

> I ought never to act except in such a way *that I can also will that my maxim should become a universal law.*

The contrast here is between policies which it would be rational only for some agents to adopt, and policies ("laws") which it would be rational for all agents whatsoever to adopt. To say that a policy is rational for some agents to adopt but not for others is to say that the reason for adopting it is a good reason for some agents but not for others. This can be the case only if the reason appeals to some state or condition that characterizes the first group of agents but not the second. For reasons which Kant has not yet explained, having to do with the difference between the phenomenal and noumenal character of agents, differentiating states and conditions are all causally determined (such as desires or inclinations). Since no man has a duty to do what lies outside his control and since our causally determined desires and inclinations lie outside our control, it follows that no one is obligated to be guided by reasons of the differentiating sort. I have no obligation, for example, to adopt a policy of charity out of a sympathetic fellow-feeling, for I cannot control whether I have that fellow-feeling.

Therefore, if there is a general principle of obligation at all, it must command me to act on reasons of the first sort: reasons, that is, that are equally good reasons for all rational agents. But in Kant's terminology a policy recommended by reasons of that sort is an "objective" policy, or "law." So we may state the general principle (if there is one) thus:

Act on policies that are universal laws. Or, putting the same principle negatively:

Never act on policies that are not universal laws. And rephrasing once more to bring out the relation to subjective maxims:

Never act in such a way that my maxim is not also fit to be a universal law. This is just the Categorical Imperative, save for the obscure notion of "willing that my maxim should become a universal law." We shall not become fully clear on that element of the formula until after our discussion of Kant's proof in chapter 2.

We have now completed our examination of the three propositions concerning duty and the Categorical Imperative which Kant extracts from them. There is still a great deal of clarifying to be done, of course, but the foundations have been laid for the central argument of the next chapter. Keep in mind that all the forgoing discussion is directed at Kant's first audience. The three propositions are, at best, reconstructions of ordinary moral consciousness. It remains to be seen whether Kant can provide arguments to persuade his more demanding second and third audiences.

6. Transition to Chapter 2 (Ak. 403–405)

Kant concludes the chapter with a brief and rather moving account of the need for a theoretical investigation and justification of the Categorical Imperative. Since ordinary men carry the highest moral principle engraved in their hearts and can only be misled by subtle speculations, why ought we to attempt a defense whose difficulty may end in misleading rather than enlightening? Kant's revealing answer is that men are endlessly beset by powerful inclinations which tempt even the strongest consciences. A coherent theory is an invaluable aid in the struggle against the inducements of desire. As Kant quite vividly puts it: "Innocence is a splendid thing, only it has the misfortune not to keep very well and to be easily misled" (Ak. 404–405).

The point is of no importance to the argument, of course, but I should like to add a reason or two to Kant's. It may be that in eighteenth-century Prussia the greatest threat to moral rectitude was the temptation of happiness, but it is otherwise today. For every man in our world who shirks duty from a weakness for self-interest, there are ten who commit evil in the name of false principles. The subjective sense of rectitude unsupported by valid arguments is a most dangerous source of evil, for it guards men against appeals to conscience. The United States in particular has been afflicted by a plague of statesmen so convinced of the rightness of their principles that they have been willing even to sacrifice their political careers for what they mistakenly thought to be right. The cure for this affliction is not, as some temperate but shallow commentators have thought, a retreat to acknowledged self-interest. Rather the only hope is a moral philosophy whose arguments can be established with more than hypothetical validity. When men's hearts are right and their reasons wrong, we can muddle through with good intentions; but when even the heart is pledged to a false cause, only right reason can restore us to the path of rectitude.

chapter two
Passage from Popular Moral Philosophy to a Metaphysic of Morals

1. Preliminary Remarks: The Structure of Chapter 2

Kant has now concluded his dialogue with his *first* audience, those who share his fundamental convictions. The arguments of chapter 1, as we have several times remarked, are expected to weigh only with those who grant the familiar moral judgments to which Kant appeals, such as that one ought to be honest in economic transactions and that it is bad for a evil man to be happy. In chapter 2 Kant directs his arguments to a second audience of those who grant the meaningfulness of moral discourse but may reject the judgments on which chapter 1 relies. In addition, as we shall see, Kant implicitly develops an argument which speaks to the total moral sceptic, the man who simply denies that there is any reason to praise, blame, or hold men responsible at all.

The thesis of chapter 2 is identical with that of chapter 1, namely, that the Categorical Imperative is a valid moral law for all rational agents. However, since Kant faces a more difficult audience, his argument must be correspondingly more complex, and chapter 2 is therefore a great deal more difficult than the relatively straightforward chapter 1. Even so, if Kant had restricted himself to an exposition of the proof of the validity of the Categorical Imperative, chapter 2 would occupy a third or a fourth of its actual length. The major portion of the text is devoted to a variety of elaborations, explanations, and correlative arguments which, though exceedingly important for Kant's moral philosophy as a whole, do not materially advance the argument of the *Groundwork*.

Chapter 2 divides more or less cleanly into four subsections. (1) Kant opens with a discussion of the inappropriateness of argument by example in moral philosophy and the need for an a priori formulation (Ak. 406–412). (2) Then he presents the proof proper, introducing it by the famous classification of types of imperatives and concluding with a demonstration that the Categorical Imperative can be derived from the mere concept of a categorical imperative in general (Ak. 412–421). At this point, strictly speaking the business of the chapter is concluded. (3) There follows a long, rich, many-sided development of the argument in which Kant gives examples of the Categorical Imperative, derives alternative formulations, and defines such central notions as moral autonomy, the self as end in itself, and the kingdom of ends (Ak. 421–436). (4) Finally, Kant reviews the argument of the section and offers a brief classification of moral philosophies based on the distinction between autonomy and heteronomy of the will. The section ends with a summary statement of what remains to be accomplished (Ak. 436–445).

2. The Need for an A Priori Moral Philosophy (Ak. 406–412)

Kant opens chapter 2 with a warning to the reader who may have misunderstood the argument of chapter 1. Although we have thus far been engaged in a reconstruction of the ordinary moral beliefs of the generality of mankind, we must not make the mistake of supposing that the argument has been inductive or that we have been generalizing on the basis of examples. "In actual fact it is absolutely impossible for experience to establish with complete certainty a single case in which the maxim of an action in other respects right has rested solely on moral grounds and on the thought of one's duty" (Ak. 407). The matters which Kant here treats rather discursively are actually fundamental to an understanding of the *Groundwork*, and this is a suitable occasion to review some more general considerations which form the background for the particular discussion of examples and the need for a priori moral philosophy. What follows may seem rather distant from ethics proper, but I will try, as trial lawyers say, to connect it up with the issue at hand.

The Inaugural Dissertation of 1770 first elaborated the characteristically Critical distinction between sensibility and intelligence as sources of representations. In that early work Kant took the view that intellect is capable by itself of yielding genuine knowledge. Only in the *Critique* was he to arrive at the conclusion that concepts without intuitions are empty, intuitions without concepts blind. In the *Dissertation* Kant makes no division in the faculty of intelligence. He refers to it indiscriminately as reason, understanding, intellect, or intelligence. But he does draw a very important distinction between two different *uses* to which the faculty of intelligence may be put.

In its merely *logical use*, intelligence performs the funtions of comparing, classifying, contrasting, and combining representations, regardless of the source from which they come. The arrangement of empirical concepts into genera and species, the classification of logical terms as singular, general, positive, negative, the combination of judgments into inferential sequences, all these are instances of the logical use of intelligence. But in its *real use* intelligence actually generates representations of objects out of its own inner resources, quite independently of sensibility and hence without empirical content. These representations, which are called pure concepts because of their lack of sensible content, apply to things as they are in themselves, for they are not limited and distorted by the subjective conditions of sense. Kant does not offer any systematic account of the pure concepts produced by the real use of intelligence, but he remarks that among their number are "possibility, existence, necessity, substance, cause, etc., with their opposites and correlates" *(Dissertation,* section 2). Through the employment of the pure concepts of intellect, we are told, reason can arrive at metaphysical knowledge of things in themselves, whereas through the employment of sensible concepts it can only achieve a scientific knowledge of things as they appear. Thus Kant thinks to compromise the conflicting claims of Leibnizean metaphysics and Newtonian science.

When he wrote the *Dissertation,* Kant seems not to have wondered how pure concepts produced by reason independently of experience could apply with the appropriate necessity and universality to things in themselves. Within two years, however, he had come to recognize the force of this question, as his famous letter of 1772 to Marcus Herz indicates. There Kant formulated for the first time the question which was to become the key to the development of the Critical Philosophy:

> In the *Dissertation* . . . I silently passed over the . . . question, how such representations [the pure concepts] which refer to an object and yet are not the result of an affection due to that object, can be possible. . . . When we ask how the understanding can form to itself completely *a priori* concepts of things in their *qualitative* determination, with which these things must of necessity agree, or formulate in regard to their possibility principles which are independent of experience, but with which experience must exactly conform,—we raise a question, that of the origin of the agreement of our faculty of understanding with the things in themselves, over which obscurity still hangs.[1]

A superficial solution to this problem must already have been developing in Kant's mind, for in the same letter he expresses the hope that a "Critique of Pure Reason" will appear later that same year containing the desired answer. Within the framework of Kant's thought, it is not hard to imagine what the solution might be. Restrict the application of the pure concepts to things as they appear, give up forever the hope of metaphysical knowledge of the supersensible, and we can account for the a priori (albeit conditioned) validity of the categories.

[1]Quoted from N. Kemp Smith, *A Commentary to Kant's "Critique of Pure Reason,"* 2d ed. (New York: The Humanities Press, 1923), pp. 219–220.

However appealing such a resolution of the problem might appear, it was not to prove satisfactory, for at some time very near the writing of the Herz letter, Kant once more became aware of the sceptical arguments of Hume.[2] The trouble with Hume's attack on our claim to knowledge, from Kant's point of view, was that it applied as forcefully to knowledge of things in space and time as it did to metaphysical knowledge of transcendent reality. Hence, having severely restricted the pure concepts to the realm of appearances, Kant was still faced with the necessity of demonstrating that representations generated by the mind itself could yield a priori knowledge even of mere appearances. The task of combating this new and more profound attack delayed the publication of the *Critique* for nearly ten years until 1781.

When the *Critique* made its appearance, Kant's theory of intelligence had undergone a significant complication. He now distinguished very sharply between the faculty of combining concepts into judgments, which he called understanding, and the faculty of combining judgments into inferences, which he called reason. The terms "intelligence" and "intellect" pretty much disappeared from the text, and, despite numerous confusions and inconsistencies of usage, Kant adhered thereafter to the division of intellectual faculties into understanding and reason.

The *Dissertation* distinction between real and logical uses of a faculty remained, but, like the faculty of intelligence itself, it had been duplicated. There were now real and merely logical employments of both understanding and reason. The logical use of understanding was assimilated to the old logical theory of judgment. In the Table of Functions of Unity in Judgment at the opening of the Transcendental Analytic, Kant organized such familiar classifications of judgments as universal, particular, singular, affirmative, negative, problematic, apodeictic, categorical, and hypothetical into a neat quadruple of triads. The pure concepts of intelligence

[2]For a more detailed discussion of the development of Kant's thought, see my book *Kant's Theory of Mental Activity* (Cambridge, Mass: Harvard University Press, 1963), pp. 8–32. On Kant's reintroduction to the arguments of Hume, and his knowledge of Hume's philosophy in general, see my article "Kant's Debt to Hume via Beattie," *Journal of the History of Ideas*, 21 (January–March 1960): 117–123.

reappeared as a Table of Categories, with the key concepts of reality, existence, substance, and causality nestled among such place fillers as unity, plurality, negation, limitation, and community.

The logical employment of reason, as contrasted with that of understanding, was now reserved specifically for the branch of Logic concerning inferences. As the various forms of judgment summarized the activity of understanding in its logical use, so the theory of the syllogism expressed reason's logical use. But reason, like understanding, has also a *real* use according to the theory of the *Critique*. It generates out of *its* inner resources a system of concepts which in various ways embody the notion of the *unconditioned*. "Uncaused cause," "necessary being," "infinite spatial or temporal totality," are all instances of the concept of the unconditioned. Just as the concepts of cause and substance cannot be abstracted from the materials of sensation but must be created by the mind a priori, so the concepts of an uncaused cause and a necessary being cannot be extrapolated from our knowledge of causes and substances but must also be created by the mind. The task of creating them is the *real use of reason*.

In order to mark the important differences between the products of the real uses of understanding and reason, Kant resurrects Plato's terminology and calls the concepts of unconditionality Ideas of Reason. Thus the Pure Concepts of Understanding and the Ideas of Reason are the two systems of representations produced a priori by the intellectual faculties of the mind. The task of the Critical Philosophy is to determine the scope and legitimacy of the application of these representations to the objects of experience.

Since the pure concepts and Ideas are not derived from experience, we must justify their application to experience before proceeding to use them. Kant adopts the legal term "deduction" as a name for the proof of the legitimacy of a concept. In the famous Deduction of the Pure Concepts of Understanding, he demonstrates that the categories have a legitimate employment in the formulation of judgments about the objects of our experience. Following Hume, he argues that we cannot provide an empirical justification of such concepts as cause and substance; nevertheless, the argument of the deduction proves that they *are* legitimate concepts. Hence it is perfectly possible to give *examples* of causes and substances, even though this possibility rests on an a priori proof.

The case is quite otherwise with the Ideas of Reason. Since objects can be objects for us only under the limiting conditions of sensibility and conception, nothing in our experience is truly *unconditioned*. Hence the Ideas, which are variations on the notion of unconditionality, cannot be instantiated in experience. We not only cannot *derive* the Idea of absolute spatial totality from our perceptual experience; we cannot even be *presented* with an instance of such totality once we have the Idea. Nor can the Ideas of a first cause and of a necessary being be exemplified in experience. For this reason Kant concludes that genuine metaphysical knowledge of a transcendent sort is impossible, for it always involves the employment of some concept of the unconditioned.

Now the concept of a free will, with its derivative notions of a free act, a morally worthy act, and an act done for the sake of duty, is an *Idea of Reason*. Kant makes this perfectly clear in the *Critique of Pure Reason*, where the Idea of Freedom turns up in the Third Antinomy under the guise of the Idea of a First Cause. Since the several key notions of Kant's moral philosophy are all Ideas of Reason, *it follows from his own argument that it is absolutely impossible ever to give a satisfactory example of any one of them in experience.* It goes without saying that the concept of a free act cannot be *derived from* experience; neither can the concepts of causality and substance. But once we possess these latter concepts, we can perfectly well give examples of them. That possibility is guaranteed by the argument of the Deduction. In the case of the Ideas of freedom and moral worth, however, it is impossible to give genuine instances of them, just as it is impossible to have an experience which is adequate to the Idea of God. That which is unconditioned simply cannot be represented *as* unconditioned within experience. Free wills always appear in experience as causally determined wills; acts done *for the sake of* duty always appear as bits of behavior *in conformity with* duty.

We are now in a position to appreciate the full significance of Kant's opening remarks in chapter 2. After the affecting tales of prudent grocers and dutiful Samaritans bowed by life's cares with which Kant has illuminated the arguments of chapter 1, it comes as something of a surprise to find him asserting flatly:

> In actual fact it is absolutely impossible for experience to establish with complete certainty a single case in which the maxim of an action in other respects right has rested solely on moral grounds and on the thought of one's duty.

The succeeding paragraphs make it sound as though Kant has simply been overcome with misanthropic scepticism about the motives of his fellowmen. The truth, however, as we have seen, is that the central doctrine of his theory of knowledge requires him to say just exactly this. Only a fool would despair of human nature because of his failure to find a truly dutiful act. Such a man might be compared to a mathematician who, setting out to test his idea of infinite length, seizes upon each long line he encounters, follows it with rising hopes, and then in an access of disappointment at always coming to the end, gives up the notion of infinity itself as a bad bet. For all we know, the right acts we observe may also be morally worthy acts (they may be done for the sake of, as well as in conformity with duty). But since those acts can be presented in experience only under the conditions of sensibility and conception, we may be certain that they will appear to us as causally determined and, hence, as lacking in moral worth.

One word of caution: when we talk of the impossibility of examples in moral philosophy, we are referring to certifiable instances of particular morally worthy acts. We can never know whether a particular man at a particular time was moved, qua noumenal agent, by the idea of duty, as well as, qua phenomenal character, by some inclination. But Kant also gives "examples" of a quite different sort, namely, examples of particular maxims which do or do not have the status of moral laws. The example of false promising in chapter 1 and the four examples of the Categorical Imperative in chapter 2 are instances of this type of exemplification. It remains to be seen whether these attempts at applying the Categorical Imperative are successful, but none of my remarks about the impossibility of examples in moral philosophy are relevant to *that* matter. It may very well be that we can demonstrate the validity of particular moral principles, even though we can never provide a certified instance of anyone *acting on* such a principle. Since Kant himself mixes these two sorts of "examples" together indiscriminately, it is particularly important that we keep them distinct.

Kant concludes the opening remarks of chapter 2 with the reminder that moral laws, if they are valid, must hold for "every rational being as such." We can never ground a satisfactory defense of them on "the special nature of human reason." In other words, the principles of morality must be known in an *unconditionally* a priori fashion, not in a merely conditionally a priori fashion as are the principles of science and mathematics. Like Logics, Ethics is absolutely universal in its validity. Hence, we shall have to derive our principles "from the general concept of a rational being as such." I have already pointed out that the difficulty of Kant's moral philosophy is due entirely to the absolute unconditionality of the results which it purports to establish. Not even the *Critique of Pure Reason* attempted so uncompromising a task.

3. The Proof of the Validity of the Categorical Imperative (Ak. 412–421)

We have now arrived at that point in the commentary which, in my Apology to the Reader, I described as "the elephant in the boa." The twenty paragraphs of *Akademie* 412–421 contain the heart of the argument of the entire *Groundwork*. In order to make any progress at all toward a clarification and reconstruction of Kant's position, it will be necessary to range rather far afield into a number of related philosophical problems. While trying as much as possible to follow the order of Kant's exposition, I shall have to say something, by way of background, about the rationalist and empiricist conceptions of causation, the nature of the will, the

distinction between reasons and causes (and the associated distinction between action and behavior), the relation of duty to inclination, the relation of reason to desire, and even the dialectical
structure of philosophical argument.

As we shall see, the root of the difficulty in this pivotal portion
of the text is Kant's commitment to a number of mutually incompatible doctrines which can neither be reconciled nor easily set
aside. I shall try to show that the contradictions are intrinsic to our
customary ways of thinking about morality and not peculiar to
Kant's own philosophical system.

The passage before us—the twelfth through the thirty-first paragraphs of chapter 2—divides naturally into four parts:

1. Pars. 12–15   Kant defines the key terms "will" and "im-
                  perative" and explains the difference be-
                  tween a holy will, which does not experience
                  principles of practical reason as imperatives,
                  and a conditioned will (like ours) which does.
2. Pars. 16–23   A lengthy discussion of the nature of impera-
                  tives, with special attention to the distinction
                  between hypothetical and categorical imper-
                  atives. It is here that we are introduced to the
                  familiar three-fold classification of Rules of
                  Skill, Counsels of Prudence, and Laws of Mo-
                  rality.
3. Pars. 24–28   The central passage, in which Kant poses the
                  question, "How are imperatives possible?"
                  The problem, Kant claims, is with Laws of
                  Morality, for he does not seem to think that
                  there is much difficulty in explaining how
                  either Rules of Skill or Counsels of Prudence
                  are possible.
4. Pars. 29–31   A very brief passage, not even 200 words
                  long, in which Kant states the formal deriva-
                  tion of the Categorical Imperative.

My plan of attack is to analyze the text in five stages. I begin with
the definition of "will" which opens paragraph 12 and use it as a
hook on which to hang associated discussions of rational causality,

action versus behavior, and reasons versus causes. Then, I explore Kant's conception of the moral condition, go into the relation of reason to desire, and connect this up with the definition and discussion of imperatives in paragraphs 12–23. Third, I explore some of the contradictions which emerge in the first and second stages of the discussion, focusing particularly on the relationship between reason and desire. Fourth, I comment directly on paragraphs 24–28 and the question, "How are imperatives possible?" And finally, I analyze and attempt to reconstruct the derivation proper of the Categorical Imperative in paragraphs 29–31.

A. The Nature of the Will (Par. 12) and Other Matters

> "Everything in nature works in accordance with laws. Only a rational being has the power to act *in accordance with his idea* of laws—that is, in accordance with principles—and only so has he a *will.*" (Ak. 412, the opening sentences of par. 12)

With this definition of "will," Kant begins his argument. As if to emphasize that this is the true starting point of the argument, he reiterates the definition in the opening sentence of chapter 3:

> Will is a kind of causality belonging to living beings so far as they are rational. (Ak. 446)

Two things about these definitions seem to me to call for immediate comment. First of all, will is described as a *power* of acting in accordance with the idea of laws or, alternatively, as a *kind of causality.* In English, this sounds as though Kant's grammar has gotten slightly garbled in the translation. We might expect Kant to claim that the will is *capable* of acting in accordance with the idea of laws, but not that the will *is* that capacity. Similarly, Kant might want to say that the will *can be determined by* causes of a certain sort, namely, rational causes or reasons, but it is a bit odd to say that will *is* a kind of causality.

The other peculiarity is that the definitions, particularly the second, link causality so closely to the concept of will that the familiar notion of a free, uncaused will appears to be a flat, logical impossibility. Now Kant may want to deny the possibility of an uncaused will, although we know that he believes in—indeed relies upon—the concept of a free will in some sense of "free." But why does he define "will" in such a way that "uncaused will" becomes a simple contradiction in terms?

It turns out that Kant really means what he appears to be saying. The grammar has not been botched in the translation, and he has good reason to reject "uncaused will" as a contradiction in terms. But we shall need some background information before we can understand this definition of will.

i. KANT'S TWO CONCEPTIONS OF CAUSALITY

In the rationalist tradition from which Kant emerged, causal connection is understood, so far as possible, on the model of the logical connection between the premises and conclusion of a deductive argument. Just as reason can grasp the relation between premises and conclusion and, grasping it, can recognize its *apodeictic* necessity, so reason should be able to grasp the relation between an event or state of affairs and its cause and, grasping it, recognize that it too is a *necessary* connection. Hence, the correct employment of reason should lead man to a knowledge of those first principles of rational knowledge which state the true and fundamental nature of the universe. It is for this reason, among others, that Plato treats the mathematical forms as most like the form of the good; for mathematics, in particular geometry, was the most perfect species of deductive reasoning available to Plato as a model for rational necessity in general.

It was common among rationalists, from Plato and Aristotle to Leibniz, to connect man's cognitive powers with the structure of the universe by claiming that man's reason is a spark of the divine Reason which created that universe. In its completed form, therefore, man's systematic knowledge mirrors the order of being, with the first, or highest, judgment asserting the existence of the first, or highest, being: God. As Aristotle argued, man knows that he has true knowledge when and only when his finite reason directly apprehends the rational structure of being. The connections among things and events are thereby seen to be necessary, not contingent, so that our knowledge of those connections has the demonstrative force of a valid syllogism.

By contrast, accumulations of sense experience can give us no more than a collection of rules of thumb, what Plato rather contemptuously calls *empiriae,* which tell us what sorts of events have been associated with one another on past occasions. Lacking a rational insight into the true, inner nature of those events, we have no idea *why* they have occurred together, and so the best we can do is to hope that the future will resemble the past sufficiently to allow us to get by. We cannot truly be said to *know* that one event causes another until we understand the essence, or inner nature, of the events sufficiently to see necessary connections between them: to see why the second *must* follow the first.

For the ancients, the obvious examples of rational knowledge came from mathematics. Repeated measurements of the areas enclosed by squares erected on the three sides of a right triangle may reveal the curious fact that the two smaller squares erected on the legs equal in area (within the limits of error of such measurements) the square erected on the hypoteneuse. And architects or surveyors may after a time come to rely upon this relationship instead of testing it again with each new right triangle. But only the Pythagorean theorem, by exhibiting the rational connection between that relationship and the properties of the right triangle in general, explains *why* the square of the hypoteneuse is equal to the sum of the squares of the adjacent sides. And only after we have comprehended the derivation of the Pythagorean theorem from the self-evident axioms of Euclid can we be said to *know* the relationship and to know that it is *necessary.*

In the seventeenth and eighteenth centuries philosophers had even more impressive instances of this sort of rational knowledge to buttress their analysis of causal connection as a kind of logical connection akin to deductive inference. The development of mathematical physics, culminating in Newton's derivation of Kepler's laws of planetary motion and Galileo's laws of terrestrial motion from a single set of axioms, transformed a mass of painstakingly accumulated observations into a rational, deductive system of knowledge. To be sure, Newton himself said, "I do not make hypotheses," meaning that he refused to speculate about the inner rational nature of substances which would explain the phenomenon of gravitation. But the contrast between the new science and the sorts of collections of instances of properties proposed by Bacon was no less striking. From Descartes's creation of analytic geometry as a science of space to Leibniz's invention of a version of the calculus as a mathematics of forces, rationalists sought to extend the rational necessity of mathematical inferences into the field of metaphysical knowledge of nature.

Against this background, we can appreciate the force of the attack which Hume launched in Book I of the *Treatise of Human Nature* and which he reiterated in sections IV, V, and VII of the *Enquiry Concerning the Human Understanding*. The essence of the relationship between cause and effect, Hume argues in *Treatise* I: iii, 2, is a *necessary connection*. He views this (in *Treatise*, I: iii, 3) as a *logically* necessary connection, which is clearly what his rationalist opponents had in mind. Hume deploys two principles to make his attack upon the validity of causal reasoning. The first principle, which he draws from his atomistic psychological theory of the contents of consciousness, is: whatever is distinguishable, is separable at least in the imagination. The second principle, which depends for its plausibility on Hume's sense data phenomenalism, is: whatever can be conceived by the imagination is at least logically possible. (As Hume puts it, "is so far possible, that it implies no contradiction nor absurdity" [*Treatise*, I: iii, 3, par. 3].) Any event which we designate as cause is always distinguishable from the event which we designate as its effect. Hence, they can be separated in the imagination, which is to say that we can imagine one event occurring without the other. For example, we can imagine raising the temperature of an enclosed volume of gas without the pressure which it exerts on the walls of the container changing (unless, of course, we have so defined temperature, pressure, and volume that Boyle's Law becomes analytic). But if we can imagine the cause without the effect, then the occurrence of the one without the other "is so far possible, that it implies no contradiction nor absurdity." Hence, their connection is not necessary in the requisite sense: it is not logically necessary.

Hume makes much of the fact that we know little or nothing of the "ultimate springs and principles" of things. In the *Enquiry* he refers repeatedly to those "secret powers," concealed from our view, which if known might explain the de facto patterns of association on which we are forced to rely. But his argument makes it clear that a detailed knowledge of atomic or subatomic structures would get us no closer to a rational grasp of the necessity of causal connection. The source of the contingency of supposed causal connections is the spatio-temporality of our experience. The parts of space and moments of time are external to one another, at least as Hume (and Leibniz and Kant) understand the matter. As Kant says in the Axioms of Intuition of the *First Critique,* space and time are extensive magnitudes. They are wholes composed of aggregations of homogeneous parts. Any object or event which occupies two or more places or times is in principle divisible into the parts which occupy the several places or times. Whatever the relation among the parts, it cannot be a logically necessary connection, for the reasons Hume advanced.

Kant accepted Hume's attack on the rationalist claim that causal connection is akin to logical necessity. In the *Critique* he developed an alternative analysis of the key concept of "necessity" in terms of the rule-governed synthesis of a diversity of perceptual elements standing in spatial, hence external and contingent, relationship to one another. Essentially he took the position that causal connection in the realm of our experience is different in kind from the logical connection between the premises and conclusion of a deductive inference. But Kant clearly retained the conviction, bred of his training in the tradition of rationalist metaphysics, that things-in-themselves stand in relations of rational necessity to one another. In a manner of speaking, he remained persuaded that some variant of Leibniz's metaphysics was true, although forever unknowable by us.[3]

[3]For a more complete discussion of Kant's theory of phenomenal causation and his relationship to Hume, see the Introduction and my book *Kant's Theory of Mental Activity.* The flavor of Kant's position is conveyed in the following sentence, added by him to the Transcendental Aesthetic in the second edition of the

ii. REASONS AS CAUSES: AN ALTERNATIVE MODE OF RATIONAL CAUSALITY

In order to develop a conception of rational causality which he can set over against the conditioned, rule-governed connections of phenomenal events, Kant draws upon a second tradition whose lineage is as ancient as the doctrine that causation is like deduction, namely, the explanation of human action in terms of the purposes it serves or the reasons for which it is done.

One of the first recorded analyses of reasons as a species of cause is to be found in Socrates's famous account in the *Phaedo* of his dissatisfaction with the scientific explanations of Anaxagoras and his own search for a better mode of explanation. The passage is intended as an introduction to the theory of forms, which does not concern us here, but in the midst of his autobiographical discourse Socrates offers the following example:

> It seemed to me that [Anaxagoras's] position was like that of a man who said that all the actions of Socrates are due to his mind, and then attempted to give the causes of my several actions by saying that the reason why I am now sitting here [in jail] is that my body is composed of bones and sinews [etc., etc.]. . . . Analogous causes might also be given of my conversing with you, sounds, air currents, streams of hearing, and so on and so forth, to the neglect of the true causes, to wit that, inasmuch as the Athenians have thought it better to condemn me, I too in my turn think it better to sit here, and more right and proper to stay where I am and submit to such punishment as they enjoin. For, by Jingo, I fancy these same sinews and bones would long since have been somewhere in Megara or Boeotia, impelled by their notion of what was best, if I had not thought it right and proper to submit to the penalty appointed by the state rather than take to my heels and run away.[4]

The appeal to purposes or reasons, as opposed to merely de facto or external causal antecedents, is by now a familiar philosophical

---

Critique of Pure Reason: "Now a thing in itself cannot be known through mere relations; and we may therefore conclude that since outer sense gives us nothing but mere relations, this sense can contain in its representation only the relation of an object to its subject, and not the inner properties of the object in itself [*und nicht das Innere was dem Objekte an sich Zukommt*]" (B67).

[4]*Phaedo*, 98B–99A, trans. R. Hackforth (New York: Cambridge University Press, 1955).

maneuver. In the *Phaedo* passage Socrates seems to imply that reasons and causes—or final and efficient causes—are compatible or complementary elements in a total explanation of an event. For Kant, as we shall see, the matter is not so simple. But it is not yet at all clear why an explanation via purposes can be said to be *rational* in the sense required by Kant. The nonrationality of causal connections in nature was demonstrated by Hume's argument that their denial is not absurd or logically impossible. In what way is the connection between a purpose and the action which fulfills or pursues it any different?

The answer lies in a fact which Kant has already used as a crucial element in the argument of the *First Critique,* namely, the double nature of our representations. As we have seen (in the Introduction to this book), the cognitively significant contents of consciousness—concepts and perceptions—have according to Kant a double objective nature. They are, at one and the same time, *events* in the objective temporal order and *representations* of events in that order. My present thought of my desk is a datable event (occurring, as near as I can make it, at 9:13 P.M. on June 16, 1972). It is *also* a representation of an extended spatio-temporal object (namely, the desk) whose beginning is probably somewhere in the year 1968 and whose end is at some time not now known to me.

It is as events located in objective time and *not* as representations that our concepts and perceptions have phenomenal causes and effects. According to the theory of causal connection defended in the Second Analogy of the *Critique,* to say of two events that the first causes the second is to say that the second follows upon the first according to a rule. In making judgments about the two events, we must (if we are to be correct) assign the first to an earlier time than the second. The rule of this temporal succession is simply the rule, or law of nature, which the mind imposes on its perceptual contents in the process of recollecting them and thereby becoming conscious of them.

As Hume so persuasively shows in the *Treatise,* there is nothing intrinsic to any event which permits us to infer, independently of experience, what its causes or effects must be. In principle, anything can cause anything. Kant's "deduction" of the concept of cause in no way rebuts Hume's claim. Although he demonstrates that the concept of necessary succession has an appropriate use within the realm of experience, Kant cannot exhibit an intrinsic or rational connection between the events designated as cause and effect. The connection remains extrinsic or external: to wit, that the two events are assigned successive objective temporal positions by the system of rules which the mind has imposed on its contents.

What is true of events in general is of course true in particular of our thoughts, which are phenomenal events in the minds of empirical egos. My thoughts must have causes reaching backward in time and effects reaching forward in time as far as I care to search; for that is simply what it means to say that my thoughts *occur*. But prior to an empirical investigation, there is in principle no way of knowing what the particular causes or effects of a thought might be, no way of even knowing the *sorts* of things that might stand in relation to a thought as its causes or effects. For all I know, the causes and effects of a thought include motions of bodies anywhere in the universe, other representations (concepts or perceptions) in my mind, or representations in consciousnesses of other empirical egos.

But the situation is entirely different when we consider thoughts in their representative function, rather than as mere temporally located mental events. A concept qua representation stands in an intrinsic and necessary relation to that which it represents. It may be impossible, independently of experience, to identify the prior causes or subsequent effects of a thought qua mental event. But it is trivially easy to identify the object or event which stands as referent of a concept in its representative function. The appropriate referent is simply that—whatever it is—of which the thought is a representation.

In order to avoid misunderstanding, let us note immediately that we are not concerned here with the existence of the referent or with the truth of some judgment whose assertion involves the use of the concept. Mental contents have a representative function insofar as they *purport* to represent something other than themselves or, if one prefers, insofar as we employ them to represent something other than themselves. So long as coherent criteria can be given for the application of the concept, it qualifies as a representation, even though in fact nothing in the world conforms to those criteria.

Now on Kant's view, the paradigmatic case of rational action is a case in which: first, I form a concept of some event, object, or state of affairs which I choose to bring into being; and second, I do something which I believe will actualize that which my concept represents. In short, I act so as to realize my end.

When I thus act, I am moved by my thoughts. But I am moved by my thoughts qua representations having cognitive significance, not by my thoughts qua mental events having temporal location and, hence, phenomenal causes and effects. The action I perform is one which I believe to be related by some causal law to the state of affairs which I have represented to myself as my end. So, for example, I make it my end to light a match, and I strike it against the side of the match box because I believe that that will cause it to light. Now, of course, my belief is a belief about a phenomenal causal connection, one which could not be deduced a priori from the concepts of a match and a match box (ignoring people who think that the concept of a match box analytically contains the notion of strikeability). But what moves me is *not* the occurrence of that belief that the striking of the match will accomplish my end. The end, the idea of the end, the idea of its being *my* end, the idea of the causal law connecting the end with an action, and my belief that I am capable of performing that action are all analytically related to one another in such a way that knowing them all, I or anyone else can deduce a priori that I shall perform that action. Indeed, if I cannot show this analytical connection, then I have failed to explain the action as an action. Or, to put the same point slightly differently, I have failed to show that the bit of behavior in question *is* an action.[5]

Since thoughts are mental events, they have phenomenal causes and effects, but there is no way a priori to determine what specific events or even what sorts of events stand in the relation of phe-

[5]All of this is a rather turgid recapitulation of ideas which have been common-place in philosophy for some time now. What I am outlining here bears a very close resemblance, for example, to R. G. Collingwood's account of "rethinking the thoughts" of an historical actor in *The Idea of History* (New York: Oxford University Press, 1946). Collingwood's distinction between the inside and the outside of an event comes ultimately from the rationalist distinction between internal and external relations. The same set of ideas can be found in the Franco-German sociological distinction between explanation in the natural sciences and under-standing *(verstehen)* in the sciences of man.

nomenal cause and phenomenal effect to thoughts. Brain states, agitations of the nervous system, movements of the planets, other thoughts—anything might be the cause of the occurrence of a thought. Hume might be right that our thoughts are connected with one another by elaborate patterns of association. Or a physiological line of investigation might prove to be the most fruitful avenue to the empirical laws governing the sequence and character of states of consciousness. But these laws of thoughts, as we might call them, are strictly irrelevant to an analysis of intentional action; for our thoughts figure in such laws as mental events, not as representations. And it is as representations (specifically as ideas of ends and as ideas of actions believed to be causally connected with ends) that our thoughts figure in the analysis of action.

In principle, any thought can, qua mental event, be a cause of any bit of human behavior. For example, the occurrence in my consciousness at one moment of the idea of a horse could, so far as anything knowable in advance of observation is concerned, be the cause of my taking hold of a glass of water and pouring its contents into my mouth at a later moment. It follows, therefore, that the occurrence in my consciousness of the thought that I am thirsty, together with the thoughts that water slakes thirst, that the slaking of thirst is my end, and that I have available a glass of water, could for all anyone knows be phenomenal causes of the occurrence at a later moment of my drinking the water. *But* as we are speaking here of the sort of causal connection which Kant explicates in the Second Analogy of the *Critique of Pure Reason*, these various thoughts could be causes of my drinking the water only insofar as they are mental events. It would be the merest coincidence that those very same thoughts, construed as cognitively significant or representational, stood in an analytic, deductive relationship to the drinking of the water construed as an act. (There is obviously an analogy in this special case to Kant's distinction between action in conformity with a law and action because of, or for the sake of, a law.) Since this distinction is the basis for virtually everything that follows, let me say a bit more about it, even at the risk of being tedious. I shall begin with an extended example from the social sciences.

When the classical economists first developed a theoretical

model of the exchanges in a free market, they posited a system of rationally self-interested agents, each intent upon maximizing his individual wealth. The economic laws relating prices, wages, rents, profits, interest, and the flow of investments could be deduced a priori precisely because the participants in the system were assumed to be rationally purposive. A consumer confronted with a choice among identical commodities could be counted upon to buy the cheaper, for that choice followed necessarily from his presumed purposes and knowledge. (Conversely, a consumer who failed to choose the cheaper goods could be assumed either not to know that they were identical or not to know their relative prices.) After a while, it became apparent that the observed behavior of economic men deviated very considerably from what the theory of the free market implied. In particular, rents for land in England over long periods of time persisted either at significantly higher or significantly lower rates than the theory predicted. In a famous chapter of his monumental *Principles of Political Economy,* John Stuart Mill attempted to account for this irritating failure of the real world to conform to the economic theory:

> [Political economists] are apt to express themselves as if they thought that competition actually does, in all cases, whatever it can be shown to be the tendency of competition to do. This is partly intelligible, if we consider that only through the principle of competition has political economy any pretension to the character of a science. So far as rents, profits, wages, prices, are determined by competition, laws may be assigned for them. Assume competition to be their exclusive regulator, and principles of broad generality and scientific precision may be laid down, according to which they will be regulated. The political economist justly deems this his proper business; and as an abstract or hypothetical science, political economy cannot be required to do, and indeed cannot do, anything more. But it would be a great misconception of the actual course of human affairs, to suppose that competition exercises in fact that unlimited sway. I am not speaking of monopolies, either natural or artificial, or of any interferences of authority with the liberty of production or exchange. Such disturbing causes have always been allowed for by political economists. I speak of cases in which there is nothing to restrain competition; no hindrance to it either in the nature of the case or in artificial obstacles; yet in which the result is not determined by competition,

but by custom or usage; competition either not taking place at all, or producing its effect in quite a different manner from that which is ordinarily assumed to be natural to it.[6]

"Custom or usage" is Mill's general term for the variety of *causes* which determine this economic behavior; by contrast, competition is analyzed in terms of a rational, prudential pursuit of the presumedly universal goal of increased wealth. The economist is not entirely frustrated by the workings of custom, as subsequent developments in that science show. But in attempting to explain or predict behavior which cannot be deduced from reasons, he is forced to rely upon patterns of recurring behavior discovered by the accumulation of observations. In effect, the "time series" which state the monthly fluctuations in inventory levels or the annual growth rate of the gross national product are the economist's sophisticated version of what Hume called "constant conjunctions of resembling instances." The elaborate mathematical models which modern economists construct differ from the classical models in requiring inputs of empirical data before they can be used to predict the course of the economy.

Now, just as Kant tends to fix upon cases of reluctant honesty or conscientious rather than warm-hearted philanthropy when he wants instances of action done for the sake of duty, so Mill focuses attention on economic behavior which deviates from what rational prudence dictates in order to exhibit the workings of custom. But if Kant's theory of phenomenal causality is correct, then it must in principle be possible to discover Hume-style causal explanations for behavior in conformity with, as well as behavior which deviates from, the dictates of rational self-interest. This is precisely the direction that psychocultural explanations of human behavior have taken in the century since Mill wrote. We are accustomed to to the notion that rational accumulation (or the Protestant ethic) is itself a cultural trait whose causes (not reasons) can be found in patterns of child rearing or in the secularization of a religious ethos or in the institutional pressures of economic development.[7]

[6]John Stuart Mill, *Principles of Political Economy*, Book II, chapter 4, par. 1.
[7]Modern economists have a complicated device for preserving the plausibility

iii. WILL AS A KIND OF CAUSALITY

Let us now return to the two definitions of will with which we began and see whether we can make some sense of them. Will, Kant says, is a kind of causality. It is the power to act in accordance with the idea of laws. It is the causality of living beings so far as they are rational (Ak. 412, 446).

Strictly speaking, the term "the will" is misleading, for it encourages us to suppose that there exists some faculty or internal engine or part of the self, which it names. This, in turn, leads us naturally into asking such questions as "What sorts of factors determine the will?" or "Is the will free?" or "Under what circumstances can the will overcome the siren lure of desire?" Kant certainly gives us every reason to suppose that such questions make sense, but his own definitions of "will" undercut them completely. For Kant, "will" is what logicians used to call a syncategorematic term. Its appropriate use is in such contexts as "to have a will."

"To have a will" means "to be a creature capable of being moved by reason." Hence, to have a will is to be a creature in whom reason can be practical (as well as theoretical). That is why immediately after the opening definition in paragraph 12, Kant goes on to say, "Will is nothing but practical reason." "To be moved by reason" means "to be moved by one's comprehension of the truth of a proposition." For reasons that we shall explore presently, the propositions by whose comprehension we are moved are always universal propositions of one sort or another. They are, in common parlance, *reasons.* Kant calls such universal propositions *laws,* and he calls the comprehension of them *principles.* So he writes (rewording the sentence slightly):

---

of rational accounts of economic behavior in the face of deviations from what the original theory of competition predicts. By assuming that economic agents maximize utility rather than money and that each agent has his own individual internally consistent utility function, they can, at least in theory, exhibit the observed behavior as a consequence of a policy of rational maximization. This intellectual exercise, which we might facetiously label "saving the noumena" (in memory of Plato), is the obverse of the search for the causes of apparently rational action.

Will is the power to act in accordance with the idea of laws—that is, in accordance with principles.(Ak. 412)

To be moved by the idea of laws is to be moved by a thought. In the terms that we have been using, it is to be moved by a thought qua representation rather than by a thought qua mental event. Now it is a completely open question *whether* any person is capable of being moved by reasons. We can ascertain easily enough whether he has ever *had* reasons for some bit of his observed behavior. That requires merely figuring out whether the behavior constitutes a rational means to some end which he might have. But it is quite another matter to determine whether he chose that end and whether he was moved by his belief that the behavior was a rational means to it. In other words, it is problematic whether any creature has a will.

As I have many times repeated, Kant's phenomenal determinism commits him to the view that *all* human behavior can be brought under Hume-style causal laws. If he is correct, then it is in principle possible to give a completely sufficient causal explanation of human behavior without ever appealing to purposes, without invoking the cognitive or intentional or representational significance of thoughts at all. Therefore, no empirical evidence could ever be offered in support of the claim that someone has a will. In short, the concept of a will, or of a being which has a will, is an Idea of Reason.

Kant himself does not usually discuss the subject in this way. He talks as though one could perfectly well give certified examples of prudential action in which men are moved by their conception of laws. The problem, he often seems to suggest, is only in showing that men are capable of being moved by reason in one special way, namely, by *pure reason* or reason uninfluenced by sensuous motives. But there are a number of passages in which he gives signs of realizing the fact that he is committed by his own epistemology to the broader position. We shall return to this problem when we come to Kant's treatment of hypothetical versus categorical imperatives.

We can now also explain the second peculiarity of Kant's definition of will, namely, that it seems to rule out *ab initio* the notion of an uncaused will. To have a will is to be capable of being moved by a rational cause rather than by the merely external, nonrational causes which connect phenomena. Freedom, as Kant explains in the opening paragraph of chapter 3, is not the absence of causation. Negatively, freedom is the absence of, or independence from, foreign or external determination. Positively, freedom is autonomy, or self-determination (Ak. 446).

B. Reason, Desire, and Imperatives (Pars. 12–23)

Immediately after defining the notion of "will," Kant draws a distinction between perfectly and imperfectly rational creatures and then launches into the well-known discussion of imperatives. Here, as in the discussion of will, we must review some background material before the theory of imperatives can be sorted out. A number of subjects must be taken up, including Kant's conception of man's moral condition and his view of the relationship between reason and desire.

i. KANT'S CONCEPTION OF THE MORAL CONDITION

Kant comes to the systematic consideration of moral philosophy with a prephilosophical picture of man's moral condition which is familiar to anyone conversant with the Pauline-Augustinian-Lutheran tradition of Christian thought. Man is a finite, fallible creature in whom there glows a spark of the divine reason but who is subject to the temptations and torments of the flesh. Men and women know what is right, either through God's revelation or by their plain, unaided reason. The moral law is simple and direct: do unto others as you would have others do unto you; be a man or woman of your word; do not lie or steal or murder or break covenants. But the flesh is weak, and we are perpetually tempted by desire and self interest to break the moral law. So pervasive is this temptation that we must never relax our vigil against it, for when we are most certain of our righteousness, we may merely be succumbing to the sin of pride.

The characteristic moral problem for Kant arises in situations where our duty is clear but our contrary inclination strong. We must struggle to overcome the inclination and do what we know to be right. Kant does not seem to be much impressed by the moral problems which arise in situations where one wants very much to do what is right but cannot figure out what that is. To many moralists, these so-called hard cases, in which gratitude conflicts with contract, or mercy with justice, are the real core of moral philosophy. But Kant's attention is focused more on world-weary men tempted by sinful self-murder or grocers who know they ought to make the right change but feel an urge to cheat. When he does turn to an apparent conflict between duties, as in the famous essay, "On the Supposed Right to Lie from Altruistic Motives," Kant makes a total botch of it. Clearly, the heart of morality for Kant is the struggle between duty and inclination.

Kant holds that all men seek happiness.[8] Not all men *deserve* happiness, however, and Kant is firmly of the conviction that in a just world, happiness will be proportioned to merit. Merit, of course, comes not merely from doing one's duty, but from doing it dutifully, that is, out of respect for the law (God's or the moral law). So Kant sees men as caught in the familiar puritan dilemma: one only deserves happiness (salvation) for acting out of dedication to the right; to do what is right in order to win eternal happiness counts for naught, morally.

ii. THE RELATION OF REASON TO DESIRE

All this is familiar enough and either depressing or uplifting depending on one's tastes in styles of culture and personality. But

[8]But not that all rational creatures do. In his treatment of the so-called Counsels of Prudence, Kant makes it appear that all *men* seek their own happiness, but his conception of happiness, as a thoroughgoingly integrated satisfaction of all our rational desires, suggests that he should have said, "All *sensuous creatures* seek their own happiness." The point is not terribly important for our purposes here, but it could become important if one wanted to work out a conditionally a priori theory of prudential morality analogous to the theory of the *First Critique*. The premise, "All men seek happiness" might be nothing more than a widely confirmed empirical generalization, whereas the premise, "All sensuous creatures possessed of reason seek the systematically integrated satisfaction of their rational desires," might be susceptible of something akin to a transcendental deduction.

Kant's discussion of duty and inclination contains a very serious inconsistency which raises large problems for his moral theory. Essentially, Kant has two completely different views of the relationship between reason and desire in men.

The first view, which we have just been rehearsing, is that desire is a failing in men, a weakness, a temptation. Desire is, to use Kant's language, a "subjective condition" to which the will is "exposed." The sentences just following the definition of "will" in paragraph 12 express this view clearly:

> But if reason solely by itself is not sufficient to determine the will; if the will is exposed also to subjective conditions (certain impulsions) which do not always harmonize with the objective ones; if, in a word, the will is not *in itself* completely in accord with reason (as actually happens in the case of men); then actions which are recognized to be objectively necessary are subjectively contingent, and the determining of such a will in accordance with objective laws is *necessitation*. (Ak. 412–413)

The other view, which is perhaps most often associated with the empiricist philosophical tradition in Great Britain, is that reason and desire perform complementary functions in the processes of deliberation, choice, and action. Desire selects the ends of our action, and reason identifies the most efficient means, taking care to consider long-run or side effects on the satisfaction of other desires as well. Since reason merely discovers the causal connections among types of events, it can at most tell me, "If you would bring about B, do A." Desire, by setting B for me as an end, impels me then actually to do A. Paraphrasing Kant's description in the *First Critique* of the relationship between concepts and intuitions, we might summarize this view as:

> Reason without desire is impotent; desire without reason is blind.

Hume rather dramatically overstates the case in the *Treatise of Human Nature*, when he delivers the famous dictum that "reason is, and ought only to be the slave of the passions, and can never pretend to any other office than to serve and obey them" (Book II, part iii, section iii). This is a misrepresentation of their relationship, as he subsequently makes clear, for the passions are as dependent upon reason for a choice of appropriate means as reason is upon the passions for the impulse of a desired end. Neither is capable of rational action without the other.

We have already had an indication of the sorts of problems which are created for Kant by his confusion of these two conceptions of reason's relation to desire. If desire is a limitation or condition upon the will, then it is, at least in principle, possible to conceive of a will which is free of such constraints. A will which did not even experience temptations would be a perfectly rational will or a "holy will." On the other hand, a will which experienced temptations and overcame them would be a morally praiseworthy will deserving of divine reward.

But if desire sets the ends of action and reason chooses the means, then it is simply nonsensical to speak of a purely rational will "unhindered" by desire. Such a notion makes no more sense than the notion of a statue so perfect in its beauty that it consists entirely of an exquisite shape unconstrained by any marble or of a vacation planned with such perfect efficiency that it is unconstrained by the limiting condition of being a vacation to anywhere in particular.

Kant wants to ask whether it is possible for pure reason to determine the will, unhindered by the intervention or limitation of sensuous inclinations. Hence, he must construe the relation in the first way, so that he can at least posit the purely rational will as a logical possibility. At the same time, however, his account of ordinary interested or prudential action assumes the second version of the relationship, in which desire selects the end and reason discovers the means.

Although Kant is confused, he is by no means unfaithful to familiar and widespread ways of thinking about choice and deliberation. Many people think of at least some of their moral problems as internal struggles between what they want to do and what they believe to be right. If we set to one side the rhetoric of cold showers, stiff backbone, and moral athleticism which reached its full flower in late Victorian English sermons, we have a perfectly plausible bit of moral phenomenology. It also seems to make good sense to describe purposive agents as using their capacity of causal reasoning to guide their actions toward ends or objects which they desire. So the confusion resides in very common conceptions of moral agency and not simply in Kant's particular view of the moral condition.

Nevertheless, we must sort the confusion out if we are to make any progress in interpreting the *Groundwork*. The first step is to remind ourselves of Kant's peculiar definition of "will." I pointed out that on Kant's own definition it is misleading to speak of "the will," as though that were the name of a power or faculty which could be moved, limited, urged, or guided by various psychic forces. Kant encourages this mistake. Consider simply the following phrases from paragraph 12:

> If reason infallibly determines the will. . . .

> If the reason solely by itself is not sufficient to determine the will. . . .

> If the will is exposed also to subjective conditions. . . .

> The will of a rational being, although it is determined by principles of reason, does not necessarily follow these principles in virtue of its own nature.

These and countless other phrases invoke images of a will which is pushed and pulled by reason and desire so that now one, now the other achieves the upper hand.

But "will" is defined by Kant as "a kind of causality belonging to living beings so far as they are rational," and it makes no sense at all to speak of a kind of causality as *itself* subject to competing causal influences. "To have a will" *means,* according to Kant, "to be capable of being moved by reason." Hence, it is true by definition that "reason infallibly determines the will," for that can only mean something like:

> Insofar as man is moved by reason (has a will), he is moved by reason,

which is a tautology.

Now someone might protest, in defense of Kant, that this is a pointlessly picky way to read the text. After all, when Kant asks, Does reason infallibly determine the *will*? he obviously means, Does reason infallibly determine the *man*? Kant's answer is, No, reason does not infallibly determine men. Sometimes a man is determined by reason, in which case he can strictly be said to "have a will," and sometimes desire determines a man, in which case he can variously be said to lack a will or to have succumbed to desire or even, without any *real* confusion, to have a will which has succumbed to desire. So beyond a terminological quibble, what, if anything, is at stake?

The answer is rather complicated, and some of it must wait until later in our discussion. Briefly, two problems of the very greatest importance come to a head in this apparently finicky insistence upon the letter of Kant's definition of will. First of all, by explaining will as rational causality, Kant makes it virtually impossible to give coherent meaning to the notion of a morally blameworthy action. A man who fails to do what he ought to do is, according to Kant, a man who has not acted rationally, which is to say, a man who has not been moved by reason. But since we could never be moved by a good reason not to be moved by reason, there is no such thing as an irrational *act*. So the immoral is reduced to the irrational, which is to say, to the involuntary and hence unblameworthy.

The second problem is that even if Kant were able to make sense out of the notion of voluntary blameworthy action, he could find no place for it within the framework of the theory of the *First Critique*. Creatures qua phenomena do not have wills, for to have a will is to be moved by reason, hence to be self-moved, rather than to be moved by "alien causes," as Kant puts it in the first paragraph of chapter 3. Now every single bit of behavior of a phenomenal being must, insofar as it occurs as an event in the realm of appearance, come under heteronymous causal laws of the sort that establish de facto nondeductive connections between events in objective time. Hence all behavior in the realm of appearance is completely determined by desire or by physiological causes or by whatever else it is that turns out to cause behavior.

It is possible, of course, that one and the same event might be construed both as causally determined qua behavior of a phenomenal being, and as rationally determined qua act by a noumenal being. That, in fact, is just the line Kant takes in chapter 3. But such a view rules out conflict between reason and desire. Instead, it construes some events as doubly determined both by desire (or other causes) qua behavior and by reason qua act. The case of the finite, fallible man who, knowing what is right, nevertheless succumbs to desire and hence is blameworthy, disappears as a metaphysical impossibility. Ironically, Kant begins chapter 2 with the assumption that cases of blameworthy action are easy to find, while cases of praiseworthy actions are impossible to certify; and he is pushed by his own metaphysics to the position that only praiseworthy actions are possible, albeit noncertifiable, whereas blameworthy actions are logically impossible.

I have pressed Kant on this issue because I think that ordinary, prephilosophical beliefs about morality, including Kant's own beliefs, are wrong and that the position implied by Kant's metaphysics is actually closer to the truth, even though he himself would have rejected it had it been presented to him. Praise and blame must be divorced from considerations of what is right and wrong. To act is to be moved by reasons; hence, praise and blame, which are an observer's response to behavior, have no role to play in the determination of action. When, as observers, we come to understand the causes of behavior, *including our own,* we must cease to judge it morally, although we may still feel admiration or disgust for it. But the cessation of moral evaluations of persons in no way affects the process of deliberation about acts, for when I deliberate, I am trying to decide *what* to do, not whether I am or will be worthy of approbation.

iii. IMPERATIVES AND MORAL PRINCIPLES (Pars. 13–15)

Despite the fact that his account of reason and desire suffers from these difficulties, some of which he would probably not have acknowledged, Kant proceeds to base his theory of imperatives on it. Paragraphs 13–15 give us the definition of imperatives and draw the distinction between perfectly and imperfectly rational wills.

> The conception of an objective principle, so far as it constrains a will, is a command (of reason), and the formula of this command is called an *Imperative.* (Ak. 413)

A perfectly good, which is to say perfectly rational, will "stand[s] quite as much under objective laws," but it is not *necessitated* to obey them because it does so naturally. So imperatives are only "formulae for expressing the relation of objective laws of willing to the subjective imperfection of the will of this or that rational being—for example, of the human will" (Ak. 414).

Moral laws are thus not commands. They are principles of practical reason which are *experienced* as commands only by creatures who might be inclined to violate them. Since Kant leans so heavily on the parallels between logic, or the principles of theoretical reason, and ethics, or the principles of practical reason, it might illuminate this conception of imperatives to try to imagine how the analogous "formulae" could arise in logic.

Suppose, then, that a logician undertakes to derive a theorem from a set of premises, using the customary rules of inference. He sets about his task, deducing the first step from the premises, then the second step from the first together with the premises, and so on, until suddenly he reaches a point at which he realizes that not the desired theorem but its contradictory is entailed by his premises! Devastated by the realization, he checks his reasoning again and again, but there can be no doubt. He wishes to establish not-q as a theorem; but p is a premise, and the penultimate step of his deduction, established by perfectly correct steps, is the conditional (if p then q).

At first our imaginary logician is utterly dejected; then he hears a small voice of temptation. "Go ahead," it urges him. "Conclude not-q. Make an exception of yourself! What harm is there in it? Oh, we all know that p and (if p then q) entail q, but you so much want to prove not-q! After all, it will only be this once." The logician is tempted, for he truly does want to prove not-q, but is still so far in possession of his reason to ask himself whether it is not improper and opposed to logic to satisfy his desire in this way (cf. Ak. 422). Perhaps, he tells himself, he could compromise, and draw *two* conclusions: q *and* not-q. But now he hears, as if from on high, a mighty voice which commands imperiously, "Thou shalt not assert q and not-q." Confronted with this imperative, which his own reason has autonomously legislated (for the voice is the voice of his reason), our logician overcomes his all too human weakness and submits himself to the objective principles of theoretical reason. With a proud sense of his dignity as a rational creature but with heavy heart nonetheless, he completes his proof with the final step:

Therefore, q.

This facetious example has several points. First of all, it helps us to understand how a perfectly rational creature would experience the principles of morality. Ordinary logicians do not suffer from the temptation to draw patently invalid conclusions. They may rage with frustration at not being able to prove theorems which they are convinced are true. But what earthly point could there by in saying "therefore not-q" when you know that it is q that follows from the premises?[9] If you were to suggest to a logician in the throes of a proof that he could simplify his task by merely employing an invalid mode of inference, he would conclude that you didn't understand what logic was about.

The second point of the example cuts the other way and reinforces what we have already said about the problem of explaining voluntarily immoral actions. Kant understands the practical employment of reason on the analogy of its theoretical employment.[10] An inconsistent willing is therefore very much like an error in formal reasoning. Since we can imagine no *good* reason for making a mistake in logic, we must treat such errors as lapses or failures of the rational faculty. They are in no plausible sense the fault of the logician, since he clearly would not have made the error had he been able to avoid it. In the same way, a violation of the principles of practical reason must be a lapse or failure of the rational faculty (and hence, in *that* sense only, a "failure of will"). Since there could never be a good reason for acting on bad reasons

[9]I am not concerned here with extraneous considerations, such as completing a doctoral dissertation, winning a Nobel prize, or publishing an article. There are well-known cases in the sciences, if not in logic and mathematics, of fudged research data and cooked experiments. The point is that those are violations of the canons of rationality for some extraneous purpose, not for the sake of obtaining the desired conclusion itself.

[10]In fact, since the *assertion* of a theoretical proposition is an act, the theoretical and practical employments of reason have a common root.

or for failing to act on reasons at all, such a lapse could hardly be the basis for moral disapprobation.

There is a third point, suggested by our example, which leads us toward the distinction between hypothetical and categorical imperatives. Kant frequently talks as though a holy or perfectly rational will would be guided only by unconditional principles of practical reason, the sorts of principles which would be experienced by a conditioned or finite will as categorical imperatives. But the distinction he has drawn, between a will which is and a will which is not completely determined by reason, is one which applies equally well to the case of prudential action motivated by conditioned principles of practical reason. Once again, Kant is misled by his tendency to see desire as a limitation on the will rather than as a source of ends toward which reason guides us.

We are all familiar with the experience of not wanting to do something that we know would be good *for us*. Dieting, exercising, going to the dentist, saving for old age—these are not policies which we are under any moral obligation to adopt. Kant to the contrary notwithstanding, each of us has a right to act self-destructively, imprudently, to neglect the precautions which will make him happier. Now we can at least imagine a perfectly prudential man, who always adopts what reason tells him is the most efficient means to the integrated satisfaction of his ends. Such a man, celebrated in the literature of classical laissez faire political economy if nowhere else, would be hindered neither by the temptations of immediate desire nor by the commands of morality. He would, therefore, not experience the conditional principles of practical reason as *imperatives*, not even as hypothetical imperatives. When presented with a valid principle of practical reason of the form, "Having E as your end, do A," he would either ignore it, if E was not his end, or do A, if it was.

iv. HYPOTHETICAL IMPERATIVES AND CATEGORICAL IMPERATIVES (Pars. 16—23)

After introducing the concept of an imperative, Kant expounds the familiar theory of hypothetical and categorical imperatives. Paragraphs 16–18 draw the distinction between the two types of imperatives and elaborate upon it a bit. Paragraph 19 attempts to connect the theory of imperatives with the doctrine of the *First Critique* by associating *three* types of imperatives with the three categories of modality (possibility, existence, necessity) and the three modal functions of unity in judgment (problematic, assertoric, apodeictic). The attempt is somewhat confused, however, as Kant subsequently acknowledged. Then each type of imperative is dealt with in a separate paragraph: imperatives of skill in paragraph 20, imperatives of prudence in paragraph 21, and imperatives of morality in paragraph 22. Finally, Kant allows himself a few terminological flourishes in paragraph 23 and brings the exposition of the types of imperatives to a close.

Most of what Kant has to say in this passage is of relatively little importance for our purpose, but there are two matters that require extended comment, namely, the form in which imperatives are stated (what Kant calls the "formula") and the nature of categorical, as opposed to hypothetical, imperatives.

Imperatives, says Kant, are "formulae for determining an action which is necessary in accordance with the principle of a will in some sense good." Recalling the lengthy discussion of maxims, policies, and reasons in our commentary on chapter 1, we can construe this to mean that an imperative is a formula which commands a policy for which there purport to be reasons which are good for some rational agent. A valid imperative is simply an imperative which commands a policy for which there really are good reasons. A valid hypothetical imperative is then a formula which commands a policy for which there are reasons which are good reasons for some, but not necessarily for all rational agents. Strictly, a hypothetical imperative is never valid per se, but rather *valid for* an agent. A valid categorical imperative is a formula which commands a policy for which there are reasons which are good reasons for all rational agents as such. Hence it can be said to be valid per se.

Kant often talks as though only valid imperatives are imperatives; so, for example, he sometimes speaks of "the only categorical imperative." But I think it is clear from his definitions that any formula which commands a policy unconditionally qualifies as a categorical imperative. A *valid* categorical imperative is one which commands a policy which is an objectively valid law of practical reason. The distinction is not especially troublesome, but it is as well to be clear about it, because we shall be focusing on the precise wording of Kant's argument when we come to the actual derivation of "the categorical imperative."

The distinction between "formula" and "policy" may also seem unnecessarily cumbersome, but I have clung to it in order to preserve Kant's conception of imperatives as rules of reason which appear as commands only to imperfectly rational creatures. Presently we shall have to consider whether the notion of an imperfectly rational creature is a plausible one either in itself or in the context of Kant's metaphysics and theory of knowledge.

Now let us take a closer look at the theory of imperatives and see whether we can clarify it. Recall the example we gave earlier of a policy:

To drink water when I am thirsty.

If a rational agent has the physical constitution of a normal human being (that is, if he is the sort of creature whose thirst can be slaked by drinking water) and if he has chosen as his purpose the slaking of his thirst, then this policy, "to drink water when I am thirsty," is a policy for the adoption of which he has a good reason. His reason, which is that the adoption of the policy will further a purpose which he has, is an equally good reason for all rational agents similarly constituted and possessed of the same purpose. It is, of course, possible that there will be agents for whom the adoption of this policy on these reasons would be irrational, namely, those agents whose thirst would not be slaked by drinking water (perhaps for physiological reasons) and those agents who have not chosen the slaking of their thirst as their purpose (perhaps because of some plan of self-mortification or for medical reasons or whatever).

There is an objectively valid principle of practical reason corresponding to this policy together with its good reasons and limiting conditions. It would, I suppose, be something like this:

Physically normal thirsty humans who seek to slake their thirst drink water.

Any perfectly rational agent who met the limiting conditions and had chosen the specified purpose as his purpose would act on this principle just as any rational logician who had adopted the premises and modes of inference of a given formal system would infer only propositions which were theorems in the system.

But since, according to Kant, we are imperfectly rational, the objectively valid principle of practical reason stated above presents itself to us in imperative form as a command of (prudential) reason. The formula expressing the principle would be something like this:

> Having it as your end to slake your thirst and being as you are a physically normal human being, drink water![11]

Now, an imperative of this sort commands absolutely. There is no other way that an imperative can command. But it is a command which is binding upon or is valid for or addresses itself to only those rational agents who meet the conditions specified in the preamble to the command. By analogy, when an army officer gives the command, "Company, Attention!" even if it is a valid command, it applies or is addressed to only those rational agents who are soldiers in that company. A member of a different company or a civilian standing nearby is not an appropriate recipient of the command. Turning the point around and expressing it in terms of excuses, if a soldier is challenged to explain why he has not obeyed the command, he can relevantly reply *either* that the command is invalid on the grounds, for example, that it exceeds the authority of the commanding officer *or* that he is not a member of the company and, hence, that the command was not addressed to him.[12]

---

[11]Since Kant gives us very few examples of the principles and formulae to which he keeps referring, I am forced to make up examples which seem to me to capture the essence of his theory. These formulations are obviously open to dispute, and since so much of my interpretation turns on them, the reader is warned to examine them closely and critically.

[12]Needless to say, he may also reply that the command was issued by someone other than himself and as such is a heteronomous command which no rational agent is under any obligation to obey. My own view is that Kant's analysis of rational agency, autonomy, and moral principles entails the doctrine which in political philosophy is known as anarchism. See my book *In Defense of Anarchism*

So the imperative "Having it as your end to slake . . . drink water!" commands absolutely; but a rational agent who has not adopted the end of slaking his thirst or whose physical constitution is such that drinking water does not slake his thirst is not bound by the imperative. It is not addressed to him. He can legitimately excuse himself from adherence to it by appealing to these facts about himself.[13]

A categorical imperative, so-called, is also a formula which expresses an absolute command. But the preamble to a categorical imperative specifies conditions which are necessarily met by all rational agents as such. Indeed, all categorical imperatives begin with the same preamble. They are all of the form:

> Being as you are a rational agent and having as your end the realization of the good, do X.

Since all and only rational agents are capable of acting, hence, of being moved by reasons and since according to Kant there is an objective good which all rational agents qua rational take as their end (the so-called obligatory ends), it follows that the principle of practical reason corresponding to such an imperative is a valid principle for all rational agents whatsoever. And, of course, the imperative is binding upon (and is experienced as a command of reason by) all imperfectly rational beings, including all human beings. No man can excuse himself from the command on the grounds that he is not a rational agent. Nor can any man deny that the realization of the good is his end. For it is a practical contradiction to deny that one is a rational agent (since denials, like all assertions, are acts), and all rational agents, or so Kant maintains, aim at the objectively good.

In paragraphs 16–19 Kant expresses all of this rather badly. The principal source of confusion is his habit of describing categorical imperatives as commanding actions without reference to ends. In

---

(New York: Harper & Row, Publishers, Harper Torchbooks , 1970). Kant, of course, did not hold this view of the implications of his moral philosophy.

[13]At Ak. 415 Kant characterizes hypothetical imperatives as either "problematic" or "assertoric," depending on whether their ends are such as men may have or do have. This is a mistake—all imperatives are apodeictic or necessary— and in the first, unpublished, Introduction to the *Critique of Judgment*, Kant corrected it. See Ak. XX, p. 200.

paragraph 16 just after the reference to desire quoted above he writes:

> A categorical imperative would be one which represented an action as objectively necessary in itself apart from its relation to a further end.

A little later on, in paragraph 19, he says:

> A hypothethical imperative thus says only that an action is good for some purpose or other, either *possible* or *actual*. In the first case it is a *problematic* practical principle; in the second case an *assertoric* practical principle. A categorical imperative, which declares an action to be objectively necessary in itself without reference to some purpose—that is, even without any further end—ranks as an *apodeictic* practical principle.

Finally, in paragraph 22, Kant repeats:

> [T]here is an imperative which, without being based on, and conditioned by, any further purpose to be attained by a certain line of conduct, enjoins this conduct immediately.

Now this way of talking just doesn't make any sense. Rational action is purposive action. It is behavior which is caused by the agent's conception of the state of affairs to be brought about *by* that behavior. Of course, I may sometimes take as my end the doing of something rather than the making of something. When I make a table, my end is the coming into being of the table. When I play the violin, my end may either be the making of a recording or the hearing of the music or simply the doing of the playing. But in each case the cause of my action is the idea of my end. That, according to Kant, is simply what it means to say that I have a will.

So a categorical imperative cannot "directly command a certain conduct without making its condition some purpose to be reached by it," for that is the same as saying that it commands an agent to engage in purposive action which has no purpose. Instead, the logic of Kant's theory of imperatives ought to lead him to define a categorical imperative as an imperative which commands us to pursue a purpose which we *must* (insofar as we are rational) adopt. Then he would be able to express his doctrine quite comfortably in terms of the categories of modality. Thus:

An imperative of skill says that an action is good to some *possible* purpose.

An imperative of prudence says that an action is good to some *actual* purpose.

An imperative of morality says that an action is good to some *necessary* purpose.

If we suppose, as I do, that Kant's analysis of will and rational agency is substantially correct, then there are three positions we can take on the subject of necessary or obligatory ends. *Either* we agree with Kant that obligatory ends can in some way be deduced from the purely formal principle of rational agency (the Categorical Imperative), even though Kant may have failed to come up with the deduction; *or* we agree with Kant (in his other mood) that an independent theory of the objectively good can be found which will provide us with the requisite obligatory ends, even though Kant may not have found it; *or* we conclude that there is nothing good in itself, that there is therefore no valid theory of the objectively good to be found, and hence that there are not and could not be any obligatory ends.

I believe that the last of these positions is true and that Kant has laid the necessary theoretical basis for proving it, even though he himself would have rejected it. Most of the difficulty of this commentary derives from my efforts to separate out the part of Kant's theory which I believe to be valid and to interpret, clarify, and defend it while at the same time I do my best to explain and account for the passages in which Kant set forth the part of his theory which I believe to be wrong.

Let me summarize our conclusions in a preliminary way: a principle of practical reason is not a policy (or maxim). Rather, it is a criterion or rule for the adoption of policies. Every principle of practical reason states the conditions under which the adoption of a policy is rational. A hypothetical principle of practical reason asserts that the adoption of a policy is rational under conditions which are not necessarily or universally met by all rational agents as such. A categorical principle of practical reason asserts that the adoption of a policy is rational under conditions which are necessarily and universally met by all rational agents as such. Hence, a categorical principle of practical reason asserts that the adoption of a policy is rational, *simpliciter*. All principles of practical reason appear to or are experienced by imperfectly rational creatures as commands, and they are expressed in formulae whose grammatical form is the imperative. If a satisfactory theory of obligatory ends can be defended, then there will be categorical principles of practical reason which specify the adoption of specific policies as rational per se. But if no such theory exists, then the only categorical principles of practical reason will be negative or purely formal principles which *rule out* the adoption of certain policies as irrational.

C. Some Difficulties in Kant's Theory of Rational Agency

Because of the complexity of the issues raised by Kant's theory of rational agency, I have been forced to put off discussion of a number of problems which arise in a consideration of the first twelve paragraphs of the pivotal portion of chapter 2 of the *Groundwork*. Before going on to an analysis of paragraphs 24–31, let us pause for a bit and take a closer look at several of those problems. In particular, I want to consider once more the puzzling relationship between reason and desire.

I pointed out earlier that the *Groundwork* contains two incompatible conceptions of the relation between desire and practical reason. The first portrays desire as a limitation upon reason, so that man is seen as tempted by desire to swerve from the path dictated by reason; the second portrays desire and reason as complementary contributors to action, with desire setting the ends and providing the impetus and reason choosing the best available means. When Kant defines "imperative," he invokes the *first* conception: in the absence of the temptations of desire or inclination, we should never experience the principles of practical reason as commands, or imperatives. When he draws the distinction between hypothetical and categorical imperatives, on the other hand, Kant appeals to the *second* conception: hypothetical imperatives command an action (more precisely, the adoption of a policy) which is necessary to the accomplishment of something desired; categorical imperatives command the adoption of a policy which is necessary without reference to something desired.[14]

The central problem of the *Groundwork* thus becomes, "How are categorical imperatives possible?" This is ambiguously construed to mean *either* "How can imperfect man shake himself loose of the constraints of desire and act as reason commands?" *or* "How can a rational agent be moved by anything other than desire?"

Unfortunately for the coherence and clarity of Kant's argument, both ways of construing the relation of desire to reason conflict with his own doctrines. Hence, even after we have successfully distinguished between them, we are left with a Hobson's choice. I should like to indicate why both views are incompatible with Kant's better philosophy and then at least suggest a third position that he might fruitfully have adopted.

First of all, let us dispose of the view that desire limits reason. From the standpoint of Kant's *First Critique* doctrine, it is mani-

[14]There are some rather complicated problems of terminology and definition in Kant's discussion about which at least something needs to be said. In paragraph 16 of chapter 2 Kant draws the distinction between hypothetical and categorical imperatives without making reference specifically to desire. Thus he says: "Hypothetical imperatives declare a possible action to be practically necessary as a means to the attainment of something else that one wills (or that one may will) [*etwas anderem, was man will (oder doch möglich ist, dass man es wolle)*]."

In paragraphs 10–23, Kant also speaks of hypothetical imperatives in terms which do not refer explicitly to desire. He refers to "a possible purpose of some will" (par. 20), a purpose which all dependent or imperfect rational beings "have by a natural necessity—the purpose, namely, of *happiness*" (par. 21), and so on. This would seem to leave it open whether the ends of conditioned beings like ourselves are determined by desire or are selected in some other way.

But elsewhere in Kant's writings on this subject he clearly identifies desire as the determinant of the ends of hypothetical imperatives. In the *Critique of Practical Reason*, for example, when he first introduces the distinction between hypothetical and categorical imperatives, he does so in the following words: "Imperatives themselves, however, when they are conditional, i.e., when they determine the will not as such but only in respect to a desired effect [*nur in Ansehung einer begehrten Wirkung*], are hypothetical imperatives, which are practical precepts but not laws" (Ak. V, 20, trans. Lewis White Beck).

Perhaps the most we can say is that *if* Kant does conceive of hypothetical imperatives as commanding actions which are necessary to the accomplishment of something desired and categorical imperatives as commanding without reference to what is desired, then he is open to the criticisms I offer below.

festly impossible for phenomenal impulses to war with noumenal reason for control of the behavior of the person qua phenomenon. All events in the phenomenal world are completely determined by preceding events in the objective temporal order. It is always in principle possible to discover scientific laws of regular succession under which human behavior (as phenomenal events) can be subsumed. Since the occurrences of thoughts, feelings, perceptions, and desires in the minds of empirical selves are also phenomenal events, it must in principle be possible to find scientific laws adequate to their prediction and explanation as well. The fable of reason and desire struggling within the breast of the good but tempted man is simply a metaphysical impossibility for Kant.

Lest anyone be tempted (as it were) to cling to this fable and Kant's metaphysics be damned, on the grounds that it accurately captures the reality of our moral experience, we should realize that the story of the struggle between reason and desire fails to do the one job it is intended for. The idea, presumably, is to lay the foundation for the practice of moral approbation and blame by portraying at least some right action as the outcome of a praiseworthy struggle and wrong action as the result of a reprehensible succumbing to temptation. But Kant's own identification of the right with the rational thoroughly undermines praise and blame. After all, if the story of the struggle is true, then there are only two possibilities: either desire is too strong for reason, in which case there is no dishonor in reason's failure so long as it did its best; or else reason is capable of overcoming desire, in which case there can be no possible explanation of why it failed to do so.[15]

Nor can we plausibly construe the situation as one in which the individual chooses not to follow reason's dictates. Kant sees choice (rightly, I think) as based upon reasons. Since he conceives of right action as action determined by reason alone, he can hardly claim that a man might have reasons for disregarding reason's dictates. So we are forced back to the conclusion that whenever a man fails

[15]Indeed, in the absence of direct access to the faculties of desire and reason, our only measure of their relative strengths is the outcome of a struggle between them. Hence, it would be self-contradictory to say *both* that we have good grounds for supposing that reason is stronger than desire *and* that reason failed to overcome desire.

to do as reason advises, desire has been too strong for him. And that relieves him of moral responsibility for his wrong action. (Strictly speaking, it shows that he didn't act at all, since action is behavior caused by reasons.)

We might expect to have more luck with Kant's second conception of the relation of reason to desire, namely, that desire sets the ends and moves us, while reason chooses the means. As Beck puts it, summarizing Kant's position:

> [Practical reason] provides the cognitive factor in the guidance of action whose *dynamis* is impulse.[16]

But there are very serious difficulties here as well. First of all, are we to suppose that reason literally is "the slave of the passions," as Hume says, or does it exercise some sort of causal influence upon action? Obviously Kant intends the latter. Were desire by itself completely to determine behavior, in the way that we may suppose reflex and instinct do in the lower animals, it would make no sense to describe reason as "guiding," or "directing" desire. But immediately we come into conflict with Kant's theory of phenomenal causality. For if reason can "guide" desire, for example, by dissuading me from eating attractive but harmful foods or by getting me to the dentist against my inclination, then it presumably can deflect a chain of phenomenal causes which would otherwise have brought about a different bit of behavior. We are invited to imagine reason as impinging on the chain of causes more or less as a force which, by acting at an angle to the path of a particle, deflects it or even (if the angle is 180 degrees) stops it altogether.

Now there are a number of philosophers who have read Kant as espousing some such view of the causal intervention of reason in the phenomenal world. Nicolai Hartmann, for example, devotes the entire third volume of his *Ethics* to expounding a theory of moral freedom which he imagines to be Kantian in spirit and which is based on the doctrine that noumenal reason can step into the chain of phenomenal causes. But this interpretation is totally contradictory to the *First Critique* position, even though

[16]Lewis White Beck, *A Commentary on Kant's "Critique of Practical Reason"* (Chicago: University of Chicago Press, 1960), p. 40.

Kant himself often lapses into talking that way.[17]

The problem is that practical reason cannot coherently be portrayed as a faculty having, as it were, a certain amount of muscle which it flexes when impulse threatens to plunge us into imprudent excesses. There is, to be sure, a familiar set of psychic experiences corresponding to the story Kant is telling, but he is wrong in fact and untrue to his own theory if he describes them as struggles between guiding reason and impetuous desire. Nor does it make any sense to portray reason as a servant pointing the shortest road for its master, desire.

The source of the confusion, so far as I can see, lies in a misunderstanding of the role of desire in action of any sort, whether prudential or moral. Action is behavior whose cause is an idea qua cognitively significant representation. It is, therefore, behavior caused by practical reason. In short, action is, in Kant's sense of the term, *willed* behavior. When we act, we choose or posit or set an end for ourselves. The choice is not determined by desire, although we may very well choose as an end something which we desire. Insofar as desires cause behavior, they do so in the phenomenal world qua mental events. The causal relationship between a desire qua mental event and a bit of behavior qua physical event is exactly like any other causal relationship between two events in the phenomenal world. Just as there is no rational connection between fire and heat or between the motion of the cue ball and the subsequent motion of an object ball, so there is no rational connection between a desire qua event and a bit of behavior qua event. If desires have an intensional structure, so that we can speak of them as cognitive representations of objects or states of affairs, then it is not—it could not be—qua representations that they cause behavior in the phenomenal world.

I have said that we choose ends. The obvious question is, do we have reasons for our choices? Is the fact that I desire some event or object a good reason for my choosing it as my end? Are there any reasons for the choice of ends which would be equally good reasons for all rational agents as such? My own view, to which I shall return at the conclusion of this commentary, is that there are

[17]I shall return to this subject when we get to chapter 3 of the *Groundwork*.

no good reasons for the choice of ends, save those which make reference to other ends already chosen and appeal to considerations of consistency, compatibility, and so forth. A man who chooses to ignore his own desires and pursue some other ends is not thereby irrational, nor is a man who sets as his end the satisfaction of one desire to the exclusion of all others, nor again is the traditional man of prudence who seeks the integrated satisfaction of all his desires. It follows, of course, that there are no ends which all rational agents as such have good reasons to choose. Ends in general are objects of choice unconstrained by principles of reason, and moral obligations are the consequences of contractual commitments among agents who choose to bind themselves to one another. Hence, there are no substantive principles of practical reason which are valid for all rational agents as such.

These remarks carry us very far from the intent of Kant's argument, although I believe that the position I have sketched follows from Kant's own theory of rational agency. In particular, as the analysis of the next bit of text will make clear, my view tends to jeopardize the all-important notion of a positive or substantive categorical imperative. If there are no reasons for the choice of ends, then there can be no reasons which would be good for all agents qua agents. One could still talk of good reasons for the adoption of policies, but all such reasons would be good only for agents having the specified ends, and so the principles expressing those reasons would be what Kant calls hypothetical rather than categorical.

The Categorical Imperative itself remains, however, for as we shall see, it is a perfectly universal negative criterion of the rationality of policies, and as such is binding on all rational agents.

D. How Are Imperatives Possible? (Pars. 24–28)

With an abruptness to which he often resorts when he has something important to say, Kant turns to the central question of the theory of imperatives:[18]

---

[18]Compare *The Critique of Pure Reason*, A104, where Kant suddenly introduces the question, "What do we mean by an object of representations?" Although Kant

The question now arises "How are all these imperatives possible?" (Ak. 417, par. 24)

The subsequent five paragraphs are extremely important and extremely obscure. Here, as elsewhere in the critical writings, Kant states his problem in such a way as to conceal, rather than to reveal, his deeper doctrine. The reasons for this obscurity are two-fold: first, Kant's familiar attempt to link up different parts of his philosophy by the repetition of certain formulae and second, the genuine confusions about reason and desire, obligatory ends, and formal versus substantive principles of reason, which we have been discussing throughout this commentary. I shall try to sort things out at least enough so that the real philosophical problems can be distinguished from the terminological or architectonic problems created by Kant's love of system.

i. The Background of the Question "How Are Imperatives Possible?"

In the Introduction to the *First Critique* Kant draws the famous pair of distinctions between analytic and synthetic judgments and judgments known a priori or a posteriori. Combining the two pairs of categories, he arrives at four possible sorts of knowledge claims,[19] namely, analytic judgments known a priori, analytic

---

tends to run on when he is discussing matters of minor importance, he can be startlingly brief in his treatment of the most crucial issues. In the present instance, for example, he spends almost three times as long on the peculiarities of Counsels of Prudence (par. 25) as he does on the entire derivation of the Categorical Imperative (pars. 29–31). I sometimes wish, when I am struggling to understand a text, that he had followed the opposite procedure.

[19]The German word for knowledge is *Erkenntnis*. Since Kant frequently uses it in the plural, and "knowledges" isn't English, Kemp Smith translates *Erkenntnisse)* as "modes of knowledge." I am hardly competent to question Kemp Smith's translation, but it seems clear to me that "knowledge claims" would be better, at least in some cases. Kant is usually not concerned with the truth of the particular propositions we assert: he doesn't care whether fire is actually hot or cold. Rather, he is interested in the general conditions which must be met in order for it even to be possible that the propositions we assert be true. "Knowledge claim," which leaves open the possibility that the claim might be false, is therefore truer to Kant's intention than "mode of knowledge," which suggests that the claim is true. Furthermore, "knowledge claim" captures the active nature of assertion in a way that is especially important for Kant's moral philosophy.

judgments known a posteriori, synthetic judgments known a posteriori, and synthetic judgments known a priori. He then asks of each type in turn, "How are judgments of this sort possible?" This means: How or under what conditions or on what grounds can a judgment of this sort be known in the manner specified? The case of analytic judgments known a priori poses no problem, according to Kant. Since the judgment merely asserts a connection between a concept and one of the elements contained within it, we can know it "a priori," which is to say, we can know it independently of experience, with the full universality and necessity asserted in the judgment.

Analytic judgments a posteriori can be evaluated in either of two ways, depending on what we understand them to assert. If we take "all bachelors are unmarried" to be asserted with necessity and universality, then that judgment can never be known a posteriori. A mere collection of instances of unmarried bachelors, however scientific, could never yield absolute universality. On the other hand, if we leave open the modality in which the judgment is asserted, then it would be possible, although fatuous, to establish an analytic judgment by appeal to experience.

Synthetic judgments known a posteriori also pose no problem, Kant says. The connection between the terms of the judgment is grounded in our experience of objects or events, in which the designata of the terms are found to be combined. However, because the establishment of such knowledge claims must wait upon experience, we can assert them neither with universality nor with necessity.

And so we arrive at the case of synthetic judgments known a priori. It is at first absolutely impossible to see how such knowledge claims could be justified. How could we know, independently of experience, that certain sorts of connections among logically distinct properties or events or objects *must* necessarily and universally obtain? How can we ever be justified, therefore, in uniting the concepts of such properties or events or objects in a judgment which asserts that their connection is necessary? In short:

How are synthetic judgments *a priori* possible?
(*Critique of Pure Reason*, B19)

Kant was enormously pleased with this way of phrasing the central problem of the critical philosophy, even though it is an extraordinarily misleading formulation.[20] He did everything in his power to squeeze the doctrine of the *Groundwork* into the same mold, at the cost of a sizeable loss in clarity. Before we can confront Kant's real doctrine in paragraphs 24–28, we must clear away some of the confusion caused by the "How . . . possible?" formula.

ii. THE MEANING OF THE QUESTION "HOW ARE IMPERATIVES POSSIBLE?" (Pars. 24–27)

Difficulties arise as soon as we try to apply the classification of judgments to the case of imperatives. It may make some sense to describe imperatives as a priori, though I doubt it. But no sense can be made of any attempt to classify them as analytic or synthetic. They are not declarative judgments. They do not assert, they command. How could they possibly be either analytic or synthetic?

To be sure, Kant does not say at this point in the text that hypothetical imperatives are analytic. Instead, he rests their possibility on the proposition, "Who wills the end, wills the means." *This* judgment, he says, is analytic, and about that he is quite correct, as we shall see shortly. But in paragraph 28, he says that the Categorical Imperative is "a synthetic a priori practical proposition," an assertion which simply makes no sense.

It would be a great deal closer to the truth to say that the principles of practical reason, which are one and all analytic, are experienced by us as either analytic or synthetic. Later on I shall, in effect, impute such a view to Kant; but that is not what he says, and we shall have to try to understand why not.

Since Kant seems to want to claim that hypothetical imperatives are analytic practical propositions and that categorical imperatives are a priori synthetic propositions, we might suppose that he would simply set aside as irrelevant the category of synthetic judgments known a posteriori. But in paragraph 26, in contrasting hypothetical with categorical imperatives, he appears to treat the

[20]For an explanation of why the "How . . . possible?" formula is misleading, how it came to be included in the *Critique,* and what Kant should have said, see my book *Kant's Theory of Mental Activity,* pp. 44–56.

former as empirical or a posteriori and the latter as a priori judgments. Here is the passage:

> Beyond all doubt, the question "How is the imperative of *morality* possible?" is the only one in need of a solution; for it is in no way hypothetical, and consequently we cannot base the objective necessity which it affirms on any presupposition, as we can with hypothetical imperatives. Only we must never forget here that it is impossible to settle *by an example*, and so empirically, whether there is any imperative of this kind at all: we must rather suspect that all imperatives which seem to be categorical may none the less be covertly hypothetical. (Ak. 419, par. 26)

The clear implication of this passage is that hypothetical imperatives can be exhibited in experience, whereas categorical imperatives cannot be. Recall the sentence which I have several times quoted, from the second paragraph of chapter 2, to the effect that "in actual fact it is absolutely impossible for experience to establish with complete certainty a single case in which the maxim of an action . . . rested solely on moral grounds and on the thought of one's duty" (Ak. 406–407).

Now there is a confusion here between two quite distinct sorts of judgments. The first are the imperatives, hypothetical or categorical, whose possibility Kant is discussing; the second are the declarative assertions that Mr. Jones or Mrs. Smith has acted on an imperative of one kind or another. Kant seems to think that statements that someone has acted on hypothetical imperatives are empirical statements, which can easily enough be proved by appeals to experience, whereas statements that someone has acted on a categorical imperative (that is, from a sense of duty) are *not* empirical statements and must be proved, if at all, by a different sort of argument. Kant would seem to have in mind the contrast between empirical concepts, whose employment can be justified by appeals to experience, and a priori concepts, whose employment requires the transcendental justification called in the *Critique* a "deduction" (cf. A84–87).

So paragraphs 24–28 convey two distinct messages with the same conclusion. The first message is:

> Hypothetical imperatives are no problem because they are analytic judgments a priori of practical reason. But categorical imperatives

require a transcendental deduction because they are synthetic judgments a priori of practical reason.

The second message is:

> Hypothetical imperatives are no problem because we can demonstrate their possibility by appeal to experience. But categorical imperatives require a transcendental deduction because no experience could suffice to demonstrate their possibility.

iii. SOME CLARIFICATIONS AND EXPLANATIONS

The several things Kant is trying to say are quite tangled together, some true, some false, and some simply confused. Let me comment on three of Kant's claims, before turning to the crucial paragraph 28 with its accompanying footnote.

a. The proposition "Who wills the end, wills the means" is analytic.

This statement is perfectly correct. It follows directly from Kant's definition of "will," and might therefore be called a theorem of the pure theory of rational agency:

> To have a will is by definition to act according to the idea of laws (Ak. 412, par. 12).
> To will an end is to be moved by the idea of a law which connects that end with some possible behavior of mine (Ak. 417, par. 24).
> Behavior connected by a law to an end is a *means* to that end (by definition).
> But to be moved to do that which is a means to some end, by the idea of the law connecting that means to that end, is simply to will the means.
> Hence, combining the foregoing steps:
> "Who wills the end, wills the means."

Two points should be noted. First, there is a great difference between "Who wills the end, wills the means," and "Who desires the end, wills the means." The former is analytic, as we have seen. The latter is synthetic and, if taken as a universal proposition, is false to boot. There are countless cases in which an agent desires some end without willing it and in which he therefore does not will the means. There is nothing in the least irrational about choosing not to will an end one desires. Indeed, the willingness to forgo ends that one desires is normally taken as a prerequisite both of prudence and of morality. Nor is the converse of the generalization true. "Who wills the means, desires the end" might appear plausible, if one makes the mistake of supposing that desire and only desire determines us to choose ends. But once we recognize that an agent is free to choose or posit ends for many reasons (or indeed, for none at all), we see that willing a means to some end in no way implies a desire for the end.[21]

The second point concerns the nature of the law connecting my behavior with my end. There are in general two possibilities. Either my behavior stands in a causal relation to my end, according to the laws governing the connection of events in the natural world; or else the occurrence of the behavior simply is my end. An example of the first is drinking water in order to slake my thirst. If I believe that there is a causal connection for creatures like myself between drinking water and diminishing thirst, then my conception of the causal law governing that connection, together with my choosing as my end the slaking of my thirst, will move me to drink the water. An example of the second is playing a tune on the violin when my end or goal simply is to play the tune, rather than to earn money by playing or even just to have the tune played (which is an end that might be attained by getting someone else to play it).

b. It can be settled by an example and so empirically whether someone has acted on a hypothetical imperative (cf. Ak. 419, par. 26).

This proposition is false according to Kant's own theory of knowledge, although he seems not to have realized it. Throughout the *Groundwork* Kant's attention is focused on cases of apparently

---

[21]"Who wills the end, wills the means" is analytic. But, "He is a creature who wills ends" or more simply, "He has a will" is a synthetic proposition. As I have already suggested, it is a proposition for which we can, in general, have no proof at all. Even the proposition "I have a will" is, according to Kant, impossible to prove. The most I can say is that I must assume its truth insofar as I undertake to act. See the discussion of chapter 3.

moral action which might, upon closer examination, turn out to be prudentially motivated. So in paragraph 26 he goes on about the possibility that "fear of disgrace, perhaps also hidden dread of other risks," might be the cause of an action which looks virtuous on the surface. But, he thinks, we can quite easily exhibit in experience bona fide cases of self-interestedly prudential action.

Not so, alas. In order to prove that a bit of behavior is a prudentially rational action, we would have to show that the agent had posited some event or state of affairs as his end, that he believed that end to be connected by a law to some possible act of his, and that he had been moved to perform that act by his conception of the law connecting the act with his end. Now there is no way in which we could demonstrate *any* of those propositions empirically, for all three are propositions about the agent qua noumenon, not about the agent qua phenomenon or appearance in the realm of experience.

First of all, there is no way of demonstrating empirically that an agent has posited some state of affairs or event as his end. We can show that he desires the end, but an agent is free to ignore a desire in choosing his ends. Second, we can give empirical evidence of the occurrence of certain thoughts in the empirical consciousness of the agent, but belief is a matter of the cognitive significance of thoughts, not of their character as temporally located mental events. Hence, unless we give a behavioral account of belief, we can offer no evidence that the agent *believed* the law connecting his behavior with the end in question. Finally, we can never show in the phenomenal world that a belief in a law caused the agent to act, because in the phenomenal world the only causal connections are law-governed regularities, in which ideas figure as mental events, not as beliefs or assertions or concepts. Furthermore, we can be sure that a causal explanation of the phenomenal sort is available for the behavior in question, for that behavior is an event, and all events, according to Kant, have phenomenal causes.

So, we are in exactly the same situation with regard to prudential action as with moral action. We can show that a man's behavior was in conformity with a rational principle of prudence, on the assumption that he chose as his end something that he desires and on the further assumption that he believes a law, the idea of which occurs in his empirical consciousness as a mental event. But we cannot show that his behavior was caused by his conception of that law. We cannot, in other words, show that he performed a prudentially rational action. Or, to put the same point in yet another way, we cannot show that his reason was practical.

Paraphrasing Kant himself, we can show that an action was *in accordance with prudence*, but not that it was *done from a sense of prudence*. So in this crucial respect, prudence and duty—or hypothetical and categorical imperatives—have exactly the same epistemological status.

c. *We must "investigate the possibility of a* categorical *imperative entirely a* priori*" (Ak. 419, par. 27), which is to say, we must provide for it a transcendental deduction.*

This proposition is true, but not entirely for the reasons Kant gives. All propositions about willing and rational agency require a transcendental justification, for they all make claims which go beyond what experience can establish. Since Kant holds that we can have no knowledge of the noumenal self or its activities, he is forced (in chapter 3) to argue for something weaker than the *truth* of his theory of rational agency. As I have already indicated, he limits himself to two claims: that the theory is logically possible and that we must assume its truth insofar as we undertake to act. The question "How are imperatives possible?" is thus interpreted as two questions. First, what would rational agency be like if there were such a thing? and how do imperatives fit into that theory? Second, how is it even logically possible that the existence of rational agency be compatible with the already established causal determinism of the phenomenal world? Chapter 2 gives an answer to the first of these questions, and chapter 3 recapitulates the answer already developed in the Antinomies of Pure Reason to the second.

iv. How Are Categorical Imperatives Possible?
(Par. 28 and Note)

Now, let us turn to paragraph 28 and the note, where Kant explains the special difficulties involved in showing that a categorical imperative is possible. I believe this bit of text to be especially confused, and if I can explicate it successfully, we shall be able to sum up our entire discussion of paragraphs 24–28 and move on to the derivation of the Categorical Imperative itself.

Kant attributes the difficulty of establishing the possibility of the Categorical Imperative to the fact that it is a synthetic a priori practical proposition. The substance of his argument is contained in the following explanatory note:

> Without presupposing a condition taken from some inclination I connect an action with the will *a priori* and therefore necessarily (although only objectively so—that is, only subject to the Idea of a reason having full power over all subjective impulses to action). Here we have a practical proposition in which the willing of an action is not derived analytically from some other willing already presupposed (for we do not possess any such perfect will), but is on the contrary connected immediately with the concept of the will of a rational being as something which is not contained in this concept. (Ak. 420, *n.* 1)

In paragraph 24, immediately after asking how imperatives are possible, Kant gives the following interpretation of the question:

> This question does not ask how we can conceive the execution of an action commanded by the imperative, but merely how we can conceive the necessitation of the will expressed by the imperative in setting us a task. (Ak. 417, par. 24)

This seems to me to be a very obscure "explanation," particularly in view of the five paragraphs which follow it. As we have seen, Kant first disposes of the case of hypothetical imperatives on the grounds that "Who wills the end, wills the means," is analytic. He then disposes of hypothetical imperatives all over again on the grounds that we can find empirically confirmed cases in which someone has acted on a hypothetical imperative. In the light of these two dispositions of the supposedly easy case of hypothetical imperatives, it is hard to see exactly what the problem is supposed to be in the "difficult" case of categorical imperatives. I can think of *three* different ways of explaining the peculiar difficulty posed by categorical imperatives. All three interpretations are supported by the text and by our general understanding of Kant's argument, but all three are incompatible with the footnote we are now considering, in which Kant seems to say what he really has in mind.

The *first* interpretation is this: categorical imperatives pose a special difficulty because we can never have evidence that anyone actually acts on them. I have already cited a number of passages in which this seems to be the problem Kant is concerned with, but the note to paragraph 28 focuses on other problems entirely. It is not the lack of evidence for bona fide dutiful action that concerns Kant here, but rather the intrinsic obscurity of the notion of a *categorical* imperative.

The *second* interpretation is this: categorical imperatives pose a special difficulty because we cannot see how practical reason can conquer sensuous impulse. In the language of paragraph 24, we cannot see, in the case of a categorical imperative, "how we can conceive the necessitation of the will expressed by the imperative in setting us a task" (Ak. 417). I have several times explained why this notion of reason struggling with impulse conflicts with Kant's own metaphysics, as set forth in the *Critique of Pure Reason*. But Kant himself rules out this interpretation, for in the footnote to paragraph 28, he says:

> Without presupposing a condition taken from some inclination I con-nect an action with the will *a priori* and therefore necessarily *(al-though objectively so—that is, only subject to the Idea of a reason having full power over all subjective impulses to action).* (Ak. 420, n. 1, emphasis added)

As the italicized parenthesis indicates, Kant is putting aside the question how reason can overcome impulse. Paraphrasing in what seems to me a correct way, I read Kant as saying:

> Even if we assume that man's reason is capable of subduing all subjec-tive motives, we still have difficulty in explaining how a *categorical* imperative is possible.

So, the second possible interpretation must be wrong.

The *third* interpretation is this: categorical imperatives pose a special problem because they are formulae expressing (in impera-tive form) principles of practical reason which make no reference to an end at which the agent aims. As Kant says in the footnote:

Here we have a practical proposition in which the willing of an action is not derived analytically from some other willing already presupposed.

In other words, hypothetical imperatives pose no problem, because they are of the form: "Having as your end E, do A which is a means to E," and the validity of an imperative of this form follows from the general analytic proposition "Who wills the end, wills the means." But categorical imperatives are of the form, "Being as you are a rational agent, do A," and the validity of such imperatives cannot be derived either from "Who wills the end, wills the means" or from any other analytic proposition. So we are puzzled as to *how* such a categorical imperative can even be conceived to constrain a will.

Now, this is the most plausible interpretation of Kant's problem, and in struggling with paragraphs 12–31 of chapter 2, I thought for a long time that it was indeed what Kant had in mind. Certainly, if it *is* what Kant meant, then he has a serious problem, for it is not merely difficult to see how such an imperative could constrain a will, it is absolutely impossible! But there are *two* reasons for rejecting this interpretation, and in the end they persuaded me that it was *not* what Kant meant. The first reason is philosophical and concerns the correct way of construing Kant's doctrine; the second is textual and concerns an otherwise mysterious parenthetical aside in the footnote we are considering.

Philosophy first: As I have already pointed out the difference between hypothetical and categorical imperatives consists in the nature of the condition or constraint which the imperative specifies. A hypothetical imperative limits its command to the class of those rational agents who have adopted some specific end, E. A categorical imperative addresses its command to the class of all rational agents as such. The preamble to every categorical imperative is the same, namely,

> Being as you are a rational agent and having as your end the realization of the good. . . .

Kant's entire moral theory depends upon his being able to show that a perfectly rational agent would necessarily take the good as his end. That, as I have so often pointed out, is why he tries to develop a theory of objective or "obligatory" ends in the *Meta-physic of Morals*. It is very important to see that there are two quite distinct questions at issue here. The first is: would a perfectly rational agent necessarily aim at the good? The second is: how are we to understand the situation of an *imperfectly* rational agent who does not always do what he would do if he were perfectly rational? The second question raises problems which are difficult enough for Kant. But if he does not answer yes to the first question, if he cannot somehow show that a perfectly rational agent necessarily aims at the objectively good, then his entire theory collapses. For in that case the objective principles of ethics will not be principles of pure practical reason, resting only on the objective canons of rationality. They will instead be principles of something other than reason, resting on God's fiat, on a benevolent sentiment, on intuition, or on some other nonrational basis. And that would thoroughly destroy the autonomy of reason which Kant sought to establish.

So on purely philosophical grounds, we ought to reject the notion that categorical imperatives pose a special problem because they are formulae expressing principles of practical reason which make no reference to an end at which the agent aims. They *do* refer to such an end, namely, the Good.

But we also have a tiny bit of textual evidence to support our rejection of this third, plausible interpretation. In the footnote which we are still discussing, Kant writes:

> Here we have a practical proposition in which the willing of an action is not derived analytically from some other willing already presupposed (FOR WE DO NOT POSSESS ANY SUCH PERFECT WILL). (Ak. 420, *n*. 1, emphasis added)

The implication of the parenthesis, which I have emphasized so heavily, seems to me perfectly unmistakable. If we did possess such a perfect will, it says, then there *would* be some other volition already presupposed (namely, the Good), from which the action commanded by the categorical imperative would be analytically derived. And in that case, of course, there would be no special problem about categorical imperatives. For they, like hypothetical imperatives, would follow from the analytic proposition, "Who wills the end, wills the means." But the Categorical Imperative would not thereby be revealed as contingent, because a perfect will could not "escape from the precept if [it were to] abandon the purpose" (Ak. 420, par. 27). It could not give up the Good as its purpose because, according to Kant, a perfect will necessarily aims at the Good.

So we come to what I believe must be the correct interpretation of the claim that categorical imperatives pose a special problem of understanding: Given an imperfectly rational agent who does not necessarily aim at the good, how is such an agent constrained by the Categorical Imperative to do that which he would necessarily do if he were perfectly rational and hence necessarily aimed at the good? According to the last sentence of the footnote, a categorical imperative connects the willing of an action "immediately with the concept of the will of a rational being as something which is not contained in this concept" (Ak. 420n).

There is no problem about hypothetical imperatives because they bind only those who acknowledge the condition (that is, the having of the specified end) under which they are valid. And there is no problem about the unconditional principles of pure practical reason, for they follow from the principle, "Who wills the end, wills the means," together with the proposition that all perfectly rational agents necessarily will the Good. But there *is* a problem about categorical imperatives, for they issue unconditional commands precisely to those imperfectly rational agents who cannot be assumed necessarily to will the Good. Their bindingness, therefore, cannot be derived analytically from the proposition "Who wills the end, wills the means."

E. The Derivation of the Categorical Imperative (Pars. 29–31)

At this point (par. 29) the argument takes a sudden, very puzzling turn, and Kant almost immediately brings it to an abrupt end. It is worth reviewing the line of the exposition in the preceding paragraphs in order to get some perspective on this unexpected twist.

The argument of chapter 2 begins in paragraph 12 with the introduction of the concept of will, or rational agency. Kant distinguishes perfectly from imperfectly rational agents and uses the distinction in paragraph 13 to define the key term "imperative." After developing a theory and classification of imperatives (pars. 14–23), he asks the crucial question "How are imperatives possible?" (par. 24). This question is not difficult to answer in the case of hypothetical imperatives, we are told (pars. 24–25), but it is exceedingly difficult to answer in the case of categorical imperatives (par. 26), both because there can be no empirical evidence of anyone's acting on a categorical imperative (par. 27) and because categorical imperatives are synthetic practical propositions a priori (par. 28 and note).

Anyone who has followed Kant's exposition to this point will obviously expect the next paragraphs to contain some sort of answer to the key question, "How are categorical imperatives possible?" What else, after all, have the previous seventeen paragraphs been leading up to?

"In this task," Kant begins, "we have first to enquire whether perhaps the mere concept of a categorical imperative may not also provide us with the formula containing the only proposition that can be a categorical imperative" (Ak. 420, par. 29). Good enough, though that seems a rather roundabout way of approaching the problem. But the remainder of the sentence leaves us hanging in midair:

> for even when we know the purport of such an absolute command, the question of its possibility will still require special and troublesome effort, which we postpone to the final chapter.

He isn't even going to try to explain how categorical imperatives are possible until chapter 3, which is some twenty-five pages further on! Instead, it turns out, he is going to pull the formula of the Categorical Imperative out of the preceding discussion as if by sleight of hand and then launch into an extended treatment of examples, alternative formulations, and countless other subsidiary matters. A careful reader may be forgiven for feeling that Kant has pulled the rug out from beneath him.

To grasp what is happening, we must remind ourselves of the

overall pattern of the *Groundwork* argument. As I pointed out in my preliminary analysis of the structure of Kant's argument, chapter 2 aims only at proving a hypothetical proposition:

> If man is capable of being moved by reason, then we all stand under the moral law.

Now strictly speaking, Kant thinks that there is no problem in showing that man is capable of being moved by reason, insofar as reason's laws take the form of *hypothetical* imperatives. He thinks the real problem is in showing that man is capable of being moved by *pure* reason. And that, as we have seen, is equivalent in his eyes to showing that *categorical* imperatives are possible. So the thesis of chapter 2 might be restated thus:

> If categorical imperatives are possible, then the Categorical Imperative (as stated in chapter 1) is valid for all rational agents.

This is just exactly what paragraphs 29–31 try to prove. In that brief passage Kant derives the formula of the only (possible) categorical imperative from an analysis of the mere concept of a categorical imperative in general. So the thesis of chapter 2, in effect, is that if man is capable of being moved by categorical imperatives, then he is bound by the Categorical Imperative.

Kant would have made the structure of his argument a good deal clearer if he had moved directly from paragraph 31 of chapter 2 into paragraph 1 of chapter 3. Instead, he took a long and fascinating detour, on which I shall comment presently. When he does finally return to the possibility of categorical imperatives, of course, he argues that the question is unanswerable, because it concerns man's nature as a noumenon, or self-in-itself. Now let us examine the derivation of the Categorical Imperative.

The entire argument consists of one paragraph:

> When I conceive a *hypothetical* imperative in general, I do not know beforehand what it will contain—until its condition is given. But if I conceive a *categorical* imperative, I know at once what it contains. For since besides the law this imperative contains only the necessity that our maxim should conform to this law, while the law, as we have seen, contains no condition to limit it, there remains nothing over to which the maxim has to conform except the universality of a law as

such; and it is this conformity alone that the imperative properly asserts to be necessary. (Ak. 420–421, par. 30)[22]

Kant's argument in this crucial paragraph is clouded by the same confusions and internal conflicts which afflict the rest of the *Groundwork*. The central problem is his impossible quest for a purely formal criterion of rational agency which will serve as a sufficient condition of the objective rightness of policies or maxims. In terms of the analysis of maxims and reasons which I advanced in my commentary on chapter 1, it is possible to reconstruct Kant's derivation of the Categorical Imperative. But it is not possible to reconstruct it in a way that gives Kant what he really wants. The argument of paragraph 30 goes something like this:

From the concept of a hypothetical imperative in general, I can derive only a schema of such an imperative, namely, "Having as your end E, do A, which is a means to E." Until I know what particular end, E, an agent has chosen (until, as Kant puts it, "the condition is given"), I cannot know which particular hypothetical imperatives are valid for him. But a categorical imperative is an imperative whose "condition" applies to all rational agents as such, namely, "Being as you are a rational agent and having the Good as your end. . . ." So, if there are any valid categorical imperatives at all, we should be able to derive them from the mere concept of a categorical imperative in general. There is no particular, empirically specifiable limiting condition that must be given in order for the imperative to be valid.

Now, if we ignore Kant's assumption that all rational agents qua rational aim at the Good (and Kant *does* ignore this part of his theory here), then we are left with the universal condition, "Being as you are a rational agent. . . ." The only possible command of reason that could follow from such a premise would be a command to be rational. In terms of maxims and reasons, this would be a command to adopt only those policies for which one had good reasons. Since we are abstracting from all particularizing conditions, this in turn must mean, "Act only on maxims for the adoption of which you have reasons which would be equally good reasons for all rational agents." As Kant puts it, "There remains nothing over to which the maxim has to conform except the universality of a law as such" (Ak. 421, par. 30).

If we were perfectly clear that this line of argument could only lead to a negative criterion of maxims, a criterion which rules some out

---

[22]To the first occurrence of the term "maxim," Kant appends a note explaining the distinction between maxims and laws. I have already discussed this note at length in my treatment of chapter 1.

as irrational but does not rule any in as objectively valid, then we would formulate the Categorical Imperative in an appropriately negative manner. It might read something like this: "Being as you are a rational agent, reject any policy which is inconsistent." (I shall explain presently what this means.) But if we cherish the illusion, as Kant did, that a positive, sufficient criterion of policies can be derived from the purely formal canons of rationality, then we will formulate the Categorical Imperative in such a way as to convey, confusedly, the impression that a purely formal criterion of consistency suffices to identify specific policies as enjoined by the canons of rationality above. In short, we will probably formulate the Categorical Imperative as:

ACT ONLY ON THAT MAXIM THROUGH WHICH YOU CAN AT THE SAME TIME WILL THAT IT SHOULD BECOME A UNIVERSAL LAW (Ak. 421, par. 31, emphasis added)

4. The Categorical Imperative:
The Alternate Formulae
(Ak. 421–436)

With the statement of the only possible Categorical Imperative, in paragraph 31, the argument of chapter 2 is completed. Kant has derived the formula of the Categorical Imperative from the concept of rational agency, thereby establishing the hypothetical proposition "If man is capable of rational agency (if man can be moved by reason), then he stands under the Categorical Imperative." The completion of the argument must await chapter 3, where Kant signals its resumption by entitling one of the subsections "How Is a Categorical Imperative Possible?" (Ak. 453).

The remainder of chapter 2, save for a brief concluding portion (Ak. 436–445), consists of elaborations on and examples of the Categorical Imperative. Kant offers a number of alternative formulae for his highest principle of practical reason and uses them to introduce discussions of autonomy, human dignity, the society of moral agents, and other subjects. Kant himself speaks of *three* formulations of the Categorical Imperative, namely, the official formula which he has just derived, the formula of humanity as an end-in-itself, and the formula of autonomy. H. J. Paton distinguishes five formulae, and I shall follow him since his division of Kant's exposition seems to me a better guide to the actual content of chapter 2.[23] The text following paragraph 31 divides in the following way:

A. Ak. 421–424: The formula of the Law of Nature, together with four examples of the application of this version of the Categorical Imperative.

B. Ak. 425–430: The formula of humanity as an end-in-itself, with a reconsideration of the same four examples in terms of this version.

C. Ak. 430–433: The formula of autonomy, or man as a giver of universal law.

D. Ak. 433–436: The formula of the Kingdom of Ends, or man as a member of an ideal society of autonomous law-givers.

The conclusion of chapter 2 is devoted to a summary of what has been said, a discussion of autonomy versus heteronymy, and a (deprecatory) classification of all other moral philosophies as species of heteronymy.[24]

---

[23]As usual, the architectonic is at work here obscuring Kant's own deeper argument. Kant claims to have only three formulae because he sees them as fitting into the thesis-antithesis-synthesis format of the Table of Categories of the *First Critique*. Roughly speaking, the first formula is supposed to be purely formal; the second formula (man as end-in-himself) is supposed to be material; and the third formula (autonomy) is then the synthesis of the first and the second. But flashy as that way of representing things may be, it is no help at all in understanding the argument, so I shall ignore it.

[24]Klaus Reich, in an essay on Kant's relationship to Greek ethical theory, calls attention to a close parallel between the three subsidiary formulae of the Categorical Imperative (that is, the formulae of universal law of nature, of man as an end-in-himself, and of the kingdom of ends) and a triad of principles proposed by Cicero in *De Officiis*. The Cicero work had been translated by Christian Garve into German and was known to Kant. A number of recent commentators on the *Groundwork*, including A. R. C. Duncan and B. E. A. Liddell, have inferred from Reich's study the conclusion that Kant intended his various subsidiary formulae to reflect Cicero's and Garve's principles and, thus, to represent in some sense "popular morality." It may very well be that something of this sort was in Kant's

A. The Formula of the Law of Nature (Ak. 421–424)

Kant indicates the provisional or hypothetical status of the remainder of chapter 2 in the paragraph just following the statement of the Categorical Imperative. "Now," he says, "if all imperatives of duty can be derived from this one imperative as a principle [that is, if we can derive all the particular commands of duty from the Categorical Imperative], then even although we leave it unsettled whether what we call duty may not be an empty concept, we shall still be able to show at least what we understand by it and what the concept means" (Ak. 421). But instead of going directly to a consideration of particular imperatives of duty, Kant introduces a second formulation of the Categorical Imperative which differs in a significant, albeit small, respect from the first formula. He writes:

> Since the universality of the law governing the production of effects constitutes what is properly called *nature* in its most general sense (nature as regards its form)—that is, the existence of things so far as determined by universal laws—the universal imperative of duty may also run as follows: *"Act as if the maxim of your action were to become through your will a universal law of nature."* (Ak. 421)

In each of the four examples which directly follow this passage, Kant appeals to the "law of nature" formula rather than to the first, official "universal law" formula. The difference is extremely

---

mind, but I find such a line of interpretation unhelpful as a guide actually to grasping the philosophical significance of Kant's formulae. For example, the formula of the law of nature, as I argue in the following pages, can truly be understood only in the light of the specific metaphysical theory of the *First Critique*, with which Cicero was of course totally unfamiliar. The formula of man as an end-in-himself, although similar to many moral injunctions from classical and biblical writings, nevertheless serves for Kant the quite specific purpose of providing an objective or obligatory end to complement the formal principle of universal law. Under the circumstances, I think it is not philosophically enlightening to emphasize the relationship between Kant's formulae and Cicero's principles. See Klaus Reich, "Kant and Greek Ethics," *Mind*, 48:338, 446; A. R. C. Duncan, *Practical Reason and Morality* (London: Nelson, 1957); B. E. A. Liddell, *Kant on the Foundation of Morality* (Bloomington, Ind.: Indiana University Press, 1970). See also T. C. Williams, *The Concept of the Categorical Imperative* (New York: Oxford University Press, 1968), chap. 3.

important, and once we understand it fully, we will be able to make much more sense out of Kant's puzzling notion of contradictory willing.

The key to a correct reading of Kant's argument, as is so often the case, can be found in the doctrine of the *First Critique*. According to Kant, my actions as a rational agent are known to me not as they are in themselves—that is, as rational actions—but as they appear to me under the forms of space, time, and the categories in the phenomenal world. In this guise, as *events*, they stand under that total system of regularities or laws which Kant calls "nature." In short, my rationally willed actions appear to me as phenomenally caused behavior. The same is, of course, true for the actions of other rational agents.[25]

If, as a rational agent, I undertake to act only on those policies which would be adopted by all rational agents insofar as they are rational, then it is as though I were to undertake to lay down laws of (phenomenal) nature which phenomenally necessitated just that behavior which would make its appearance if all rational agents acted on rational policies. For example, suppose that I conclude that the canons of practical reason require me to keep my promises. This is equivalent to concluding that all rational agents, insofar as they are rational, will adopt the policy of keeping their promises. But since all such promise keepings will appear in the phenomenal world as instances of promise keeping behavior,[26] this is equivalent in turn to acting as though the policy of my action "were to become through [my] will a universal law of [phenomenal] nature."

We are now in a position to explain one of the central notions of Kant's moral theory, namely, the notion of inconsistent or contradictory willing. Since the Categorical Imperative is a negative criterion of the rationality of policies, or maxims, no matter what

[25]I have already explored the theoretical problems which are raised for Kant's Critical Philosophy by the postulation of more than one rational agent in the field of appearance. For the present purposes, however, let us put those problems to one side.

[26]Where an instance of promise keeping behavior is an event which is in conformity with the principle of promise keeping, but not as such an act done from the policy of promise keeping.

extravagant claims Kant makes for it, we must concentrate on the sorts of policies which it rules *out*. To put the point as simply as possible, the Categorical Imperative rules out the adoption of policies or sets of policies which are internally inconsistent and, hence, impossible to carry out as specified. For example, a company which announced as its hiring policy, "We are an equal opportunity employer: no women, blacks, or Indians need apply," would be guilty of inconsistent willing. The policy (or pair of policies) thus announced cannot be carried out, because the first part will be violated if the second part is followed and vice versa.[27]

Now, Kant obviously thinks that in all or most cases of contradictory willing, some self-serving motive is at work. The promise maker who breaks a promise when it serves his interests, the grocer who cheats on the change, the magistrate who gives preferential treatment to his relatives, all are persons who adopt a general policy and then violate it to suit their own needs. But it should be obvious that *any* inconsistency in willing is ruled out by the Categorical Imperative, even if it is occasioned by altruism rather than egoism. The tax official who adopts the policy of collecting exactly what each citizen owes and then shuts his eyes to a bit of cheating by a poor widow is as guilty of contradictory willing as though he had taken a bribe to fudge the returns of a wealthy industrialist. In each case, remember, the contradiction consists in adopting policies which cannot consistently be carried out. There is nothing inconsistent about a policy of collecting exactly what the tax law requires, and there is nothing inconsistent about a policy of bending the law for deserving widows (assuming that one has not already adopted some other incompatible policy, such as upholding the law to the letter). But it is inconsistent to adopt *both* the policy of collecting what the law requires *and* bending the law for deserving widows.

The beauty of the Law of Nature formulation of the Categorical Imperative is that it permits Kant to exhibit a volitional inconsistency as a physical impossibility. To explain this point, let us con-

[27]Note: The Categorical Imperative does not tell us that it is irrational to bar women, blacks, or Indians from a job. It only tells us that it is irrational to adopt as one's policy *both* the principle of equal opportunity *and* the exclusions.

sider an example drawn from the game by which Kant is said to have supported himself in his youth—billiards.[28] Suppose that I agree to play a game of billiards with a friend. As we customarily understand the situation, there are two sets of "laws" which govern the play, namely, the laws of physics and the rules of billiards. The laws of physics, which I cannot, of course, violate even if I should wish to, specify that the collisions of balls will be such that the sum of the momenta of the several objects is preserved, that the direction and speed of the several balls conforms to the parallogram of forces, and so forth. The rules of billiards specify that I may not move a ball with my hand (save to spot it at the appropriate times), that my opponent and I must play in turn, and so on.

Now, imagine that my opponent and I both possessed what devotees of ESP call "psychokinetic ability," so that we "played" by moving the balls about the table at will, merely by thinking of the path we wanted them to take. In that case, if we wished to play billiards as we know the game, we would have to add a special set of rules to the regular rules of billiards, namely, Newton's Laws of Motion. In short, what are now laws of nature would become rules of the game. It would be against the rules to strike the object ball squarely with the cue ball and then have the object ball describe a figure eight before coming to rest. It would also be against the rules to make a ball without any spin on it rebound from a cushion in such a way that the angle of incidence did not equal the angle of reflection, and so forth.

Under these fanciful conditions, cheating would consist in adopting Newton's Laws of Motion as one's policy and also adopting some other, inconsistent rule of motion as one's policy on a particular shot. And now the force of the "Law of Nature" formula becomes evident. For even if I were God, I could not create a world which embodied as its Laws of Motion both Newton's Laws and the incompatible laws which I had made my policy for the cheating shot. There could not be a system of nature in which

[28]The evidence is rather slender that Kant actually made money at billiards, but, considering the greyness of his popular reputation, I feel some hyperbole may be permitted by way of a correction.

reaction was both always equal to and sometimes not equal to action or in which force always equalled but also sometimes did not equal mass times acceleration. So the principle, "Act as if the maxim of your action were to become through your will a universal law of nature," would quite effectively bar one from cheating at this game of psychokinetic billiards.

What is clear in this example based upon the familiar laws of motion is, according to Kant, also true, though perhaps less clear, in cases involving unfamiliar laws of behavior. To act as though the maxim of my action were to become a universal law for all rational agents is to act as though the maxim of my action were, through my will, to be transformed into a law of nature. But an inconsistent set of policies could never be transformed into a possible system of nature. So the "law of nature" formula, like the universal law formula, rules out inconsistent willing.[29]

We come now to the passage which I have several times referred to, somewhat facetiously, as the Famous Four Examples. These applications of the Categorical Imperative have received a quite disproportionate amount of attention, and I shall try not to add too many more pages to the literature on them. Two of the examples are simply no good at all, a third fails, although in an interesting manner, and only one—the example of false promising

[29]On this matter of the impossibility of an inconsistent system of natural laws, as on so many matters, Hume anticipated Kant. In his *Enquiry Concerning the Human Understanding*, with which Kant was quite familiar, Hume has a famous discussion of miracles (chap. 10) which shows that the concept of a miracle is epistemologically inconsistent. A miracle is, by definition, an event which contravenes the laws of nature. Now all laws of nature, Hume argues, are generalizations from the past regularity of our experience. So there are only two possibilities: either the evidence for the universality of the law is stronger than the evidence for the occurrence of the "miraculous" event, in which case we conclude that the offending event did not happen, or the evidence for the occurrence of the "miracle" is stronger than the evidence for the universality of the law, in which case we alter the conception of the laws of nature to fit the event (thereby depriving it of its miraculous character). But to demonstrate the occurrence of a miracle per se, we would have to produce evidence which *both* supported the universality of the law *and* demonstrated the occurrence of the exception. That is logically impossible, and, therefore, so are "miracles." A similar argument, translated into the Kantian language of "succession according to a rule in objective time," could be constructed to show why Kant's epistemology rules out an inconsistent system of nature.

—can be salvaged by appropriate alterations. Nevertheless, I think we shall learn a good deal about the nature of rational willing from an analysis of all four.

First of all, let me repeat the observation I made during my introductory remarks about reading Kant. There is a considerable difference in philosophy between genuine proof and what might be called hypothetical argument. Philosophers frequently flesh out their works by showing how familiar concepts, doctrines, or beliefs can be given "natural" interpretations in the special terms of their systems. They don't exactly *deduce* the favored doctrines from their principles; they just fit them in, so to speak. The discovery of a natural-looking place for familiar ideas in the system is taken as a sort of subsidiary confirmation of the theory. The criterion used is plausibility rather than validity. Aristotle's account of the virtues in Books III–V of the *Nichomachean Ethics* is a good example of this sort of exercise. So is Hobbes's brilliant redefinition of psychological predicates in chapter 6 of *Leviathan*. The best modern example I know is Sidgwick's attempt, in *Methods of Ethics,* to exhibit the conventional morality of English society as a corollary of his particular brand of utilitarianism.

Kant is excessively fond of this sort of exercise. In the *Critique of Pure Reason* it takes such forms as the attempt to squeeze his own special theory of matter into the section entitled The Anticipations of Perception.[30] In the *Metaphysic of Morals,* it appears as a typical recapitulation in terms of the Critical Philosophy of such virtues and vices as beneficence, avarice, gratitude, suicide, and (my favorite) "self-stupefaction through the immoderate use of food and drink." Kant firmly believes that it is wrong to commit suicide and right, indeed obligatory, to develop one's natural talents. So, quite naturally, he hopes to confirm these beliefs by appeal to the Categorical Imperative. Although he is inventive in searching for the needed arguments, his effort is trebly misguided, for in the first place, his beliefs are false; in the second place, his arguments are invalid; and worst of all, he misleads us as to the meaning of the Categorical Imperative. Let us take a look at the examples one by one.

---

[30]See *Kant's Theory of Mental Activity,* pp. 232–238.

i. THE EXAMPLE OF SUICIDE

A man feels sick of life as the result of a series of misfortunes that has mounted to the point of despair, but he is still so far in possession of his reason as to ask himself whether taking his own life may not be contrary to his duty to himself. He now applies the test "Can the maxim of my action really become a universal law of nature?" His maxim is "From self-love I make it my principle to shorten my life if its continuance threatens more evil than it promises pleasure." The only further question to ask is whether this principle of self-love can become a universal law of nature. It is then seen at once that a system of nature by whose law the very same feeling whose function [*Bestimmung*] is to stimulate the furtherance of life should actually destroy life would contradict itself and consequently could not subsist as a system of nature. Hence this maxim cannot possibly hold as a universal law of nature and is therefore entirely opposed to the supreme principle of all duty. (Ak. 421–422)

The argument is a *reductio,* designed to show that a policy of hedonistic suicide (so to speak) violates the criteria laid down in the Law of Nature formula. The major and fatal flaw in the argument, of course, is that Kant simply assumes the existence of a natural purpose which God or Nature has assigned to the inclination to self-love. But let us clear up a few preliminary matters before examining the argument proper.

First of all, some readers may be tempted to object that a man committing suicide might have other policies in mind than the one Kant attributes to his imaginary subject. That is quite true and irrelevant. The Categorical Imperative is supposed to be a criterion of the rationality of policies, not a standard for evaluating men or acts. Kant's aim is to sketch a plausible setting for a policy and then test it against his criterion. Another potential suicide, guided by a different policy, would require a separate consideration. One could only rule out an *act* by showing that every possible policy enjoining it conflicted with the Categorical Imperative.[31]

The second point concerns Kant's statement of the policy in question. I have already discussed this at some length. The policy proper is:

[31]See C. I. Lewis, *The Ground and Nature of the Right* (New York: Columbia University Press, 1955).

> To shorten my life if its continuance threatens more evil than it promises pleasure.

Kant cites a reason for adopting it, namely "from self-love." But one could easily find other reasons for which such a policy might be adopted, including even the (misguided) conviction that it was morally obligatory for each individual to maximize his own sum of pleasure by any means however distasteful, including suicide if necessary. In order for Kant to develop the desired contradiction, however, he must somehow incorporate the "principle" of self-love into the maxim itself, rather than treating it as a reason for choosing the maxim. Something like the following might capture Kant's intention:

> To shorten my life if its continuance threatens to frustrate my impulse to self-love.

Now, by the judicious deployment of some rather powerful assumptions, we can exhibit a contradiction between this policy and Nature's purpose. Briefly, we assume that Nature implants the feeling of self-love in us for the purpose of causing us to improve our lives. We assume further that the improvement of life always means at least its continuation, if nothing else.[32] Now we see that the proposed suicide maxim could never become part of a system of natural laws which also embodied these "purposes" of "Nature." For in any such system of laws, one and the same feeling of self-love would under certain circumstances be the cause of both the termination and the prolongation of life. But that is impossible. As Kant says, such a state of affairs "could not subsist as a system of nature." Hence, the policy is "entirely opposed to the supreme principle of all duty."

The same point can be made in terms of the first formula of the Categorical Imperative, provided we assume that Nature's purposes are our purposes. The problem with the argument, aside from some unclarity about the "desire" of self-love, is that there is just no sense at all to be made of the notion of Nature's purposes.

---

[32] A dubious assumption, though one familiar in philosophical circles. See Spinoza's treatment of *Conatus* in his *Ethics*.

Kant knows as much, of course. No better treatment of the subject can be found than in Kant's *Critique of Teleological Judgment*. But he cannot resist the temptation to draw his own moral convictions out of the Categorical Imperative.

This first example is, be it noted, a ruling-out rather than a ruling-in. Even with the aid of natural teleology Kant cannot alter the negative logical form of the criterion enunciated in the Categorical Imperative.

ii. THE EXAMPLE OF FALSE PROMISING

Another finds himself driven to borrowing money because of need. He well knows that he will not be able to pay it back; but he sees too that he will get no loan unless he gives a firm promise to pay it back within a fixed time. He is inclined to make such a promise; but he has still enough conscience to ask "is it not unlawful and contrary to duty to get out of difficulties in this way?" Supposing, however, he did resolve to do so, the maxim of his action would run thus: "Whenever I believe myself short of money, I will borrow money and promise to pay it back, though I know that this will never be done." Now this principle of self-love or personal advantage is perhaps quite compatible with my own entire future welfare; only there remains the question "Is it right?" I therefore transform the demand of self-love into a universal law and frame my question thus: "How would things stand if my maxim became a universal law?" I then see straight away that this maxim can never rank as a universal law of nature and be self-consistent, but must necessarily contradict itself. For the universality of a law that every one believing himself to be in need can make any promise he pleases with the intention not to keep it would make promising, and the very purpose of promising, itself impossible, since no one would believe he was being promised anything, but would laugh at utterances of this kind as empty shams. (Ak. 422)

The example of false promising is, for Kant's purpose, the most important example in the entire *Groundwork*. Like the Second Analogy in the *Critique of Pure Reason*, it tends to be underemphasized because it appears as just one of a number of examples. But since Kant's moral theory is (in my judgment) essentially a contract theory of obligation, false promising or breach of contract must necessarily go to the heart of his doctrine.

Let us again begin by dealing with some subsidiary obstacles to an adequate appreciation of Kant's thought. First, I repeat what

I said about the suicide example: Kant is not assuming that the maxim he cites is the only maxim on the basis of which one might make false promises. The entire example is a test of the policy, "Whenever I believe myself, etc., etc.," which we can rephrase as:

> To borrow money and promise to repay it, when I believe myself to need it, even though I know that I shall not do so.

Other policies which might lead to the same actions require an independent evaluation.

Second, let us ignore the reference to self-love. Kant's aim is to distinguish moral from merely prudential objections to the policy. But in light of the treatment of self-love in the example of suicide, the reference here is misleading.

Finally, let us once more observe that the argument actually given by Kant is hopelessly inadequate. I dealt with its inadequacies in my commentary on chapter 1, where virtually the same example is used by Kant. The contradictory nature of the policy cannot possibly be demonstrated by appeal to the contingent fact —if, indeed, it is a fact—that people tend to disbelieve a persistent promise breaker.

The key to correct understanding of this example, and thereby to an understanding of Kant's moral philosophy as a whole, is the concept of a social activity governed by rules which specify a system of expectations, commitments, burdens, and rewards attached to the roles defined in the activity. I have in mind what John Rawls, in a somewhat different context, calls a *practice* or an *institution*.[33] Contradictory willing, in the most general sense, is the adoption of a policy or set of policies which is internally inconsistent. From the standpoint of moral philosophy, the most important kind of contradictory willing is the case in which I commit myself to the adoption, with others, of a collective policy, thereby establishing a practice or institution, and then privately adopt another policy which contradicts it. For example, I and my fellows adopt a collective policy of binding our future actions by certain ritual utterances ("I promise"), and then I also adopt the policy of breaking my promises under circumstances not allowed in the

---

[33]Cf. *A Theory of Justice* (Cambridge, Mass.: Harvard University Press, 1971), pp. 54–56.

rules of the original, collective policy. The contradiction consists simply in the logical impossibility of acting in all possible situations on both policies.

Kant assumes, on no very good grounds, that men always violate their commitments for self-interested reasons. But, of course, that need not be so, as I have already pointed out. The irrationality consists not in succumbing to the temptations of self-love but in adopting incompatible policies.

In the example before us, we must assume that men have either explicitly or tacitly adopted a practice of promising. I say "a" practice of promising, because there is no one such practice. Endlessly many different, specific, consistent practices of promising can be generated merely by varying the rules which dictate to whom, to what extent, and in the face of what circumstances one is bound to do what one has promised. We may assume that the practice before us rules out borrowing money one knows one cannot repay. We may also assume—and this is, of course, crucial —that the protagonist of Kant's example has actually endorsed such a practice. Under those assumptions, his policies are contradictory, for the policy embodied in the practice of promising conflicts with the policy on the basis of which he attempts to borrow money. The irrationality lies in the internal inconsistency of the policies themselves, not in the danger that he will be laughed at when next he tries to borrow money.

There are, I think, two things which mislead Kant in his treatment of false promising. First, he does not see that a contradiction in willing can occur only if one has adopted a practice of promising. It is obviously possible for an individual to abstain from any practice of promising at all, and it is perhaps even possible for an entire society to exist for an extended period of time without any developed practice of promising.[34] But second, Kant doesn't see that there are many possible practices of promising, not just one. There is no reason at all to assume that societies must adopt one

[34]It isn't really clear to me whether this is, in fact, possible. In the case of the analogous practice of truth telling, I think one could maintain that *some* system of rules of truth telling is built into language per se, so that someone who literally rejected any rules of truth telling could be said not to be speaking, in the strict sense of the term. Whether one could extend that argument to cover promising is an interesting question to which I don't have an answer.

of these rather than another, and a little experience of various social circles, let alone anthropological reports of quite different cultures, teaches us that promising practices vary widely.

It is rather tricky to translate this example of contradictory willing into the language of the Law of Nature formula. Since Kant holds that all social interactions appear in nature as causally determined behavior, it must, in principle, be possible first to give nonintentional characterizations of that behavior and then to discover natural laws governing it. The contradiction implicit in a policy of false promising then becomes an internal conflict in the system of natural laws covering the relevant behavior. In the light of recent philosophical discussions concerning the possibility of a behavioral account of linguistic performance, it is obviously very much open to debate whether a Kantian-style program could be carried out. I simply am not competent even to offer an opinion on that question, but I am quite confident both that Kant's epistemology entails that one can and that his moral philosophy presupposes that one can.

The example of false promising is crucial to Kant's theory because, as I shall suggest in the concluding chapter of this commentary, a contractual theory of moral obligation is the most plausible way of construing the argument of the *Groundwork*. When Kant tries to draw in duties which do not arise out of contractual commitments, he is forced to make ad hoc assumptions about natural purposes on the objectively good. The most powerful passages of the text, such as those dealing with autonomy and the Kingdom of Ends, clearly rely upon a contractual theory of obligation.

To repeat, the Categorical Imperative in its first and second forms lays down a criterion of practical rationality. The criterion is negative: it rules out contradictory willing. What this means, concretely, is that it is irrational to adopt a set of policies which so conflict with one another that it is logically impossible to carry them out in toto. Inconsistent policies may be either imprudent or immoral (or both). In the former case, I adopt on my own a set of policies which are logically incompatible. For example, I adopt both the policy of holding my caloric intake for a period of one month to 1,200 calories per day and also the policy of eating chocolate sundaes when I feel a powerful craving for sweets. In the latter case, I commit myself, to other rational agents, to act on a set of policies and also adopt a policy inconsistent with that set of policies. In a narrow sense of "promising," the practice of promising is only one of many practices I and others might collectively adopt. But in a loose sense, all contracting might be spoken of as promising. In this looser sense, immorality consists simply in some sort of breach of promise. It now becomes clear, I think, why Kant's moral philosophy is commonly said to provide a theoretical foundation for classical liberal political theory.

iii. The Example of Cultivating One's Talents

> "A third finds in himself a talent . . . etc., etc." (Ak. 422–423)

Nothing much need be said about this argument for cultivating one's talents. Considering the oppressive odor of relentless moralism which clings to the passage, it is just as well that the argument is so obviously bad. As in the case of suicide, Kant appeals to a doctrine of natural purposes. There is no doubt that if we adopt the policy of pursuing all the purposes to which our inherited talents might be put, then it is inconsistent also to fail to develop those talents. But no one stands under any obligation to take on such a set of purposes, and in their absence he can consistently allow his talents to remain fallow.

iv. The Example of Beneficence

> Yet a *fourth* is himself flourishing, but he sees others who have to struggle with great hardships (and whom he could easily help); and he thinks "What does it matter to me? Let every one be as happy as Heaven wills or as he can make himself; I won't deprive him of anything; I won't even envy him; only I have no wish to contribute anything to his well-being or to his support in distress!" Now admittedly if such an attitude were a universal law of nature, mankind could get on perfectly well—better no doubt than if everybody prates about sympathy and goodwill, and even takes pains, on occasion, to practise them, but on the other hand cheats where he can, traffics in

human rights, or violates them in other ways. But although it is possible that a universal law of nature could subsist in harmony with this maxim, yet it is impossible to *will* that such a principle should hold everywhere as a law of nature. For a will which decided in this way would be in conflict with itself, since many a situation might arise in which the man needed love and sympathy from others, and in which, by such a law of nature sprung from his own will, he would rob himself of all hope of the help he wants for himself. (Ak. 423)

This is a rather instructive example, though not so important as the example of promise keeping. Note, by the way, that the two examples of duties to oneself (suicide and the cultivation of talents) are quite uninteresting, requiring as they do an illegitimate appeal to natural purpose. The two examples of duties to others, by contrast, go to the heart of Kant's moral theory.

Kant is, of course, quite aware that a man, upon carefully estimating his present and probable future situation, might choose to forfeit such help as he could get from others in return for the help which, in all consistency, he would be required to give to them. Such a choice, presumably, would be prudent for any man whose present and probable future circumstances were much better than average. So the supposed contradiction does not arise from the mere fact that each of us might like to be the recipient of someone else's beneficence.

The point is that in every situation in which a man finds himself, he necessarily wills such means as are requisite to his ends. That is analytically contained in the notion of willing an end. Now, *if* he ever needs the aid of others and *if* it should somehow be possible for him to determine the actions of those others by his will, then it would be inconsistent for him to will that they should not help him. But in willing that the policy of selfishness should be a universal law of nature, that is exactly what he would be doing. He would be in the position of willing two policies which conflicted with one another.

I must confess that when I first expounded this interpretation to a graduate class in moral philosophy at Columbia University in the fall of 1965, I thought that it was (within the framework of Kant's philosophy) a valid argument. However, a graduate student, whose name I unfortunately do not know, raised the following counterargument: Suppose an individual adopts it as his policy never to set for himself an end whose achievement appears to require the cooperation of others and to forswear any ends he has adopted as soon as it turns out that such cooperation is needed. Under these circumstances, he could consistently will that his maxim of selfishness should be a universal law of nature, for he could be certain a priori that he would never find himself willing an end which that natural law obstructed. This curious policy, which in the ancient world was espoused by such Stoic philosophers as Epictetus, is perfectly consonant with the Categorical Imperative in both its first and second formulations.

Thus we see that of the original four examples, only the example of false promising can be shown to be a valid application of the Categorical Imperative and then only after suitable alterations and reinterpretations.

There is another way of looking at the four examples which enables us to see what Kant is trying to accomplish in the *Groundwork*. All willing, he holds, involves an end, the concept of which moves us to act. Kant is trying to show that certain maxims of action are ruled out, and others certified as objective principles of practical reason, by the criterion of the Categorical Imperative. In terms of the distinction with which he begins the *Groundwork*, Kant is trying to show that the *form* of valid principles entails something about their *content*. There are three ways, he suggests, in which this can be done.

The first way is to appeal to ends which we *must* have and which we cannot, therefore, consistently choose to frustrate. In the first and third examples, Kant quite unjustifiably appeals to the notion of natural purpose in an attempt to prove that we must adopt the furtherance of life and the cultivation of our talents as our ends.

The second way is to point to a practice in which we are already engaged. Since the practice has a system of rules or policies built into it, it is obviously self-contradictory to make violation of the rules one's maxim. In the second example Kant takes this tack, but as we saw, the argument will not suffice to establish any policies as unconditionally required. The most we can show is that *if* one chooses to engage in a practice, *then* it is irrational to violate its rules. Whether we should engage in promising or any other practice is a question which the Categorical Imperative cannot decide.

The third way is to appeal to the fact that as rational agents we must necessarily have some ends or others. In the fourth example Kant tries to show that this analytic truth entails the objective validity of a certain substantive policy, namely, the policy of beneficence. But as the stoic objection shows, it is not true that a policy of beneficence can be deduced from the Categorical Imperative. From the mere fact that I have ends, I cannot deduce either the policy of beneficence or the policy of selfishness.

In view of the failure of these three different strategies for drawing substantive conclusions from formal premises, it is not surprising that Kant fell back upon the notion of obligatory ends. Later in chapter 2, as we shall see, he had one last crack at this impossible problem with no greater success.

In the last paragraph of his treatment of the four examples Kant briefly touches upon one of the most vexing implications of his moral theory. The allusion is indirect at best, but the passage is worth looking at because it is so rare for Kant to acknowledge the problem at all. The question is this: what are we actually doing when we engage in inconsistent willing and, thereby, commit a "transgression of a duty"? Thus far, Kant has concentrated on analyzing the structure of rational agency. Is immoral action then some sort of irrational agency? What could that actually be? According to Kant:

> [W]e in fact do not will that our maxim should become a universal law—since this is impossible for us—but rather that its opposite should remain a law universally: we only take the liberty of making an *exception* to it for ourselves (or even just for this once) to the advantage of our inclination. Consequently if we weighed it all up from one and the same point of view—that of reason—we should find a contradiction in our own will, the contradiction that a certain principle should be objectively necessary as a universal law and yet subjectively should not hold universally but should admit of exceptions. (Ak. 424)

Note what Kant says: it is impossible for us to will a contradictory maxim! If we take this statement seriously, as I believe we must, then it follows that *immoral action*, in the strict sense of the phrase, is impossible. For immoral action is irrational action, and action is by definition behavior originated by reason in its practical employment. There can be mistakes, lapses, errors in action as in calculation. But just as we would not say of a mathematician, in the strict sense, that he had "added" two and two to get five, but rather that he had failed to add two and two; so we could not say of a man that he had, in the strict sense, "acted" inconsistently, but only that he had failed to act. (It would, on this construction, be redundant to say that he had "acted consistently.")

Kant tries to avoid this conclusion, which he would find totally unacceptable, by invoking the distinction between the noumenal and phenomenal standpoints. He puts it this way:

> Since . . . we first consider our action from the point of view[35] of a will wholly in accord with reason, and then consider precisely the same action from the point of view of a will affected by inclination, there is here actually no contradiction, but rather an opposition of inclination to the precept of reason [antagonismus]. (Ak. 424)

The best we can say for this is that it is a good try. But it remains a mystery how we can blame a man for the fact that his inclinations sometimes overcome him. As I have several times observed, either reason is stronger than inclination, in which case it will win and the agent will act on consistent maxims; or inclination is stronger than reason, and through no fault of his own the agent will be prevented from (in the strict sense) acting at all. There is no solution for this problem within the framework of Kant's moral philosophy, a fact which I believe does not count against Kant.

B. The Formula of Humanity as an End-in-Itself (Ak. 425–430)

Having set forth the Categorical Imperative in two formulae designed to exhibit its character as a formal principle of rational agency, Kant now sets about the task of deriving some substantive content for it. After two and a half pages of what is really a review of matter previously discussed (Ak. 525–527), he begins his argument.

Ends which we adopt because of some special characteristic of our nature or in satisfaction of some desire are, of course, contin-

---

[35] *Gesichtspunkt.* In chapter 3 Kant uses the term *Standpunkt*, but I think the reference is clear.

gent and relative, for they are ends only for those agents who have that characteristic or desire. This is true whether the ends are self-serving (satisfaction of desire) or other-regarding (the happiness of others because of a sympathy for them). The value which we assign to such ends (their "worth") is relative to the desire which someone has for them. As such, they are "grounds only of hypothetical imperatives" (Ak. 428).[36]

But, Kant continues:

> Suppose, however, there were something *whose existence* has *in itself* an absolute value, something which as *an end in itself* could be a ground of determinate laws; then in it, and in it alone, would there be the ground of a possible categorical imperative—that is, of a practical law. (Ak. 428)

There is no doubt that Kant is correct. *If* he could establish the absolute or objective worth of something, if he could make sense of the notion of something as an "end in itself," *then* he would have the basis for demonstrating the unconditional validity of substantive principles of practical reason. To put the point in terms of good reasons: if a policy is an efficient means for the accomplishment of my end, then I have a good reason to adopt it, and that reason is a good reason for any rational agent who has the same end. If there is an end which is in itself good, then that is a good reason for its adoption as an end by every rational agent, and any policies which are efficient means to such an end will thereby be good policies for every rational agent.

How might Kant go about demonstrating the existence of an end in itself? Strictly speaking, he offers no argument at all. He just begins the next paragraph flatly with the words, "Now I say that man, and in general every rational being *exists* as an end in himself, *not merely as a means* for arbitrary use by this or that will" (Ak. 428). But I think we can construe Kant as offering an indirect argument by elimination. In effect, Kant argues, if there were nothing of absolute value, then there could be no supreme principle of practical reason, for there would then be no end which all rational agents were obligated to take as their end. Now products

[36]In the language of a twentieth-century moral philosopher, Ralph Barton Perry, "value [that is, worth] is any object of any interest." Perry, of course, can derive only a theory of conditional imperatives from such a premise.

of our will, states of affairs, and things which we employ for our several purposes are clearly only of relative value. That is, their value is relative to the purposes for which they are employed or the desire which they satisfy.

Nothing remains, therefore, save persons themselves—that is, rational agents—to serve as ends in themselves. So Kant reformulates the Categorical Imperative in one of the most famous propositions in all moral philosophy:

> *Act in such a way that you always treat humanity, whether in your own person or in the person of any other, never simply as a means, but always at the same time as an end.* (Ak. 429)

Everyone who reads this passage must feel some sympathetic echo in himself, some sense that whatever the merits of the Categorical Imperative, here at least Kant has touched the very heart of morality. And yet, upon reflection, I find it very difficult to tell what Kant means by the injunction to treat humanity as an end-in-itself, and I find it even more difficult to discover an interpretation that can serve the philosophical purpose for which Kant has introduced it.

Kant is searching, let us remember, for something that is an obligatory or objective end for all rational agents as such. This "end-in-itself" is to be contrasted with the myriad "ends-for-someone" which ground merely hypothetical imperatives. Now, in what sense can a moral agent—whether myself or another—be an *end* of my action? Can a person *be* my purpose? No. The question makes no grammatical sense. Can a moral agent be something I choose to bring into existence? Perhaps, in the sense of siring or bearing children, but even in that marginal case, Kant might wish to argue in Christian fashion that parents produce children, not moral agents per se. Can a moral agent be that for the sake of which I do something? Not in the ordinary sense of that phrase. When I say, for example, that I took my son to the dentist *for his sake*, I mean that I did it in order to further his well-being. My end was his happiness, which I assume is his end too, insofar as he is capable of choosing ends. So I did what I did for the sake of his purpose. It was *his end* which I took as my end, not *him*.

Presumably, what Kant means by treating humanity as an end-in-itself is that I must never fail to take account of the fact that I am dealing with rational moral agents rather than things. In short, I must keep it in mind that *they* have purposes too. This in turn involves respecting their purposes, rather than ignoring them.

Now, however true this injunction may be—and I believe it is the very bedrock of morality—we are still without the substantive criterion that Kant seeks. For consider: either respecting the purposes of other moral agents means making their purposes my own, in which case I am implicated in their pursuit of immoral ends; or it means making their *moral* purposes my own, and I am left to discover a criterion for distinguishing good from bad purposes. But the formula of humanity as an end-in-itself was supposed to provide just that criterion.

When Kant applies the formula of man as end-in-itself to the four examples of the Categorical Imperative, it becomes clear that he does mean for us to treat other agents' ends as our own.[37] In reviewing the example of false promising, for example, he argues:

> For the man whom I seek to use for my own purposes by such a promise cannot possibly agree with my way of behaving to him, and so cannot himself share the end of the action. (Ak. 429–430)

Later on, he says of the duty of beneficence:

> Now humanity could no doubt subsist if everybody contributed nothing to the happiness of others but at the same time refrained from deliberately impairing their happiness. This is, however, merely to agree negatively and not positively with *humanity as an end in itself*

---

[37]Kant's unclarity about his meaning is revealed by the imprecision with which he expresses himself. In the space of a page and a half he uses four different phrases to state his principle, no two of which are obviously synonymous. He first says that "man [*der Mensch*] and in general every rational being [*jedes vernünftige Wesen*] exists as an end in himself." Then he speaks of "objective ends—that is, things whose existence is in itself an end [*Dinge, deren Dasein an sich selbst Zweck ist*]." In the next paragraph he says that the ground of the Categorical Imperative is that "rational nature [*vernünftige Natur*] exists as an end in itself." And finally, when he actually states the third formula, he says we must treat "humanity [*menschheit*] . . . never simply as a means." Thus, Kant says that man, every rational creature, the existence of rational creatures, rational nature, and humanity, is an end in itself. If this seems simply to be a terminological quibble without moral significance, we may reflect that one might urge eugenic schemes in the interest of "rational nature" which could hardly be justified in the name of "every rational creature" or of "humanity."

unless every one endeavours also, so far as in him lies, to further the ends of others. For the ends of a subject who is an end in himself must, if this conception is to have its *full* effect in me, be also, as far as possible, *my* ends. (Ak. 430)

The only way to draw substantive moral conclusions from an argument of this sort is to show that the purely formal constraints of collective, unanimous, contractual agreement, when added to the constraint of bare consistency, suffice to rule out all but one set of substantive principles. Kant seems not to have understood this problem clearly enough to attempt such a demonstration. John Rawls, if I understand him correctly, has offered just such an argument in his work, *A Theory of Justice*, to which I have already referred. This is not the place to ask whether Rawls is successful, but in an indirect way, I consider his formulation of the problem a kind of confirmation of the interpretation of the *Groundwork* which I am setting forth here.

C. The Formula of Autonomy (Ak. 430–433)

After enunciating both a formal and a material version of the Categorical Imperative, Kant follows his familiar architectonic custom by attempting a synthesis of the two. The result is the formula of autonomy. In the passage before us Kant does not state the formula in proper imperative form. Instead, he simply refers to it as "the Idea of the will of every rational being as a will which makes universal law" (Ak. 431). Later on, however, he gives us a correct formulation of the principle, thus:

> Never to choose except in such a way that in the same volition the maxims of your choice are also present as universal law. (Ak. 440)[38]

---

[38]The original German is rather difficult to translate. Kant wrote, "nicht anders zu wählen als so, dass die Maximen seiner Wahl in demselben Wollen zugleich als allgemeines Gesetz mit begriffin seien." Here are the ways in which four translators render the sentence:

L. W. Beck: Never choose except in such a way that the maxims of the choice are comprehended in the same volition as a universal law.

H. J. Paton: Never to choose except in such a way that in the same volition the maxims of your choice are also present as universal law.

I find Kant's treatment of the principle of autonomy perplexing for two reasons, only one of which is legitimate for a commentator. First, and quite legitimately, the argument is obscure. Like the argument for the first formulation of the Categorical Imperative, it relies on a dubious appeal to the elimination of alternatives, so that one is left with the feeling that Kant has pulled yet another rabbit out of his hat. But my real problem is that in this passage, despite some very strong contrary indications, Kant turns out *not* to be saying what I personally want him to say. As the title of this commentary indicates, I believe that the notion of autonomy—at least, as I understand it—is the key to Kant's moral philosophy. In the second paragraph of his discussion of the formula of autonomy, Kant gives what I consider the classic explication of the concept of autonomy. He writes:

> The will is therefore not merely subject to the law, but is so subject that it must be considered as also *making the law* for itself *and precisely on this account* as first of all subject to the law (of which it can regard itself as the author). (Ak. 431, second emphasis added)

The words which I have italicized in this passage are the heart of the concept of autonomy. From them, I believe, flow the most far-reaching consequences for politics as well as for ethics.[39] But in the next paragraph, which contains the core of Kant's argument, it becomes clear that acting only on laws that one has given to oneself and being bound by them only because one has so given them is not at all what Kant has in mind! Instead, the argument

C. J. Friedrich: Always so to choose that in the same act of willing the maxims of this choice are formulated as a general law.

B. E. A. Liddell: Always choose according to maxims which you can think of as becoming universal laws by your choice.

The problem is the phrase "zugleich . . . mit begriffin seien." Beck and Paton are closest to the German, but it seems to me that Liddell comes closer to Kant's intention. Compare this rather obscure formulation with the much better statement of the formula of autonomy in the *Critique of Practical Reason:* "So act that the maxim of your will can always at the same time be valid as a principle of a giving of universal law [*einer allgemeinen Gesetzgebung*]" (K.p.V., Ak. V, 30).

[39]See my book *In Defense of Anarchism* (New York: Harper & Row, Publishers, 1970).

for the formula of autonomy turns on the notion of legislating disinterestedly, that is to say, legislating independently of or in abstraction from the particular interests of the agent. This is, to be sure, a crucial notion for Kant, but I find it unsettling to have Kant put it forward as an explication of autonomy, rather than of objectivity or of universality.

Let us first look at the argument of the text, especially as it appears in paragraphs 3 and 4 of this subsection. Then I shall say a few words about the passage quoted above from paragraph 2 and try to explain why I consider it so important.

Kant begins by pointing out that thus far the various formulations of the Categorical Imperative have all abstracted from or eliminated from consideration any interest as an incentive to the performance of the actions commanded. The reason, of course, is that if a command rests its claim, so to speak, on the agent's possession of some interest, then it cannot possibly be a categorical command. The agent could always excuse himself from obeying the command if he happened not to have the interest on which the command was based. Since there is no interest that must necessarily be possessed by every rational agent as such, it follows that no command based on an interest can ever be categorical.

But, Kant says, none of the formulations of the Categorical Imperative advanced thus far place this *disinterestedness* of the agent at the center of attention. To be sure, we can infer the agent's disinterestedness from the formula of universal law. Indeed, since Kant holds that all five formulae are equivalent, it ought to be possible to infer any one from any other. But in the notion of an agent making universal law, Kant feels that he has captured the independence from interest in an especially satisfactory way.

Briefly, the point is this. If we think of the agent as standing under laws, even under universal laws, we must recognize that he might be "bound" or obligated by the law for any number of reasons, including some interest of his. He might be generous out of the hope that he would be doubly repaid or honest for fear of punishment by the civil authorities or, of course, he might obey the moral law out of duty, in which case only would he be worthy of our esteem.

But when we imagine this same agent as *making* universal law, we capture directly the quality of disinterestedness which characterizes true morality. Consider: If a man is to make a law which shall be binding upon all rational agents, he must in his lawmaking abstract from every particular interest that he or any other agent might possess; otherwise, his law would be binding only on those agents who shared the interest. For example, a law based upon an interest in happiness (such as the Principle of Utility) might be valid for all human beings, insofar as they happen to desire happiness. But it would not be a truly *universal* law, for it is at least logically possible that a rational agent should exist who does not desire happiness. So the command, "Act as though you were legislating universal law through the adoption of your maxim," turns out to be a command to be disinterested, to abstract from all interest in one's deliberations. And this quality of disinterestedness, Kant thinks, is the quintessence of morality.

The argument for autonomy, so far as I understand it, goes something like this: If there is a valid categorical imperative, then we must submit to it because we have ourselves legislated it; for the only other reason for submission would be some interest we had, and in that case our obedience would be conditional and the imperative hypothetical. So a categorical imperative can only move me insofar as I will it myself. If I have an unconditional obligation at all, it can only be to laws I have legislated myself. Any other laws are merely hypothetical for me. Needless to say, it remains open whether there can be a valid categorical imperative, but if there can be—if pure reason is to be practical at all—then it (pure reason) must be autonomous.

The trouble with this argument is that it is opaque at the most important point. If a man is not the author of the universal law he obeys, Kant tells us, then he cannot be bound to it categorically. Good enough. But he wants also to claim that if a man *is* the author of the universal law which he obeys, then he *is* bound to it categorically. If we ask *why* this latter proposition is true, we are not given an analysis of self-legislation and commitment. Instead, we are told (what is perfectly true), that if a man is *not* categorically bound when he is self-legislating, then he is not categorically bound at all, and, hence, there is no categorical imperative. So when we ask for an explanation of the central notion of autonomy, we are merely told it must be the source of unconditional obligation since heteronomy has already been eliminated, and nothing else remains but autonomy.

In the passage I quoted above, Kant goes beyond this purely indirect argument. The will, he says, "is not only subject to the law but is so subject that it must be considered as also *making the law* for itself and only precisely on this account as first of all subject to the law" (Ak. 431). But if we ask why being self-legislative constitutes a ground of unconditional obligation to the law one has legislated, Kant gives us no answer.

Kant's unclarity here stems directly from his commitment to two incompatible doctrines. On the one hand, he believes that there are objective, substantive, categorical moral principles which all rational agents, insofar as they are rational, acknowledge and obey. If this is true, then the notion of self-legislation seems vacuous. On the other hand, he believes (I think correctly) that rational agents are bound to substantive policies only insofar as they have freely chosen those policies. But if this is true, then one must give up the belief in objective substantive principles and recognize that the substance or content of moral principles derives from collective commitments to freely chosen ends.

Here, as elsewhere, Kant's practice is better than his profession. He is right that all rational agents are bound by objective laws, but those laws are purely formal criteria of the rationality of policies. They suffice only to rule out inconsistent policies, not to rule in any particular consistent ones. Kant is right also that men are bound by substantive policies only insofar as and only because they have legislated those policies themselves. But he is wrong to think that those substantive policies would necessarily be willed by all rational agents insofar as they are rational.

D. The Formula of the Kingdom of Ends (Ak. 433–436)

Kant's lengthy exposition of his conception of moral agents as autonomous rational creatures, bound by the laws they have themselves legislated, comes to a fitting climax in his presentation of the notion of an ideal *kingdom of ends*. Everything that is best in Kant's moral philosophy comes together here with everything that is most fundamentally unsatisfactory. In the literature of classical liberal political philosophy, the only text that equals these eleven paragraphs in profundity or importance is Rousseau's *Social Contract*, which was, of course, Kant's source and inspiration. As for the discussion of market price and human dignity with which this subsection closes, I think it can fairly claim to be one of the few truly sublime passages in the corpus of Western moral philosophy.

Thus far, Kant's attention has been focused almost entirely on the nature and workings of *a* rational moral agent. Despite occasional examples of something rightly or wrongly done by one agent to another (such as giving the correct change or making a false promise), there has been until this point no direct consideration of the relationship between rational moral agents. Now, Kant attempts to complete his theory by introducing the idea of a moral community of rational agents, each of whom is both subject to and a source of the laws of the community. Despite his use of the term "kingdom" [*Reich*], carrying as it does an implicit reference to the kingdom of heaven, Kant is obviously thinking of the sort of community which Rousseau says is brought into being by the social contract and which Rousseau calls a republic.

The passage from Rousseau is worth quoting, since it echoes so clearly in Kant's words. In chapter 6 of the *Social Contract*, Rousseau writes:

> [The social compact] produces a moral and collective body, composed of as many members as there are votes in the assembly, which from this act receives its unity, its common self, its life, and its will. This public person, which is thus formed by the union of all other persons, took formerly the name of "city" and now takes that of "republic" or "body politic." It is called by its members "state" when it is passive, "Sovereign" when in activity, and whenever it is compared with other bodies of a similar kind, it is denominated "power." The associates take collectively the name of "people," and separately, that of "citizens," as participating in the sovereign authority, and of "subjects," because they are subjected to the laws of the State.[40]

---

[40]From the anonymous eighteenth-century translation modernized and reprinted by Charles Frankel in his edition of *The Social Contract* (New York: Hafner Publishing Company, 1947).

The central point in this passage, of course, is the claim that each member of the republic brought into being by the social compact must be conceived as bearing a double relation to the laws of the republic. As a participant in the sovereign or legislating body he is *active;* as a subject of the state, bound by its laws, he is *passive.*

Kant's introduction of the concept of a kingdom of moral agents forces us to confront once again the problem which I discussed in the Introduction to this commentary, namely, what sort of direct interaction, if any, can there be between two noumenal moral agents? In view of the unmistakable reference to Rousseau's conception of a moral republic, we must ask whether Kant meant us to imagine the Kingdom of Ends as a community whose members enact binding law through a process of collective deliberation.

The answer is clearly no. The members of the Kingdom of Ends achieve unanimity in their moral legislation not by collective deliberation, but by each one independently legislating for himself, as though he were legislating for all, an objective law required by the canons of pure reason. Since the laws of reason are everywhere and always one, we can be a priori certain that by a preestablished harmony, all the members of the Kingdom of Ends legislate identically the same law. To be sure, they may speak to one another, but their communication is accidental to, not essential to, the achievement of unanimity and objectivity. We may compare these moral agents to mathematicians, seated together in a great hall, independently of one another solving the same problem. They arrive at identical answers, of course, and assuming perfect rationality, no one will have any need to consult the others. Each can perfectly well think of himself as proceeding as though he were laying down a solution binding upon the entire congress of mathematicians, for if his solution were not perfectly acceptable to every perfectly rational mathematician, whatever his interests, prejudices, or character, it would not be acceptable to himself.

We have returned, by an extremely roundabout route, to an old metaphysical problem that absorbed Kant's philosophical attention very considerably in the period before he began work on the *Critique of Pure Reason.* The reader may have been puzzled, some hundred pages back, by my excursion into the eighteenth-century dispute over internal and external relations of substances. At the beginning of my discussion of Kant's conception of rational agency, I referred to the unsuccessful search for a rationalist theory of causality modeled on the relation between premises and conclusions of a deductive argument. I suggested that in response to Hume's successful attack, Kant had shifted to the notion of purpose as a way of preserving the rationality of the causality of will. At that point, it may have been difficult to see the connection between the dispute over internal relations and the theory of rational purposiveness, but now I hope that I can connect the two up.

One of the theses of Leibniz's metaphysics is the claim that substances never actually exert any causal influence upon one another. Their external relations, Leibniz held, are virtual, not real. Only the internal relations among the several states of the single substance (or monad) are real. The fit between a monad's representations of the world and the state of the world is explained not in the most obvious way, as a result of the world's impact upon the monad, but rather indirectly by appeal to the omnipotent benevolence of God. God has arranged things so that there is a virtual identity between the internal "representations" in the consciousness of each substance and the external states of affairs purportedly represented.

Kant devoted a good deal of his early philosophical work to this question of the reality or nonreality of the causal relationships between substances. In the *Inaugural Dissertation* he argues that in order for a multiplicity of substances to form a *world*, it must be possible that there be real interactions between the substances. As he puts it, "actual influences do not pertain to the essence but to the state, and the transeunt forces themselves, which are the causes of the influxes, suppose some principle by which it may be possible that the states of the several things whose subsistence is none the less independent each from the other should be related to one another mutually as grounded determinations."[41] Otherwise, he concludes, while we might make a "whole of representation" (by thinking of the plurality of substances in a single thought), we could not make a "representation of a whole."

---

[41] *Inaugural Dissertation*, Section I, § 2, II, in *Kant, Selected Pre-Critical Writings*, trans. G. B. Kerford and D. E. Walford (New York: Barnes & Noble, 1968).

I should like to suggest that this metaphysical problem of the relationship among noumenal substances in a "world" or unified whole is fundamentally the same as the problem of the relationship among autonomous moral agents in a realm of ends. And strange as it may seem, after his long trek away from Leibniz's unsatisfactory doctrine of a preestablished harmony between subjective representations and objective states of affairs, Kant at this final stage in his moral philosophy returns to his metaphysical starting point. Once again, we are offered a theory of noumenal substances—moral agents this time—among whom there is no real *influxus*, but merely a virtual *influxus* achieved by a preestablished harmony.

If we try to imagine an assembly of autonomous persons, met to determine the laws of their community, we can conjure up no appropriate dialogue among them. Each would rise in turn, as at a Quaker meeting, and declaim to no one in particular some formulation or other of the Categorical Imperative. There would be no disagreements among them, for by hypothesis they are all rational. Nor would it be necessary to adjudicate conflicts of private interest, for like the citizens of Rousseau's republic, each of whom "has a general will," they would abstract from private interest insofar as they conceived themselves to be making universal law. Odd as it may seem, although each would know himself to be bound to treat the others as ends in themselves, no one would need to communicate with any other, for they would all know a priori that their several acts of moral legislation were formally identical.

It wouldn't work, of course. Since the Categorical Imperative is only a necessary condition for the objective validity of principles, it cannot by itself identify a set of substantive principles as universally binding. In order for a community of rational agents actually to bind themselves to a set of laws, some genuine communication would be necessary. Out of that collective deliberation, there might issue a unanimous commitment to a substantive policy or practice, governed but not determined by the formal constraint of consistency. The communication *(influxus)* would be essential rather than accidental because in its absence no substantive policy would acquire the status of law. The process of legislation would thus *create* the law, not *discover* it (as a logician may be said to "discover" laws of logic).

Let me turn now to the beautiful discussion of the distinction between price and dignity with which Kant concludes his treatment of the realm of ends.[42] Since Kant is usually read as a defender of liberal capitalist society and since the harshest criticism of capitalism from the early nineteenth century to the present has been its tendency to reduce persons to the status of objects worth whatever the market will pay for their labor, it is only fair to point out that no one, not even Marx in the manuscripts of 1844, has defended more eloquently the principle that persons are above price. Moral agents, Kant reminds us, have no equivalent by which they can be replaced. They possess a *Würde*, a dignity, by virtue of their capacity for moral agency. Talents, skills, traits of character are marketable, but moral agency is irreplaceable.

5. Conclusion of Chapter 2
(Ak. 436–445)

The remainder of chapter 2, although lengthy, requires little comment. First, Kant makes a half-hearted attempt to bring the

---

[42]There is another subject of great importance in Kant's account of the Kingdom of Ends which I am simply passing over in silence, namely, the conception of the Kingdom of Ends as a whole "of the personal ends which each [person] may set before himself" as well as of "rational beings as ends in themselves." Kant seems to think that in a kingdom of ends, in which each person treated others as ends by respecting their particular ends while pursuing his own particular ends, there would arise, at least as an ideal, a perfectly harmonious community combining justice with happiness. I take it that Kant is striving to explicate this conception in the Introduction to the *Critique of Judgment* when he speaks of "the unification of the law-giving [*Gesetzgebungen*] of understanding and reason through the faculty of judgment" (Ak. V, 195; see also Ak. 436*n*). But I simply don't understand Kant's thought on this subject well enough to say anything coherent about it. Once again, let me refer the reader to Rawls's *A Theory of Justice*, which can be construed as the working out of an idea very similar to Kant's.

three major formulations of the Categorical Imperative under the categories of quantity (unity, plurality, totality).[43] Then, thinking better of it, he launches instead into a connected summary of the material of chapter 2. With great skill he discursively expounds the five formulae, so that although nothing essentially new is added to their derivation, the connections among them are exhibited more clearly.[44]

After summarizing his three (or five) formulae and their interrelations, Kant goes on to the well-known discussion of autonomy and heteronomy. He makes it quite clear that by heteronomy he means bondage to *objects* outside the self, rather than bondage to other *wills*. The bondage may arise out of desire, as for pleasure or happiness, or it may arise out of a rational conception, such as the principle of perfection. Autonomy, then, is freedom from bondage to external objects. As Kant puts it,

> Autonomy of the will is the property the will has of being a law to itself (independently of every property belonging to the objects of volition). (Ak. 440)

Kant concludes chapter 2 with a brief statement of the stage at which the argument has arrived. The entire section, he says, is "merely analytical," like the first (Ak. 445). It seeks to establish the hypothetical proposition:

> [If one] takes morality to be something, and not merely a chimerical Idea without truth, [then he] must at the same time admit the principle [The Categorical Imperative] we have put forward. (Ak. 445)

Kant's opponents in chapter 2 are the defenders of the other moral theories which have been put forward. They are one and all

[43]Kant, it will be remembered, speaks of *three* formulae rather than *five*. The formula of the law of nature and the formula of the realm of ends are treated as subsidiary to, or included within, the formulae of universal law and autonomy, respectively.

[44]Note, incidentally, that the formula of the law of nature is explicitly said to rest on an "analogy" between the universal connection of things in nature, which is the form of nature, and the universality of the moral law, which is the form of the laws of the will (Ak. 437). This is undoubtedly the reason why Beck adds the words "By analogy" in his translation of the law of nature formula (Ak. 421). Nevertheless, I think my somewhat more complicated explication of that formula is truer to Kant's own philosophy. "By analogy," after all, is a rather feeble justification for so powerful a principle as the second formula.

guilty of heteronomy. Once they recognize that morality presupposes autonomy, they must either retreat to a total scepticism or else acknowledge the Categorical Imperative as the first principle of all rational agency.

Let me attempt an alternative summary of Kant's argument thus far, in terms of the general outline of the *Groundwork* that I sketched at the end of the Introduction to this commentary.

> Either man is merely a natural creature whose behavior is totally determined by the laws of nature, or else he has the capacity to be moved in some way other than by the causality of natural objects.
>
> If he is indeed merely a natural creature (as a number of philosophers, such as Hobbes and Hume, have maintained), then moral discourse must be either descriptive (Hobbes) or expressive (Hume), for it would make no sense to give reasons to a creature which was incapable of being moved by them qua reasons. (He might, of course, be moved by them qua verbal events, but they would then be a species of natural causes.)
>
> If, on the other hand, man can be moved by some species of causality other than the causality of nature, then it must be reason that moves him. (Kant doesn't prove this step in his argument. He obviously believes that there are no other plausible alternatives to natural causality. In particular, he rejects the notion that man, as a moral agent, simply is *uncaused*—free in the sense that Lucretian atoms are free when they swerve unaccountably and randomly.) To be moved by reason, that is, by my idea or conception of laws, is to have a will. It is also to have a practical, as opposed to a merely theoretical, reason.
>
> Now, there are two ways in which a man can be moved by reason. Insofar as he is moved by his rational conception of the connection between some possible action and an end in which he takes an interest, his action is prudential, or instrumental. The principles governing his action are neither descriptive nor expressive, but imperative. They are, however, condi-

tioned or hypothetical imperatives, for they bind him only under the condition that he take as his ends the ends at which they aim. We can say of a man who is moved by his conception of a hypothetical imperative that in him *reason is practical*.

Insofar as a man is moved by his conception of a principle that abstracts from all ends in which he might take an interest, insofar, therefore, as he acts on principles which must be equally valid for all rational agents as such, his action is moral. The principles governing his action are also imperative, but they are unconditioned or categorical, for they are limited by no specification or particular ends. The highest such principle —indeed, in some sense the only such principle—is the Categorical Imperative or moral law, as enunciated in chapter 1 and explicated in all its variations in chapter 2. We can say of a man who is moved by his conception of the Categorical Imperative that in him *pure reason is practical*.

Now, we can rebut those philosophers who portray man as nothing more than a creature of nature by showing that insofar as they undertake to act, or even to speak meaningfully about the problem of man's nature, they must assume that they are capable of rational agency as well as of natural behavior. This rebuttal will be developed in chapter 3.

And we can rebut those defenders of competing moral philosophies who believe that moral discourse is both meaningful and neither descriptive nor expressive by showing that moral precepts and evaluations presuppose autonomy rather than heteronomy. In short, we can show that the Categorical Imperative is the only principle that can consistently be defended by those who defend any sort of morality at all. This has been done in chapters 1 and 2.

But we are still left with the opponent who grants that *reason can be practical,* while denying that *pure reason can be practical.* In short, we must find a rebuttal to the old and familiar doctrine that moral discourse, insofar as it is meaningful, reduces to prudential discourse about instrumental actions. (Hobbes can also be read as espousing this view, and one finds it in the utilitarian or hedonist tradition from Epicurus and Lucretius to Bentham.) To these moral sceptics, Kant has an answer, I believe, but it is obscured in chapter 2 by his too hasty assertion that hypothetical imperatives pose no significant problem. Briefly, the materials are available in chapter 2 for a proof that if man can be moved by his conception of hypothetical imperatives, then he is capable of being moved by his conception of the Categorical Imperative. And if he is *capable* of being moved by his conception of the Categorical Imperative, then he is bound absolutely to obey it, for the Categorical Imperative is nothing other than the fundamental principle of rational agency as such.

The program of chapter 2 would be completely successful—both the opposed moral philosophers and the moral sceptic would be defeated, if Kant could demonstrate that the pure a priori principles of rational agency (the Categorical Imperative and its associated formulae) specified a set of substantive policies as objectively required of all rational agents. For then he would be able to say to his second and third audiences, "If you hold that some moral principles or other are valid or if you merely hold that men are capable of prudentially rational action, then you must acknowledge the moral system that I have set forth as unconditionally, objectively, universally valid."

But Kant cannot demonstrate that the Categorical Imperative specifies any substantive policies as objectively valid. The Categorical Imperative is a purely formal, necessary condition of the validity of policies. There is no substantive, objective criterion of the validity of policies.

So, Kant has proved that if reason can be practical at all, then it is bound by the Categorical Imperative. But that proof yields much less than he hopes or believes it does. The Categorical Imperative by itself can give us neither a system of moral principles binding upon each rational agent nor a system of laws for the governance of a republic of rational agents.

chapter three

Passage from a Metaphysic of Morals to a Critique of Pure Practical Reason

1. Preliminary Remarks:
The Purpose and Organization of
Chapter 3

There is a good deal less to chapter 3 than meets the eye. Kant's many remarks, scattered throughout the *Groundwork,* about what remains to be accomplished in chapter 3 prepare us for some major theoretical advance that will carry the argument significantly beyond what has been demonstrated in chapters 1 and 2. In fact, however, for perfectly good reasons, grounded in the conclusions of the *Critique of Pure Reason,* Kant spends most of this last chapter of the *Groundwork* disabusing us of our hopes and explaining to us why we can never discover answers to those questions of the metaphysic of morals which are most fundamental.

The general structure of the *Groundwork,* it will be recalled, is this: chapter 1 proves that the Categorical Imperative is the principle implicitly presupposed by all those who share certain plausible and widely held convictions about the nature of man's responsibilities and moral merit; chapter 2 proves that if man is capable of rational agency, then the Categorical Imperative is the necessary first principle of his choice and action (it also argues that man experiences the moral law as an imperative because of his imperfect rationality, a claim which figures prominently in chapter 3); chapter 3, therefore, ideally should prove that man is capable of rational agency. This proposition, taken together with the thesis of chapter 2, would permit Kant to conclude that the Moral Law written in the hearts of ordinary men is universally, objectively, absolutely binding upon all rational creatures, man included.

Unfortunately, theoretical reason can never establish the proposition that man is capable of rational agency. So chapter 3 settles for a number of lesser theses, which, though they do not together add up to the desired conclusion, nonetheless take us to what Kant calls "the extreme limit of all moral enquiry." Indeed, somewhat in imitation of the *Critique of Pure Reason*, which concludes by exposing the dialectical errors of an overextended reason, Kant ends the *Groundwork* with almost ten pages of repeated insistences that philosophy *cannot* provide a theoretical demonstration of man's capacity for rational agency.

The substitute propositions with which Kant requires us to be content are, as I have earlier indicated, two in number:

1. that it is at least logically possible that man should be capable of rational agency;
2. that man, insofar as he deliberates, chooses, and undertakes to act, must necessarily presuppose a capacity for rational agency.

Although Kant does not himself claim a dialectical victory over all possible opponents, preferring to represent his argument as discursive in character, I think we may properly construe chapter 3 as a dialectical strategy designed to force any antagonist into a choice between silence and acquiescence. If Kant can prove both the logical possibility of rational agency and the practical necessity of presupposing its reality, then the moral sceptic is reduced to asserting that he is not acting. But as I pointed out in my introductory analysis of the structure of the *Groundwork*, the assertion of a proposition is an act, an exercise of the capacity for rational agency. To construe assertion otherwise is to reduce it to the mere exhibition of verbal or other physical behavior, which can certainly be explained without the presupposition of rational agency but which also is devoid of the cognitive significance that is the essence of the assertion of propositions. So we may imagine Kant speaking thus to his three audiences:

> To you fellow men who share with me the common convictions about what is right and wrong, about who is to be esteemed and who condemned, I ask you to notice that we all implicitly accept and employ the Categorical Imperative in our ordinary moral reasoning (chapter 1).

> To you rival moral philosophers, who acknowledge the appropriateness of moral distinctions but trace them up to principles other than the Categorical Imperative, see that your principles are all infected with a heteronomy that reduces them beneath the dignity of morality to the level of mere hypothetical imperatives (chapter 2, the more superficial argument).

> To you moral sceptics who deny the meaningfulness of all distinctly moral discourse, insisting that man acts only prudentially in pursuit of some interest, see that even prudential action presupposes a capacity for rational agency from which the objective validity of the Categorical Imperative can be deduced (chapter 2, the deeper argument).

> And if thereby any among you foolish enough to deny man's capacity even for prudentially rational action, insisting that man is purely a creature of nature who *behaves* in accordance with the laws of nature but does not *act* in accordance with the laws of reason, I put to you the following challenge: Either step forward and state your views, in which case you perform a linguistic act and *eo ipso* refute yourself, or else retire from the field in silence, in which case I claim victory (chapter 3).

If one holds, as I do, that dialectical refutation is the proper mode of philosophical argument, and not a second-best tactic to which one retreats when direct proofs cannot be found, then the ability either to persuade or to silence every possible antagonist must be recognized as the ultimate philosophical victory. Kant himself is rather diffident about the dialectical character of the argument of chapter 3, and he therefore concludes the *Groundwork* with an apology rather than with the note of the triumph that he has earned.

Chapter 3, unlike chapters 1 and 2, is divided into a number of subsections which accurately indicate the structure of Kant's exposition. My commentary will therefore simply follow Kant's organization of the text. The major task of the chapter, of course, is to demonstrate the logical possibility of rational agency or, in somewhat more familiar terms, to show that freedom and determinism are compatible. Kant's treatment of this subject in the *Groundwork* is entirely inadequate, as he himself must have realized, and we shall have to introduce a rather heavy dose of *First Critique* material to explain how Kant overcomes the apparent contradiction between the two.

2. The Concept of Freedom
Is the Key to Explain
Autonomy of the Will (Ak. 446–447)

The ostensible purpose of chapter 3 is to introduce the concept of freedom, explore its connections with the concepts of rational agency, duty, and autonomy, and then establish the precise limits of our knowledge of man's freedom. Kant's actual discussion, however, though it is a useful supplement to the materials of chapter 2, is rather anticlimactic, for it immediately transpires that "freedom" is synonymous with "(a capacity for) rational agency," which, in turn, is synonymous with "practical reason." Since the treatment of will and rational agency in chapter 2 has already established Kant's principal theses on this topic, the discussion of freedom is at best an elaboration of material previously covered.

Kant opens chapter 3 with a negative definition of freedom as that species of causality which operates "independently of *determination* by alien causes" (Ak. 446). There are, Kant suggests, three possibilities if the matter is viewed in the broadest way possible. Either the activity (or behavior) of a thing is "determined to activity by the influence of alien [*fremder*] causes," or the thing acts "independently of *determination* by alien causes," or, finally, the activity of the thing is undetermined. The last of these, mere causelessness, is rejected out of hand by Kant as "self-contradictory." The first is *natural necessity* of the sort which governs the behavior of substances in the spatio-temporal world of human experience. The second, by elimination Kant says, must be *freedom.* So in a negative sense, freedom is "that property of [the causality of living beings] by which it can be effective independently of foreign causes determining it" (Ak. 446, chap. 3, par. 1).

Kant's move here has historical resonances and significances which may not be immediately obvious to the modern reader, although I assume they would have been apparent to a reader in Kant's own time. In Book II of the *Physics*, Aristotle laid the foundations for the famous and long influential distinction between natural and unnatural motion. It is worth quoting the passage at length:

> Of things that exist, some exist by nature, some from other causes.
> "By nature" the animals and their parts exist, and the plants and the simple bodies (earth, fire, air, water)—for we say that these and the like exist "by nature."
> All the things mentioned present a feature in which they differ from things which are *not* constituted by nature. Each of them has *within itself* a principle of motion and of stationariness (in respect of place, or of growth and decrease, or by way of alteration). On the other hand, a bed and a coat and anything else of that sort, *qua* receiving these designations—i.e. insofar as they are products of art —have no innate impulse to change. But insofar as they happen to be composed of stone or of earth or of a mixture of the two, they *do* have such an impulse, and just to that extent—which seems to indicate that *nature is a source or cause of being moved and of being at rest in that to which it belongs primarily,* in virtue of itself and not in virtue of a concomitant attribute.[1]

Things which had a "nature" were said to exhibit "natural motion" (insofar as the motion was motion qua natural thing, as Aristotle would, of course, point out). They had an internal source of motion—falling down toward the center of the universe in the

[1]*Physics*, II, 1, 192b, 5–23, trans. R. P. Hardie and R. K. Gaye (New York: Oxford University Press, 1930).

case of water and earth, rising to the heavens in the case of fire and air, growth and reproduction in the case of plants, locomotion in the case of animals, and so forth. The motion originated within the natural thing by virtue of some feature of its essence or natural form. Thus, a plant might have locomotion imposed upon it (by an animal which picked it up and carried it, say) but its processes of photosynthesis, cell growth, and reproduction arose from its inner and natural structure as a plant. The heavenly bodies too exhibit natural motion, it was supposed, although Aristotle mistakenly thought the motion to be circular rather than elliptical.

Although Aristotle's distinction between natural and unnatural motion is not equivalent to the distinction between living and nonliving things, living things most strikingly exhibit what he considered natural motion. Animals initiate their own movements, or so it must seem to a systematic, common sense observer like Aristotle. Artificial things, on the other hand, such as machines, move only when an external force is applied to them.

In the two millennia following Aristotle and particularly during the half millennium preceding Kant, the distinction between natural and unnatural motion was progressively eliminated. The elimination, of course, was carried out at the expense of "natural motion," for the new physics of Kepler, Galileo, and Newton portrayed the motions of terrestrial and heavenly bodies as traceable to the imposition of an external force (gravity). The elimination of the distinction was completed by Descartes's widely quoted assertion that animals lacking reason could be conceived, in a manner of speaking, as divinely created machines.[2]

In effect, Kant accepts Descartes's view that animal motion, as traceable to external causes, is "machine-like" or "unnatural." Indeed, he carries the view even further, for the doctrine of the *Critique* commits him, contrary to Descartes, to the view that even speech has its phenomenal—hence, external or "foreign"—

[2]See his *Discourse on the Method,* part 5: "From this aspect the body is regarded as a machine which, having been made by the hands of God, is incomparably better arranged, and possesses in itself movements which are much more admirable, than any of those which can be invented by man" *(Philosophical Works of Descartes,* trans. E. S. Haldane and G. R. T. Ross, vol. I, rep. ed. [New York: Cambridge University Press, 1931], p. 116).

causes. But Kant reintroduces the ancient distinction by means of his own distinction between appearances and reality. In the realm of appearances, all causes are foreign, all causality, therefore, at base irrational. But in the realm of things-in-themselves we can at least conceive of a causality that is internal to the agent and rational. That causality, on which Kant's entire conception of moral agency rests, is *freedom*.

Kant now (Ak. 446–447, par. 2) very quickly derives autonomy from freedom and the Categorical Imperative from autonomy. The derivation as presented is rather facile, almost glib, but since it is merely a recapitulation of the lengthier analysis in chapter 2, we need not cavil. The derivation allows Kant to summarize his argument in these words:

> Consequently if freedom of the will is presupposed, morality, together with its principle, follows by mere analysis of the concept of freedom. (Ak. 447)

The remainder of this brief first subsection may be puzzling to the reader, and a few words about it are, therefore, called for. When Kant first drew the distinction between analytic and synthetic judgments in the Introduction to the *First Critique*, he argued that the connection between subject and predicate which is asserted in a synthetic judgment must rest upon some "third thing" in which the two terms are grounded.[3] Ordinary synthetic empirical judgments were said to rest upon the experience of the object, a "third thing" in which the terms of the judgment were perceived to be connected. Synthetic judgments known a priori posed the real problem, of course, because one could not, *ex hypothesi*, justify them by appeal to experience. Kant's conclusion in the Analytic was that the *conditions of a possible experience in general* serve as the third thing in which the terms of the judgment are united.

Kant was very taken with this rather artificial way of expressing his problem and he continued to use it in the *Groundwork*, where it really doesn't fit very comfortably. So he repeats that the Categorical Imperative is a synthetic proposition and then says

[3]For the phrase "a third something" (*ein Drittes*), see A155.

that "the positive concept of freedom furnishes [the] third term" in which the terms of the proposition are found to be united. But, he says, "what this third term is to which freedom directs us and of which we have an Idea *a priori,* we are not yet in a position to show here straight away, nor can we as yet make intelligible the deduction of the concept of freedom from pure practical reason and so the possibility of a categorical imperative" (Ak. 447).

Harking back to my commentary on the derivation of the Categorical Imperative in chapter 2 and particularly to my remarks on Kant's first footnote to Ak. 420, I should like very briefly to suggest a clarification of this obscure passage. First of all, the synthetic proposition in question is *not* the Moral Law per se. That principle is an analytic proposition derived from an analysis of the concept of rational agency. It is supposed to provide a substantive, positive criterion of the rationality of policies according to Kant; but, if the criticisms by myself and many others are correct, it actually provides only a formal, negative criterion. In all events, a perfectly rational agent necessarily employs the Moral Law as his criterion in choosing policies, just as a perfectly rational mathematician necessarily employs the laws of logic in deriving conclusions from his premises.

The synthetic proposition in question is the Categorical Imperative: that is to say, the command which reason issues to a creature that can be influenced by sensuous causes and, hence, cannot be presumed necessarily to conform to the principles of reason. The Categorical Imperative is synthetic because in it "the willing of an action is not derived from some other willing already presupposed (for we do not possess any such perfect will)" (Ak. 420*n*). It is asserted a priori inasmuch as it is asserted with apodeictic necessity. Thus, the question, "How is a Categorical Imperative possible?" which Kant raised in chapter 2 and which he conceives as an instance of the more general question, "How are synthetic judgments a priori possible?" must be interpreted to mean, "Why does a sensuously conditioned creature experience a rule of reason as an absolute command; and how, inasmuch as it is a sensuously conditioned creature, can it stand under an unconditional obligation to be moved by such a rule of reason?"

Let me emphasize that so far as I can make out, Kant does not think that there is any puzzle in the case of a perfectly rational creature. For him, the Moral Law is simply the principle on which he acts, and he could no more deviate from it than Jesus could sin. The problem is for the creature who, in Alexander Pope's words, is

> *Plac'd on this isthmus of a middle state,*
> *A being darkly wise, and rudely great:*
> *With too much knowledge for the Sceptic side,*
> *With too much weakness for the Stoic's pride,*
> *He hangs between; in doubt to act, to rest,*
> *In doubt to deem himself a God, or Beast.*[4]

3. Freedom Must Be Presupposed as a Property of the Will of All Rational Beings (Ak. 447–448)

In this brief subsection Kant argues for two propositions: first, that we must ascribe freedom to all rational agents, not merely to men; and second, that "every being who cannot act except *under the Idea of freedom* is by this alone—from a practical point of view—really free." The first proposition is obviously true, and Kant mentions it merely to stop an unthinking reader from supposing that the argument of the *Groundwork* depends upon any peculiarly human inner feelings or "alleged experiences" of freedom. The second proposition is crucial to the argument of the book and merits a closer look. It is one of the two lesser propositions which are substituted by Kant for the unprovable assertion that man is free.

As I understand him, Kant is arguing that we *cannot* exhaustively divide all propositions into those which can in principle be known by us and those which have no cognitive significance or

[4] *Essay on Man*, Epistle 2.

value whatsoever.[5] There remain classes of propositions which play a legitimate cognitive role even though they do not meet the conditions of theoretical knowledge established by the *Critique of Pure Reason*. Among these propositions are moral principles, judgments of beauty (whose special status is analyzed in the *Third Critique*), and the proposition which concerns us here, namely, *that insofar as I (or my reason) undertake to act, I must regard myself as free*. Kant offers very little argument for this claim, but he appears to consider it an analytic consequence of the notion of an agent deliberating, choosing, and acting. If I may paraphrase what I take to be Kant's point: when I act, I conceive myself to be confronted by alternative policies from among which I shall choose; as a rational agent, I give myself reasons for my choices, and that implicitly involves me in the appeal to general principles, or laws. Now, if I conceive myself to be determined by "alien influences" (Ak. 448) in the selection of my principles of choice, then I do not really conceive myself to be acting on reasons at all, for a reason is only *my* reason insofar as I recognize its rational merits and choose to be moved by it *because of* my recognition of its merits.[6] Since freedom is the capacity to be moved by one's conception of laws, a rational being must regard himself as free insofar as he is practical, that is, insofar as he attempts to act.

One might imagine that in the absence of a theoretical proof of the fact of freedom, this practical argument would suffice, but not for Kant. As long as we can make room for freedom in the world only by limiting the causal necessity of science, we may not rest content. Thus far, it would seem that an action can be attributed to the rational agency of a free will only by denying its subordination to the scientific system of natural necessity. And Kant will have none of that!

[5]This is, roughly speaking, the tack taken by the logical positivists and also by Hume in the famous exhortation to "commit to the flames" any work of philosophy which does not contain either "abstract reasoning concerning quantity or number" or "experimental reasoning concerning matter of fact and existence." (The last paragraph of the *Enquiry Concerning the Human Understanding*.)

[6]This is the meaning of Kant's assertion, at Ak. 431, that "the will is therefore not merely subject to the law, but is so subject that it must be considered as also *making the law* for itself and precisely on this account as first of all subject to the law."

> [I]f the thought of freedom is self-contradictory or incompatible with nature—a concept which is equally necessary—freedom would have to be completely abandoned in favour of natural necessity. (Ak. 456)

So in answering the question, "How is a categorical imperative possible?" Kant must demonstrate that the practical postulate of freedom is logically compatible with the transcendentally established theoretical fact of thoroughgoing natural necessity. Kant turns to this task in the next subsection of chapter 3.

4. The Interest Attached to the Ideas of Morality (Ak. 448–453)

All of Kant's major philosophical moves originate in the distinction between appearance and reality. In the *Inaugural Dissertation*, he employs the distinction for the first time as a stratagem to resolve the antinomous contradictions between Newtonian physics and Leibnizean metaphysics. In the *Critique of Pure Reason* he refines the distinction and makes it his principal weapon against the scepticism of Hume and the "Idealism" of Berkeley. In the Preface to the Second Edition of the *Critique* (written, it should be noted, only a year or two after the publication of the *Groundwork*) Kant says of himself,

> I have therefore found it necessary to deny *knowledge,* in order to make room for *faith.* (Bxxx)

Now he is ready to cash in on that exchange. Both the resolution of the conflict between freedom and natural determinism and the explanation of how a rule of reason can appear to us men as a Categorical Imperative will turn out to be corollaries of Kant's distinction between the realm of appearances and the realm of things-in-themselves.

In the present section of the text Kant explains the distinction in terms of the "two standpoints" from which each man must view himself. As he says at Ak. 450, we "take one standpoint when by means of freedom we conceive ourselves as causes acting a priori, and another standpoint when we contemplate ourselves with references to our actions as effects which we see before our eyes." Kant goes on in the next paragraph to give a very brief summary of the doctrine of the *Critique*. Rather disingenuously, he observes that the doctrine requires no "subtle reflexion," and that even "the most ordinary intelligence [grasps it]—no doubt in its own fashion through some obscure discrimination of the power of judgment known to it as feeling."

Well, maybe so. But as one who has struggled for twenty years now both to understand and to teach the *Critique*, I have my doubts about its easy availability to "the most ordinary intelligence." At all events, the doctrine of the two standpoints won't do by itself. In order to understand how one and the same bit of behavior can consistently be construed both as a free, rational act and as a spatio-temporal event necessitated by "alien causes" in the order of nature, we must return for a bit to the *First Critique* and rehearse some of its central theses. In particular, we need to look at the analysis of phenomenal causality which extends throughout the Analytic, culminating in the Second Analogy, and at the lengthy discussion of the conflict between freedom and determinism in the resolution of the third Antinomy in the Transcendental Dialectic.

Briefly, let us recall that according to Kant, the objective causally connected order of events in space and time is an order generated by the transcendental ego in, by, and through its act of bringing to consciousness the given contents of its sensible manifold of intuition. In order to bring the data of sense to consciousness, the understanding must unify them (or "synthesize" them) in a single consciousness. The rules by which the understanding performs this creative activity are, in their objective reflection in the reorganized data of sense, simply the laws of nature. Thus, the very same synthetic unity of the manifold of the data of sense is, on its subjective side, the unity of consciousness and, on its objective side, the order of nature. As Kant puts it with a conscious dramatic flair at the close to the Deduction of the Pure Concepts of the Understanding in the First Edition:

> However exaggerated and absurd it may sound, to say that the under-
> standing is itself the source of the laws of nature, and so of its formal
> unity, such an assertion is none the less correct, and is in keeping with
> the object to which it refers, namely experience. (Ak. 127)

In particular, the *temporal* order of events in nature is mind-
imposed. Time is the form of inner sense, not an order of things-in-
themselves or their states. Indeed, it is precisely the extensive
character of space and time, the fact that the parts of space and
time are external to one another, that makes the objects at different regions of space and events at different times also external to
one another and, hence, capable of bearing only external or foreign relations to one another. Once one acknowledges the spatio-
temporality of events, the rationalist ideal of necessary causal connections modeled on the internal relation of a deductive conclusion to its premises is doomed. That is why Leibniz portrays space
and time as external relations of substances and their states and
denies the reality of substantial interaction.

In the Transcendental Dialectic, Kant confronts head-on the
apparent contradiction between the claims of natural necessity
and freedom. The Antinomies, it will be recalled, are presented as
a series of opposed propositions, each of which seems capable of
defending itself by defeating its opponents. Broadly speaking, the
thesis of each Antinomy represents the "Dogmatic" or rationalist
position, and the antithesis represents the "sceptical" or empiricist
side of the dispute. For reasons of architectonic neatness, the third
Antinomy conflates two quite distinct questions: whether there is
a First Cause of the universe (an ancient cosmological question
associated with proofs for the existence of God) and whether man
is *free* rather than, or even as well as, determined by the laws of
nature (a metaphysical issue associated with the issue of responsibility and moral agency).

The thesis and antithesis of the Antinomy are stated thus (A445
= B473).

THESIS	ANTITHESIS
Causality in accordance with laws of nature is not the only causality from which the appearances of the world can one and all be derived.	There is no freedom; everything in the world takes place solely in accordance with laws of nature.

To explain these appearances it is
necessary to assume that there is
also another causality, that of freedom.

The resolution of all four antinomies hinges in the *Critique*, as
it did in the *Inaugural Dissertation*, where some of these same
Antinomies made their first appearance, on the distinction between appearance and reality. Formally speaking, the Antinomies
are all arguments based upon an enthymeme, or unexpressed
premise, namely, the assumption that all our assertions univocally
refer to the one and only realm there is, the realm of real existence
or things-in-themselves. The antinomies can be resolved, Kant
argues, only by rejecting this premise, and drawing a distinction
between things-as-they-appear and things-in-themselves. It then
becomes clear that *both* the thesis and the antithesis of the Third
Antinomy are true (or, more correctly, that the antithesis is true
and the thesis at least logically possible), but true of different
realms. The antithesis asserts a true proposition about the realm
of appearances; it is, in fact, nothing other than the law of causality
proven in the Second Analogy of the Analytic of Principles. The
thesis is a logically possible assertion about things-in-themselves.
We cannot know whether it is true or false because to do so we
should have to be given things-in-themselves as objects for us, and
under the limiting conditions of our sensibility they would be
given only as appearance, not as things-in-themselves.

But this formulaic resolution of the conflict will not suffice, any
more than the facile reference to "two standpoints" in the
Groundwork. Perhaps we cannot know that man qua noumenon
is capable of freedom, but we must at least insist on understanding
how my causally determined behavior can legitimately be construed as even a *possible* effect of my rational agency. Let us put
the point as forcefully and specifically as possible: when I pull the
trigger of the gun in my hand and slay my enemy, the full majesty
of the *Critique of Pure Reason* stands behind the claim that my
behavior was determined by alien causes which can, in principle,
be traced back to moments in time before I or my parents or,
indeed, the human race had yet appeared on the face of the earth.
If the Second Analogy means anything, it means that there exist,

to be found, laws of human phenomenal behavior as precise as those by which astronomers calculate the location of Sirius, the dog star, in the year 4004 B.C. or A.D. 10001. By the same token, the attribution of freedom and moral responsibility is vacuous unless one is prepared to maintain that I could have refrained from pulling the trigger: not that I could have refrained had I chosen or that I could have refrained had I wished, but simply that I could have refrained.

Now, is it not a flat contradiction to make *both* of these claims? To say that I could have refrained from pulling the trigger is to say that there could have been a complete sequence of causally connected precursors of my behavior which determined me *not* to shoot, just as there was in fact such a sequence which *did* determine me to shoot. There is no real contingency in the phenomenal world, according to Kant. Empirical possibility, actuality, and necessity, he says in the Postulates of Empirical Thought, are distinguished from one another only subjectively. The terms refer to the degree of perfection of our knowledge, not to the objective status of the events themselves. To the ideal scientist, all events would be seen to be empirically necessary.

From a number of things that he says in his discussion of the Third Antinomy, one might suppose that Kant sees the noumenal self as stepping into the ongoing flow of phenomenal events from time to time to perform an act which initiates an entirely new chain of causally connected effects. Practical freedom, he says, presupposes a causality "which can . . . begin a series of events *entirely of itself*" (A535 =B563). But, for a number of reasons, this interpretation must be rejected. First of all, Kant explicitly denies it.[7] That of itself is not decisive, for I have just quoted a passage that seems to support the interpretation. But the crucial reason is that Kant's own theory in the *First Critique* rules out any new beginnings in the field of appearance. Although I have already

[7]Since this is not a book on the *First Critique*, I will omit the proof texts from my exposition. The reader who wishes to pursue the question further may look, for example, at A541, where Kant says that the effects of free actions, insofar as they appear in the phenomenal world, "are only possible as a continuation of the series of natural causes," or at A543, where he repeats that "everything which happens is merely a continuation of the series."

several times explained why this is so, it is worth repeating the point, so that no one can harbor the illusion that there is room in Kant's philosophy for occasional appearances by a *noumenon ex machina* on the stage of life. According to Kant, an event is something that happens. To happen is to be assigned a date or position in the objective time order and thereby to be time-related as after, before, or contemporaneous with each other thing that happens. The objectivity of the time order consists in the rule-governed character of the order, and, of course, Kant argues that it is the transcendental ego itself that imposes that rule-governed order through its activity of synthesis. In the realm of appearances causality is simply rule-governed temporal succession. Hence, to say of two events that the first precedes the second in objective time is the same thing as to say that the first causes the second.

Now, when some action of mine is located in objective time, its time relations are determined not only to what follows it in the time order (its effects), but also to what precedes it in that order (its causes). To say of an event, therefore, that it initiates a new series of events in the field of appearance is to say that it bears no time relations at all to the events which do not succeed it. But since objective time is what mathematicians call a well-ordering of events, that is impossible. So we can put aside any notion of freedom as a kind of intervention in the order of events.

The key to a correct interpretation of Kant's argument is the crucial fact that time itself is merely a form of appearances, not an order of things-in-themselves. As Kant says,

> Now this acting subject would not, in its intelligible character, stand under any conditions of time; time is only a condition of appearances, not of things in themselves. (A539 = B567)

What Kant has done, of course, is to resurrect the old conception of God as standing eternally and unchangingly outside the temporal order of the created universe. The extratemporality of God was used by Augustine (and others) as a device for making freedom in the world compatible with transcendent foreknowledge. In a curious reversal Kant uses a new version of this notion as a device for making transcendent freedom compatible with determinism (and hence, in principle, foreknowledge) in the world!

The point is that the noumenal subject's free, rational, atemporal agency appears in the phenomenal world as a series of behaviors causally determined by preceding events in that same phenomenal world. The entire "empirical character" of a man's will is the appearance of his "intelligible character." As appearance, it comes under the laws of nature, so that

> if we could exhaustively investigate all the appearances of men's wills, there would not be found a single human action which we could not predict with certainty, and recognise as proceeding necessarily from its antecedent conditions. (A550=B578)

In itself, the noumenal subject is not thus constrained by prior, external conditions. Indeed, Kant tells us—and I find this very dark, I must confess—that the noumenal subject's agency does not strictly begin or end at all, for it is outside of time. Here are a number of statements, extracted from A539=B567 through A552 =B580. They make Kant's position perfectly unambiguous, even though we may still not really understand what he means:

> In this subject no *action* would *begin* or *cease*.

> Inasmuch as it [the subject] is *noumenon*, nothing *happens* in it.

> Pure reason, as a purely intelligible faculty, is not subject to the form of time, nor consequently to the conditions of succession in time. The causality of reason in its intelligible character does not, in producing an effect, *arise* or begin to be at a certain time.

It should now be clear, as I have, in fact, already remarked, why Kant lays such great emphasis upon the moral agent's choice of general policies or principles and so little emphasis even in his examples on the contextual complexities of particular moral decisions. As Kant portrays him, the moral agent is an atemporal practical reason, timelessly legislating universal laws whose appearance in experience unfolds as a spatio-temporal series of behaviors. Kant could make sense of particular context-bound choices only by retreating to the notion that the agent steps into the phenomenal world and alters the ongoing stream of events. This essentially *miraculous* interpretation of moral agency would allow Kant to make a place for freedom, but only through the unacceptable forfeiture of natural determinism.

We are still where we began, with my finger on the trigger, my enemy dead, and Kant saying, "You could have done otherwise." What can this possibly mean? My pulling of the trigger is a bit of behavior which follows, according to the laws of nature, from my empirical character. That empirical character, in turn, is the effect of previous natural causes including my genetic inheritance, my environment, and my own previous behavior. It may be true that my empirical character is, from a transcendental point of view, the appearance of my intelligible character as rational agent. And it may even be true, as Kant says, that "a different intelligible character would have given a different empirical character" (A556 = B584). But since my empirical character itself is the effect of previous causes lying as far back in phenomenal time as the observations and inferences of science can reach, what right have we to suppose that a "different intelligible character" could appear as an empirical character *which would not pull the trigger?* If I cannot prove that the appropriate intelligible character *could* appear as an empirical character which wouldn't pull the trigger, then I cannot even make *sense* of the claim that I could have behaved differently. And in that case, I cannot be held morally responsible for killing my enemy.

Kant has the materials for an answer to this crucial question, and he comes within an ace of actually stating it; but he does not, so we must supply the answer for him. I am myself persuaded that it is what he intended, but I cannot produce a text in which he says it flat out.

The clue to the answer is the fact that the noumenal subject, which in the practical employment of its reason is a moral agent, is also in the theoretical employment of its reason the transcendental ego which synthesizes the spatio-temporal world of events and objects. Not merely the empirical character, but the entire order of nature is the product of the activity of reason.[8] To say that

---

[8]And now we finally see why Kant's entire theory depends upon identifying the transcendental ego, the noumenal self, the moral self, and the empirical self as one and the same entity under various guises or in various functions. See the discussion of the four selves in Kant's philosophy.

I could have behaved differently is literally to say that I (the transcendental ego) could have synthesized the phenomenal world in such a way that I (the empirical self) would have been determined according to the laws of nature to behave in the way that I (the moral self) chose as a policy rational for all rational agents and, hence, right.

We now see the full force of the "law of nature" formula of the Categorical Imperative. Not only must I act as though the maxim of my action were by my will to become a universal law of nature, I am accountable for my actions precisely because it is at least logically possible that I could have created a different system of nature in which the right act would occur as a causally determined event.

Well, Kant didn't say he was going to explain how man's freedom worked. He only said he would show that freedom is logically possible. Most readers, I imagine, will feel as I do that this logical possibility is a trifle bare of their taste. But nothing short of the "solution" I have sketched will really do the trick; and, as Sherlock Holmes once observed, when you have eliminated all else, what remains (assuming it is possible), however improbable, must be true.

5. How Is a Categorical Imperative Possible? (Ak. 453–455)

And so Kant finally returns to the question which he first raised in paragraphs 24–28 of chapter 2: How is a Categorical Imperative possible? In my commentary on chapter 2, I observed that Kant's argument would have been a good deal clearer if he had cut directly from the formulation of the Categorial Imperative at Ak. 421 to the beginning of chapter 3. Nevertheless, he chose to interpolate a long discussion of the Categorical Imperative in all its forms and varieties, so only now, at the end of the *Groundwork*, do we complete the formal argument.

To repeat, the problem is *not* to explain how the Moral Law is possible. That question, Kant thinks, has been answered by the analysis of rational agency in chapter 2 (together with the explication of the concept of freedom at the beginning of chapter 3). Since the Moral Law follows analytically from the nature of reason, a purely rational creature would act always and necessarily in accord with it. Kant says flatly, "If I were solely a member of the intelligible world, all my actions would be in perfect conformity with the principle of the autonomy of a pure will" (Ak. 453). In the next paragraph he repeats, "if I were solely a member of the intelligible world, all my actions *would* invariably accord with the autonomy of the will" (Ak. 454).

But I am, at one and the same time, a member of the intelligible world and "a member of the sensible world." My will is affected by sensuous desires. Hence, I experience the moral law *not* merely as a principle of rational agency derived analytically from the nature of reason, but also as a *command* telling me, qua sensuously conditioned being, what I OUGHT to do.

Thus the "third thing" in which the Categorical Imperative is grounded[9] is *not* the "positive concept of freedom," as Kant claims, but rather the fact that man experiences himself and his actions as conditioned appearances, while nonetheless conceiving of himself and his actions as unconditioned by external constraints. This fact is a "third thing" because it could never be inferred from the mere concept of a rational agent. As the *First Critique* shows, it can only be inferred, by means of a complex and lengthy argument, from the premise of the unity of consciousness.

I think we can agree that this is a really brilliant attempt on Kant's part to tie together the major elements of his moral and epistemological theories, to establish the absolute bindingness of the commands of morality, and to account for certain central and puzzling facts of moral experience. But I don't think it works. There are, so far as I can see, three serious difficulties with Kant's position.

First, it leaves unresolved the dilemma I mentioned earlier:

[9]See above, my commentary on the first subsection of chapter 3.

either reason is too weak to overcome sensuous inclination, in which case we cannot hold the agent responsible (but the explanation of the possibility of freedom presumably rules this alternative out), or reason is strong enough to overcome sensuous inclination, in which case it will (but this makes nonsense of the *imperative* character of the Categorical Imperative). Kant's explanation of the possibility of a categorical imperative assumes that there is a struggle between duty and inclination, the outcome of which is in some sense genuinely open. But that assumption just cannot be made consistent with the rest of Kant's philosophy.

The second difficulty, which I have already discussed, is the problem of evil. Since a purely rational agent would necessarily act in accordance with the moral law, it is impossible for Kant to explain how such an agent could ever *be responsible for* a wrong act. Again we are faced with an irresoluble dilemma: either the agent did it, in which case the act must be right, or he didn't do it, in which case he can't be blamed.

Finally, even if we accept Kant's account of the two standpoints, there remains the old question, "Why should I be moral?" That is to say, why should I grant the primacy of the noumenal over the phenomenal and identify with what Kant assumes is the higher or better self? In the last paragraph of the present subsection he rather touchingly expresses his conviction that "there is no one, not even the most hardened scoundrel—provided only he is accustomed to use reason in other ways—who, when presented with examples of honesty in purpose, of faithfulness to good maxims, of sympathy, and of kindness towards all . . . does not wish that he too might be a man of like spirit" (Ak. 454). Would that Kant were right! The world would be a more bearable place if the evil men in it knew in their hearts that they were evil!

All of these difficulties are in some sense internal to Kant's own theory. Even if he could resolve them, he would still be faced with the greatest difficulty of all, namely, that the only moral law derivable from the nature of reason is a purely formal law of self-consistency which suffices to rule out inconsistent policies but does not, and cannot, serve to select some specific consistent policies rather than others. Let me repeat one more time that in order to find a sufficient criterion for the purely rational selection of specific policies, Kant would have to drive a system of objective and obligatory ends a priori from the concept of rational agency as such. He does not present such a derivation, although he tries in his account of man as an end in himself; manifestly he cannot find such a derivation, since the task is an impossible one; and therefore the Categorical Imperative can never be, as Kant wanted it to be, an a priori valid substantive test of the rightness or wrongness of every possible human policy.

6. The Extreme Limit of Practical Philosophy (Ak. 455–463)

In this long subsection Kant clearly and skillfully rehearses the argument of chapter 3. His primary aim appears to be to emphasize two points, both of which have been made before. First, in any conflict between the claims of freedom and natural determinism, freedom must give way. And second, the nature of man's cognitive powers absolutely rules out any knowledge of or further insight into man's noumenal (intelligible) character and rational agency. Again and again Kant hammers it home that reason can never explain how pure reason can be practical. "Where determination by Laws of nature comes to an end," he says, "all explanation comes to an end as well" (Ak. 459).

It is easy enough to see why Kant emphasizes so heavily a point which he has already made quite adequately. Kant thinks that just as there is a natural temptation to suppose with Descartes that the self's theoretical awareness of itself constitutes a special and more perfect kind of knowledge through which we can know the self as it truly is; so also there is a natural temptation to suppose that the self's practical awareness of itself constitutes a special and more perfect kind of knowledge through which we can know the self as it truly is. In the former case, the temptation leads to subjective idealism, against which Kant took special pains to argue in the *First Critique*. In the latter case, the temptation leads to spurious accounts of man's rational agency, on which are then based theoretical claims about the noumenal character of man. Since Kant's entire philosophy rests on a thoroughgoing distinction between knowable appearance and unknowable reality, it is crucially important for him to defend that distinction precisely at the two points where it is most likely to be blurred, namely, reason's theoretical self-awareness and reason's practical self-awareness. It is perhaps worth noting that the strongest reassertions of the distinction in the *First Critique*, namely, General Observation II to the Transcendental Aesthetic and the Refutation of Idealism in the Transcendental Analytic, were added by Kant to the second edition at roughly the time that he was writing the *Groundwork*.

7. Concluding Note (Ak. 463)

Lest the reader, in his frustration at the limits imposed upon his inquiry, direct his reproach at the doctrine of the *Groundwork*, Kant concludes with an apology. Reason ceaselessly pursues the unconditioned, both in its theoretical and in its practical employment. But all explanation requires a condition or premise on which to rest.

> Thus is it no discredit to our deduction of the supreme principle of morality, but rather a reproach which must be brought against reason as such, that it cannot make comprehensible the absolute necessity of an unconditioned practical law (such as the categorical imperative must be). For its unwillingness to do this by means of a condition— namely, by basing this necessity on some underlying interest—reason cannot be blamed, since in that case there would be no moral law, that is, no supreme law of freedom. And thus, while we do not comprehend the practical unconditioned necessity of the moral imperative, we do comprehend its *incomprehensibility*. This is all that can fairly be asked of a philosophy which presses forward in its principles to the very limit of human reason.

conclusion

Some Speculations
on the Groundwork
of Morals and Politics

I have gambled my time and energy on a philosophical reconstruction of the *Groundwork*, and those of you who have followed me this far have gambled your time and attention on its results. In this brief concluding chapter I should like to cut myself entirely loose from the constraints of the text and indicate what in Kant seems to me to be of lasting value. Even if you have found my particular reconstruction suggestive or helpful, you may, of course, disagree completely with these final remarks. Nevertheless, I am encouraged by the fact that a number of other philosophers in the fields of moral and political theory appear to be thinking along similar lines, and so these speculations may be of some interest.

What I shall do, therefore, is first rehearse those elements in Kant's moral theory which I believe to be true or, at least, aimed in the right direction, then indicate those other elements which seem to me clearly to be wrong, and after that adumbrate the sort of pure moral theory which I should like to be able to defend but for which I do not now have adequate arguments. I shall conclude with some very speculative observations designed to indicate the limitations of pure moral theory in general and to point the way toward the larger theory which I think is ultimately required.

1. What Is Right
in the *Groundwork*?

Kant's great achievement in the *Groundwork*, to my way of think-ing, is his analysis of the nature of rational agency. In my study of the text I first began to think that I might understand what Kant was driving at when I finally figured out the meaning of his strange and unsettling definition of will. Until that time, I had somewhat dimly imagined "the will" as an elusive faculty of the mind or self, subject to influences of varying sorts and capable, on occasion, of "acting freely." This notion made no particular sense to me, but I could not see how to get rid of it without also giving up the notions of responsibility and action. Once I saw that "will" is not the name of a mental faculty—indeed, is not the name of anything at all—but rather is a term whose appropriate use is as a compo-nent of such phrases as "to have a will," then I could understand Kant's claim that to have a will simply means to be capable of being moved by reason rather than by natural causes. In short, will is a kind of causality, but rational causality, causality through rea-son, rather than nonrational or de facto causality. Thus freedom, I saw, is not a property of the will, one which it might conceivably lack or lose or fail to exercise upon occasion. To be free is simply to have a will, which, in turn, is simply to be moved by reason. "Free will" is redundant, as is "rational will" and "will moved by reason."

To be moved by reason, as I understand Kant, is to be moved by one's conception of a rational connection between an end that one has posited for oneself and a bit of behavior which either is an instance of or else will accomplish that end. It follows from the formal demands of reason for consistency that such a conception takes the form of a general policy. It is for Kant mysterious that men are capable of being moved in this way, although it is, in some sense, equally mysterious that natural events stand in the sort of causal relationship to one another that he analyzed in the *First Critique*. But I think Kant was absolutely correct to insist that if will is anything at all, if freedom is anything at all, if men are capable of acting, if they can be said to be responsible in any significant sense, then reason must be practical.

The highest principle of practical reason, as of theoretical reason, is consistency. Since for reason to be practical man must be moved by a conception of general policies, it follows that consistency in the realm of practical reason means the consistent application of policies that one has adopted together with the adoption of consistent policies. Inconsistency is either the failure to treat alike those cases which one's policy defines as relevantly alike, or else it is the adoption of several policies which, taken conjointly, constitute an inconsistent policy.

The second great accomplishment of Kant's moral philosophy is the absolutely uncompromising articulation of the conflict between the natural and rational interpretations of human behavior or, as it is usually referred to, the conflict between free will and determinism. I am persuaded that Kant's central intuition is totally correct, namely, that an adequate foundation for moral theory requires some coherent way of understanding men's actions *both* as causally determined, predictable, natural events *and* as rationally initiated, policy-directed actions. None of the familiar dodges, relaxations of the conflict, or reinterpretations designed to dissolve the problem will do. Neither Hume's "solution," as recently resurrected, nor, heaven knows, some misconstrual of the notion of indeterminacy in physics nor, most important, the notion that purposive action and nonpurposive behavior occur side by side in the natural world without overlapping. If any sense is to be made of responsibility and action, then one and the same bit of behavior which can be explained physiologically, predicted statistically, and brought within the scope of a scientific theory must also be capable of being consistently understood as issuing from the autonomous action of practical reason.

I do not think that Kant's interpretation of this problem is adequate, for a number of reasons that I shall indicate presently, but no other moral philosopher in the entire Western tradition has grasped so clearly and unflinchingly the existence of the conflict and the absolute necessity for some resolution of it.

Finally, Kant has given us, in his doctrine of the Kingdom of Ends, at least some of the elements of a theory of rational community and, thereby, of the origins of moral and political obligation. Later on, I shall explain why I think that obligation is rooted in communities of rational agents rather than in the nature of reason itself. Suffice it to say that when the theological overtones are eliminated, Kant's conception of the Kingdom of Ends is the closest we come in classical ethical literature to a satisfactory understanding of a moral community.[1]

2. What Is Wrong
in the *Groundwork*?

Three of the absolutely central tenets of Kant's moral theory are, in my judgment, either just plain wrong or else seriously unsatisfactory. By the time one has jettisoned them, what remains can hardly be called *Kant's* moral philosophy; but what remains is, I am convinced, very close to the truth in ethics.

First of all, Kant began his investigations completely convinced that there are objective, universally valid *substantive* principles of practical reason. In short, he believed that some policies were simply right and others simply wrong. His views on these matters, although rather strict and unbending for modern tastes, were in his own day quite conventional. One finds the details spelled out in the second part of the *Metaphysic of Morals*. Half of the confusion, obscurity, and ultimate internal inconsistency of the *Groundwork* can be traced to Kant's dogged unwillingness to give up this conviction, even in the face of the contrary implications of his own theory.

As I have several times suggested, Kant's conception of the

---

[1]The best account I know is that recently articulated by John Rawls in *A Theory of Justice* (Cambridge, Mass.: Harvard University Press, 1971). Rawls in a number of places acknowledges his debt to Kant.

nature of a moral principle requires him to distinguish between its form and its matter or end. Strictly speaking, the *Groundwork* shouldn't deal with the substance of moral principles at all; that is reserved for the second part of the *Metaphysic of Morals,* where the doctrine of obligatory ends is added to what we might call the doctrine of obligatory form, to yield supposedly objective and universal substantive principles of obligation. But the blatant inadequacy of the theory of obligatory ends leads Kant to attempt the impossible feat of deriving obligatory ends from the purely formal principle expressed as the Categorical Imperative. All of this I have tried to clarify in my commentary on the examples and alternative formulations of the Categorical Imperative in chapter 2.

The real truth of the matter, I think, is that Kant fails to find a plausible argument for the validity of substantive moral principles because there simply are no such principles! Since it may seem bizarre for me simultaneously to announce myself a follower in some sort of Kant and also to champion what appears to be a crude moral scepticism, let me anticipate the last part of this chapter a bit by way of clarification. I am persuaded that moral obligations, strictly so-called, arise from freely chosen contractual commitments between or among rational agents who have entered into some continuing and organized interaction with one another. Where such contractual commitments do not exist, cannot plausibly be construed as having been tacitly entered into, and cannot even be supposed to be the sort that *would* be entered into if the persons were to attempt some collective agreement, then no moral obligations bind one person to another.

It may be protested that, at the very least, this view runs completely contrary to the moral convictions that I or I and my friends or members of my social class or Americans or Western man, or civilized man, or all known societies have held. (I am never quite sure what the scope of "ordinary moral opinions" is supposed to be.) But strange as it may seem, I don't think this is so. Consider for a moment the familiar case of the Good Samaritan. If I encounter a man by the side of the road, sorely in need of help, my natural response is to think that I have some sort of obligation to help him, particularly if none of the usual countervailing considerations (conflicting obligations, prudential interests) obtain. But suppose that this man looks up at me and says, "I am dying. I desperately need and want your help. I implore you to assist me. But in all honesty I must tell you that if our positions were reversed, I would not lift a finger for you." My moral intuition tells me that I should then be relieved of my obligation to help him. And that, in turn, suggests that my initial sense of obligation stems from a quasi-contractual understanding or, at least, from an expectation that we would arrive at some contractual agreement if we were in a position to explore the matter of the rules governing our interactions.

There is, in fact, a spectrum of types of relationships among agents, ranging from explicit contractual arrangements at one end, of the sort that perhaps only exist in various short-lived utopian settlements; through highly articulated patterns of repeated social interaction among face-to-face acquaintances, of a sort to give rise to legitimate quasi-contractual understandings and expectations; along ever more attenuated interactions where less and less is known by the participants about the intentions, undertakings, commitments, and character of those with whom they come in contact; finally to the confrontations we might imagine between rational agents who represent utterly dissimilar forms of life. In this last case there are simply no substantive principles which can be assumed to bind the agents in their interactions, for if we do not even know what attitude others take toward their continued existence, we cannot anticipate even the most general outlines of the policies of mutual interaction to which they might be prepared to commit themselves. We would only know that they had ends and adopted policies, for that is analytically entailed by being a rational agent.

There is one way in which absolutely universal substantive policies might be derived from an analysis of rational agency as such. If one can show that the purely formal characteristics of rational agency and the purely formal characteristics of the contracting situation, taken together, rule out all but one set of principles, and if one can show further that a community of rational agents, engaged in a search for mutually acceptable principles, would necessarily, insofar as all the participants acted rationally, agree upon that one set, then one would have a purely a priori demonstration of the universal validity of that set of principles. This, I take it, is what Kant would have liked to show for his kingdom of ends, and it is also, as I understand it, the underlying intention of John Rawls's derivation of the principles of justice. For reasons which would carry us beyond the scope of this book, I believe Rawls's derivation to be incorrect. But he appears to be the only philosopher other than Kant who has even understood the problem correctly and seen what was needed.

The second tenet of Kant's moral philosophy which must be rejected is his conception of the moral life as a struggle between duty and inclination and, more generally, his account of the relationship between the rational and the affective elements in man. Here again, I have already explained why Kant's own theory of noumenal and phenomenal man comes into conflict with his portrayal of the self as a battleground for the two elements. If Kant takes his own account of natural causation seriously and if he clings to the distinction between appearance and reality on which his entire philosophy rests, then he simply cannot maintain that reason wrestles with inclination for control of man's actions. The drama of conscience must be construed, as, in fact, later psychologists and sociologists have construed it, as a causally determined psychocultural phenomenon entirely explainable, at least in principle, by the natural laws of physiology, psychology, society, and history. It ought to be possible to predict the socioeconomic and historical circumstances in which persons of strong conscience will appear, to predict the forms that their internal struggles will take, and even, if science were sufficiently successful, to predict the outcomes of particular conflicts between conscience and temptation.

Once again, I am convinced that Kant's theory is better than his presystematic beliefs. (This, indeed, is why I find him a worthwhile gamble for the task of philosophical reconstruction.) Surely the struggles of conscience, as we know them, *are* causally determined, as are all the other events of the natural world. It ought not to be so difficult today to see that this is so, although in Kant's own time the inadequacy of psychological theory made such a claim an act of metaphysical faith. Once we have recognized that antisocial behavior is rooted in the circumstances of heredity and childhood environment, it is only sentimental of us to deny that prosocial or socially acceptable behavior also is. If we are to preserve the notions of practical rationality, autonomy, and responsibility, we shall have to stop thinking of the responsible man as one whose reason o'ermasters his passion and search instead for a way of construing causally determined behavior as *also* rational and, hence, free.

But, and this is the third major weakness of Kant's theory, the resolution of the conflict between freedom and determinism with which we are presented in the Third Antinomy of the Transcendental Dialectic simply won't do. It depends upon a literal acceptance of the distinction between appearance and reality and an equally literal acceptance of the doctrine that I—my noumenal self, which is to say, my transcendental ego—choose and legislate the laws of nature. Even if we could get over the intriguing problem of the relationship within a single realm of nature of the phenomenal appearances of several transcendental egos, Kant's theory would still be just plain incredible. Is there anyone, I wonder, who actually *believes* that his character or personality is the appearance to himself of the law-giver of nature? I confess that I do not even know what it would mean to say that I believed such a thing!

Kant is correct in claiming that each of us conceives of himself in two different and apparently incompatible ways: as subject of action, deliberating, choosing, and determining himself to act by means of reasons; and as natural creature subject to nonrational laws of physiology and behavior, subsumable as an instance of inductive generalizations, predictable, a part of nature rather than either a knower of it or a doer in it. The distinction is an ancient one, as I have already noted, but Kant was right to say that it requires a full-scale metaphysical explication before we are justified in employing it to account for the nature of rational agency.

I do not have a metaphysical account of the relationship between natural and rational man to offer in place of Kant's theory of appearance and reality. Indeed, I do not even have any clear idea how to set about developing such an account. But I am dead certain that we need one, and I suspect that Kant's estimate of the magnitude of the undertaking is correct as well.

3. Suggestions for a Sketch
of a Pure Moral Theory

In the Preface to my book *In Defense of Anarchism,* I remarked
that the argument of that essay presupposed an entire moral theory, which at that time I was quite unprepared to articulate. It was
clear to me even then that the first step in the development of
such a theory would be an encounter with Kant, and this commentary has been that encounter. Although I am still a long way from
any sort of satisfactory full-scale theory of the foundations of morals and politics, I can at least now see the direction in which I
believe enlightenment can be found. Those who have read my
earlier essay will see from what follows that I have altered my
views in ways which require, at the very least, some significant
revision of the argument of *In Defense of Anarchism.* [2]

Briefly then, man is a rational agent in Kant's sense of that term.
He is capable of moving himself to act by the conception of a
rational connection between some act that he can perform and
some end that he had adopted as his own. The adoption, or posit-
ing, of ends is a nonrational process determined neither by reason
nor by desire. There are, in principle, no ends that reason requires
and no ends that it rules out. The fundamental principle of rationality is consistency and in conformity with that principle rational
agents, insofar as they are rational, choose a system of consistent
policies and act on them in a formally consistent way. Rational
agents also choose consistent ends, although not necessarily ends
which are integrated or harmonious in some richer, substantive
sense.

To choose an end is (analytically) to commit oneself to its actuali-
zation and, thereby, to those policies which are rationally con-

---

[2]This is not the place to attempt that revision, but I should like at least to give
credit to a former student, Mr. Andrej Rapaczynski, whose exceedingly acute
criticisms of some lectures I gave on political theory at Columbia University in the
late sixties first forced me to recognize the change in my position.

nected with it. (Needless to say, although the connection between the policy and the end is deductive, the empirical knowledge on which the policy rests is not, and so the familiar distinction between the subjectively right or rational and the objectively right or rational is preserved.) Those ends which one posits by oneself, treating other persons as external to the process of choice, give rise to what are commonly called principles of prudence. Those ends which one posits collectively with other rational agents, through a process of rational discourse culminating in unanimous agreement, give rise to what are commonly called moral principles.[3]

There is, at base, no difference between moral and political obligation. All obligations are grounded in the collective commitments of a society of rational agents. There is no special sort of commitment, distinct from others, which gives rise to a legitimate state, nor are there obligations whose ultimate source is other than a collective commitment. Hence, political philosophy so-called is merely a branch of moral philosophy, or, what would perhaps be more accurate, morals and politics are indistinguishable.

Thus far, I have been speaking only of obligations strictly so-called. But most of the time persons find themselves associated in ongoing institutionally organized patterns of interaction which neither in fact nor in plausible fiction can be traced to an original contractual agreement. In such cases, limited or partial obligations exist, the scope and force of which correspond to the degree to which the quasi-contractual situation approximates to the pure case of explicit collective commitment.

There is absolutely no substantive limitation to the character of the ends to which a society of rational agents may choose collectively to commit itself. They may choose a system of thoroughgoing, alienating mutual hostility, such as laissez faire capitalism, or a system of reciprocal cooperation and communal intimacy or, indeed, a system of regulated reciprocal murder, such as the institution of dueling essentially was. So long as the agreement is ex-

[3]Principles of altruism (both positive *and* negative) are not essentially different from self-regarding principles in the nature of their adoption, for neither arise out of a process of rational community. See my book *The Poverty of Liberalism* (Boston: Beacon Press, 1968), chap. 5, for a discussion of the conception underlying this point.

plicit, consistent, unanimous, and confined only to those who actually participate in the choice of the system, there is no rational,
which is to say, no moral ground for selecting one system rather
than another.

This much, I believe, should be susceptible of a priori proof in
the Kantian manner. Indeed, as Kant correctly insisted, in the
realm of moral philosophy, nothing but a priori proof has any value
whatsoever. There is another principle, half formal and half substantive so to speak, which it seems to me ought also to be capable
of a priori proof, but I cannot at all see how this can be done. The
principle, roughly speaking, is that whenever I encounter another
rational agent with whom I can expect to have more than passing
contact, I ought to attempt to establish rational discourse with him
for the purpose of discovering what principles, if any, we can
collectively agree upon to govern our interactions. Needless to
say, there may be few or no such principles, but I believe that I
have an obligation at least to attempt to explore the question. This,
I think, is what Kant was really getting at when he said that each
of us should treat other rational agents as ends in themselves and
not simply as means.

I treat a man as a means merely when I construe his behavior,
for my purposes, as nothing more than events in the natural world.
I treat him as a means also when I construe him as a rational
participant in a value-maximizing game confined to the realization of egoistic values (whether the game is one of pure competition, mixed competition and cooperation, or pure cooperation,
and even whether the ends he pursues are egoistic or altruistic!
See *The Poverty of Liberalism,* chap. 5). But I treat him as an end
in himself—as a rational agent per se—insofar as I undertake to
arrive with him at mutually agreeable principles to which we can
commit ourselves.

It is obvious that this principle goes a big step beyond what I
have so far sketched as the basis of morals. It is one thing to say
that I am obligated to abide by those principles to which I have
freely committed myself or even to say that I am *only* obligated
insofar as I have freely committed myself. But it is quite something
else to claim that I have a standing procedural obligation, as it
were, to broaden the scope of my commitments by transforming

my interactions with other persons into elements of rational community grounded in collective commitments. This latter claim, if it can be sustained, prohibits a rational agent from taking the position that he will refuse to explore the possibility of collective commitments with other rational agents and (in all consistency) accept whatever evil consequences may redound to him thereby. My intuition is that this procedural principle must have some purely a priori rational proof and that it is thus not merely the expression of an attitude that I (and perhaps others) might wish to embody in our lives. But just because the principle is categorical rather than hypothetical, just because it seems to go beyond merely articulating the nature of formal rationality, I am unclear about whether a proof for it should be discoverable.

These remarks raise many more questions than they answer. Even if principles that I have adumbrated were clarified and specified to the point that some reasonable judgment could be formed about their plausibility, I would still have to explore the nature and status of what I have rather easily referred to as "a priori proof." Nevertheless, I have roughed out this sketch because it is what lies behind the detailed textual analysis in the body of the commentary.

4. Limitations of
Pure Moral Theory:
Intimations of Mortality

But all this is only half the story. So far, I have spoken as though men could, for the purposes of moral theory, be understood in the manner that Kant conceives noumenal persons: as timeless, purely rational agents capable of abstracting from the limitations and particularities of their empirical characters. In the tradition of moral philosophy to which my own remarks belong, the accidents of birth and death, the phenomena of growth and parenthood, the facts of the social origins of personality itself, in short, what Erik

Erikson calls the life cycle, are treated as mere intrusions or embarrassments or marginal imperfections requiring a recognition that here, as elsewhere, pure theory does not quite fit the real world.

In the sort of social contract theory out of which my conception of collective commitment grows, there is, in principle, no difference between being born into a society and becoming a naturalized member of it. Death and emigration are treated as morally equivalent, assuming that one leaves no unfulfilled obligations when one emigrates. Children are treated as simply prerational until such time as they are factually or legally rational agents capable of entering the compact. The relationship of parent to child and grandchild, insofar as it enters into discussion at all, is subsumed under the heading of problems of social savings and gets mixed in with such related questions as how long a future a firm should project in making calculations of profitability. Michael Oakeshott has captured something of the craziness of this conception of human existence in his brilliant, corruscatingly funny essay, "Rationalism in Politics." Characterizing the Rationalist (who turns out to be almost every philosopher in the Western tradition except Oakeshott himself!), he writes:

> He has no sense of the cumulation of experience, only of the readiness of experience when it has been converted into a formula: the past is significant to him only as an encumbrance. . . . Intellectually, his ambition is not so much to share the experience of the race as to be demonstrably a self-made man. And this gives to his intellectual and practical activities an almost preternatural deliberateness and self-consciousness, depriving them of any element of passivity, removing from them all sense of rhythm and continuity and dissolving them into a succession of climacterics, each to be surmounted by a *tour de raison*. His mind has no atmosphere, no changes of season and temperature; his intellectual processes, so far as possible, are insulated from all external influence and go on in the void. . . . With an almost poetic fancy, he strives to live each day as if it were his first, and he believes that to form a habit is to fail.[4]

How shall we come to terms with the fact that each of us is an historically, culturally, socially located individual who is born into

[4]*Rationalism in Politics and Other Essays* (New York: Basic Books, Inc., 1962), pp. 2–3.

the world, develops a coherent personality through processes of growth, identification, internalization, represssion, and sublimation, lives out his life in a social realm which is, in some sense, a collective human creation, actualizes some portion of himself in his children, grows old, and dies? What is the relationship between each person's human personality and his pure rational agency? Neither ignoring the question, as moral philosophers so often do, nor denying the reality of moral agency, as historical or cultural determinists are prone to do, is a satisfactory answer. Kant's rather rudimentary attempt at an answer by way of the formula that the empirical character is the appearance of the noumenal character, at least has the virtue of recognizing the urgency of the problem.

We have returned by these speculations to the root conflict between freedom and determinism, but the problem now takes on a new appearance. On the one side is the autonomy of the rational agent, legislating through his independent choice a system of principles to which he is rationally bound. On the other side is the historicity of human personality, rooted in a particular moment of the endless life-cycle. We shall have a complete moral theory only when we fully understand this riddle of the human condition.

73 74 75   12 11 10 9 8 7 6 5 4 3 2 1